THE
DIVER'S REFERENCE
DICTIONARY

A BEST PUBLICATION

BEST PUBLISHING COMPANY . . . SAN PEDRO, CALIFORNIA

Copyright ©1986, by Best Publishing Company
POB 1978, San Pedro, CA, USA 90732

Library of Congress Cataloging in Publication Data:
Best Publisher
The Diver's Reference Dictionary

International Standard Book Number:
ISBN 0-941332-03-9

Printed and bound in the United States of America.

CONTENTS

PREFACE

The Diver's Reference Dictionary has been designed to fill a gap in available underwater literature. We must confess that writing it produced more difficulties then were first envisaged; and we are painfully aware that we may have left out some words.

The language of the diver runs from the scientific idioms of the researcher, to the technical vernaculars of the commercial diving engineer, to the earthy argot of sport enthusiasts. It is a rich medley of vocabularies, some in use since the Great Greek era, some born only yesterday.

This reference dictionary is an effort to make the language of the industry more understandable to people who, upon hearing it, feel more confusion than comprehension. There has been no effort to define every word, term or phrase, nor to describe every device, facility or tool, but there should be enough here to help anyone follow most conversations.

Some of the difficulties were obvious; providing hundreds of facts and, at the same time, trying to ensure accuracy despite human and typographical errors, for example. Then there was the problem of deciding what to leave out. This is always a difficulty with dictionaries, but in the case of diving, which touches on sport, commercial and scientific subjects, this becomes a very real problem. The greatest problem, however, was trying to produce a dictionary for people of differing standards. We hope that, in spite of all these factors, we have struck a reasonable balance.

DEFINITIONS OF
DIVING WORDS AND PHRASES

-A-

AAAS
American Association for the Advancement of Science.

AAG
Association of American Geographers.

abaft [uh•baft]
On a vessel, toward the stern in relation to a part of the vessel such as the mast; aft; to the rear.

abandon [uh•ban•dun]
To cease work on a well which is non productive, plug off the well, and salvage all recoverable equipment; to leave a vessel.

abdomen [ab•doe•mun]
The part of the body located between the diaphragm and the pelvis; the cavity that contains the abdominal organs (viscera).

abeam [uh•beem]
On a vessel, abreast; at right angles to the keel.

aboard [uh•bord]
On the deck or in the hold of a vessel; in or upon a vessel.

abort [uh•bort]
To terminate a dive task or procedure ahead of schedule or before completion.

abort profile [uh•bort pro•fyle]
Decompression schedule used to bring a diver safely to the surface when a dive must be aborted.

abreast [uh•brest]
Lying or moving side by side, or opposite.

abrid [uh•brid]
The lining of a hole in which a pintle works. (See: pintles.)

A.B.S.
American Bureau of Shipping.

absolute zero pressure [ab•so•loot zee•roe presh•ur]
The theoretical absence of all pressure, normally expressed as zero pounds per square inch absolute (p.s.i.a.).

absorbent [ab•zor•bunt]
A substance capable of taking something into itself; as with rebreathers capable of removing carbon dioxide from expired breath. (See: rebreather.)

absorption [ab•zorp•shun]
Taking in, as through pores; soaking in or up.

abyssal [uh•biss•ul]
Referring to the deep sea (roughly 8,000 to 19,000 ft. or 2400 to 5800 meters) where temperature does not exceed 39° F (4° C); describes marine organisms especially adapted to great pressures, low temperatures and lack of light.

abyssal hill [uh•biss•ul hill]
Relatively small topographic feature of deep ocean floor, ranging from 2,000 to 3,000 ft. high and a few miles wide.

abyssal plain [uh•biss•ul playn]
Large area of ocean bottom covered by marine sediments, characterized by flatness and gentle slope.

acapnia [uh•kap•nee•uh]
Lack of carbon dioxide in the blood.

accelerator [ak•sell•ur•ay•tur]
A chemical (calcium chloride or sodium chloride) which may be added to cement slurry to reduce its setting time. (See: slurry.)

accelerometer [ak•sell•ur•ahm•uh•tur]
A device which measures the forces of acceleration acting upon a body.

accommodation [uh•kahm•oh•day•shun]
In photography, and in physiology in relation to the eye, the forcus of the lens for near objects.

accretion [uh•kree•shun]
Natural accretion is the gradual buildup of land over a long period of time by the action of the forces of nature; artificial accretion is a similar build-up of land by an act of man, such as that formed by a breakwater.

accumulator [uh•kyoo•myoo•lay•tur]
On an oil rig, used to actuate the blow out preventer fittings on a well head; a pressure container charged with nitrogen into which fluid is pumped, thus compressing the nitrogen to a high pressure (1500 to 2000 p.s.i. working pressure), forcing fluid out of the accumulator and operating the packers. (See: blow out preventer stack, packers.)

acid bottle [ass•ud baht•ul]
A glass tube run into a hole in a steel container to record deviation from the vertical by the use of hydrofluoric acid; in oil well drilling operations, usually replaced by more sophisticated instruments.

acidosis [ass•uh•dose•us]
Clinical term indicating an increase in the acidity of the blood.

acid treatment [ass•ud treet•munt]
The technique of increasing production from a limestone reservoir by pumping acid into the formation to increase the permeability around the well bore. (See: permeability.)

ACMRR
Advisory Committee on Marine Resources Research of the Food and Agriculture Organization of the United Nations.

acoustic [uh•koo•stik]
Pertaining to sound or the sense of hearing.

acoustic beacon
(See: beacon.)

ACSM
American Congress on Surveying and Mapping.

actinometer [ak•tuh•nahm•uh•tur]
Any instrument used to measure the intensity of radiant energy.

adaptation [a•dap•tay•shun]
Involuntary adjustment of the eye to a decrease in the ambient level of light; the fitness of an organism for its environment.

adapter [uh•dap•tur]
A piece of equipment to get from one type or size connection to another.

adenitis [a•den•eye•tus]
Inflammation of a gland; frequently refers to inflammation of lymph nodes.

adiabatic process [a•dee•uh•bat•ik prah•sess]
A change of state in a system in which there is no transfer of heat or mass across the boundaries of the system.

adrenalin [uh•dren•uh•lun]
A proprietary brand of epinephrine, a hormone secreted by the adrenal gland.

adrift [uh•drift]
Loose from mooring or not held fast.

adsorption [ad•zorp•shun]
The assimilation of gas or vapor by the surface of a solid.

advance of a beach [ad•vans uv uh beech]
A continuing seaward movement of the shore line.

aerobe [air•ob]
A microorganism the lives in contact with the air and absorbs oxygen from it.

aerobic [air•oh•bik]
1. Of the nature of an aerobe; 2. Of or produced by aerobes.

aerobiosis [air•oh•bv•oh•sis]
Life in and by means of air or oxygen.

aerodontalgia [air•oh•don•tall•jee•uh]
Pain in a tooth caused by changes in ambient pressure. (See: barodontalgia.)

aeroembolism [air•oh•em•bo•liz•'m]
Obsolete term for altitude decompression sickness, no longer used in altitude medicine; obstruction of blood vessels by gas bubbles.

aerophagia [air•oh•faje•ee•uh]
Air ingestion (swallowed air).

afferent [uh•fair•unt]
Carrying toward a center or main part; nerves that carry impulses toward the central nervous system or toward ganglia.

A frame [Ay fraym]
On a vessel, used to fairlead the cable overhead off the deck and back to the winch; a device for heavy lifting over the bow or stern of a barge or vessel. (See: fairlead.)

AFT [aft]
Describing the after section of a vessel, or things to the rear of amidship and near the stern.

aftercooler [aff•tur•kool•ur]
A device for lowering the temperature of compressed air after the final stage of compression.

after perpendicular [aff•tur pur•pen•dik•yoo•lur]
The vertical line intersecting the load waterline at the after end of the stern post. (See: stern)

agar [ay•gar]
Extract obtained from several kinds of red algae; used in medicine as an ingredient in the preparation of a medium for the growth of bacteria.

aggradation [ag•ruh•day•shun]
The geologic process by means of which various parts of the surface of the earth are raised or built up by the deposition of material eroded from other sections.

aggregate [ag•ruh•gut]
A mixture of substances, separable by mechanical means.

AGI
American Geological Institute.

aground [a•grownd]
Touching bottom.

AIBS
American Institute of Biological Sciences.

air [air]
A naturally occurring gas mixture comprising approximately four-fifths nitrogen, one-fifth oxygen, and various trace gases.

airblast [air blast]
The air shock wave created by an explosion.

air carbon-arc cutting [air kahr•bun-ahrk kut•ing]
An arc-cutting process wherein the severing of metals is effected by melting with the heat of an arc between an electrode and the base metal, and an air stream is used to facilitate cutting.

air cleaner [air kleen•ur]
A device for filtering, cleaning, and removing dust from the air admitted to a unit, such as an engine or air compressor.

air compressor
(See: compressor.)

air dive [air dyv]
A dive using compressed air as a breathing mixture.

air embolism [air em•bo•liz•um]
A pathologic condition occurring in the body when bubbles of air are forced into the circulation and gain access to the arterial system, causing blockage of blood flow and leading to local hypoxia and cellular death. (See: hypoxia.)

air gap [air gap]
A system of blasting where a charge is suspended in a hole and the hole tightly stemmed to allow a time lapse between detonation and failure of the rock.

air holes [air holz]
On a vessel, small holes cut into longitudinals and floors of confined compartments in order to permit venting while pumping the compartment.

air in gut [air in gut]
Swallowed or trapped air in the stomach or large bowel, expanding on ascent.

air lift [air lift]
The technique of injecting compressed air into the fluid column in a well or pipe to stimulate the flow of fluid; also used by divers in the management of underwater cargoes. (See: gas lift.)

air lock [air lahk]
A bubble of air trapped in a fluid circuit which interferes with normal circulation of the fluid.

air lock [air lahk]
A small chamber with outer and inner hatches that allow divers to swim out by equalizing chamber pressure with ambient sea pressure.

algae [al•jee]
Marine and fresh-water plants ranging from microscopic unicellular plants to giant kelps; singular form; alga.

alimentary [al•ee•men•teri]
Of or pertaining to nutrition.

alist [uh•list]
Listing or canted to one side; said of a vessel not on an even keel.

alkalinity [al•kuh•lin•tee]
In sea water, the excess of hydroxyl ions over hydrogen ions.

allergen [al•ur•jen]
A substance that causes sensitivity; something that induces allergy.

alloy [al•oy]
A mixture of different metals.

alluvium [uh•loov•ee•um]
Soil deposited by flowing water

alternating current (AC) [all•tur•nay•ting kurr•unt]
The kind of electricity which reverses its direction periodically; for 60 cycle current, the current goes in one direction and then in the other direction 60 times in the same second, changing direction 120 times in one second.

alternobaric [all•tur•no•bare•ik]
Refers to outward gas pressure on the tympannic membrane of the ear during diving ascent, or lowered ambient pressure.

altitude chamber [al•tuh•tood chaym•bur]
A chamber capable of simulating the environmental conditions experienced at altitude.

altitude correction [al•tuh•tood kur•rek•shun]
Adjustment to decompression schedules necessitated by the reduced barometric pressure prevailing at altitude.

altitude/depth sonar [al•tuh•tood/depth so•nahr]
A type of sonar that measures the distance from a submersible to the ocean surface or to the ocean bottom, using upward and downward transducers and a graphic recorder.

altitude diving
(See: dive at altitude.)

altocumulus [al•toe•kyoo•myoo•lus]
A cloud layer (mean height 6,500 - 20,000 feet) composed of flattened globular masses, arranged in groups, lines or waves.

altostratus [al•toe•strat•us]
A sheet of gray or bluish cloud sometimes composed of a compact mass of dark gray clouds of fibrous structure, at other times thin.

aluminum [uh•lum•uh•num]
A metal noted for its lightness; often alloyed with small quantities of other metals.

alveolar [al•vee•oh•lur]
A small depression or pertinent to an alveolus.

alveolar air [al•vee•oh•lur air]
The mixture of gases collected by having the subject first execute a normal expiration and then exhale as much additional air (which comes from the alveoli of the lungs) into the collecting device as possible. Its composition is fairly constant at rest. Exercise increases the carbon dioxide above, and voluntary overbreathing decreases it below 5.5%.

alveolar exchange [al•vee•oh•lur eks•chaynj]
Diffusion of oxygen into the blood, and removal of carbon dioxide from the blood, in the alveoli of the lungs.

alveolar ventilation [al•vee•oh•lur ven•tul•ay•shun]
The product of the respiratory frequency and the difference between the expired volume per breath and the dead space; the volume of inspired gas that ventilates the alveoli; total ventilation minus dead space ventilation.

alveoli [al•vee•oh•lee]
A cluster of air sacs at the end of the bronchial trees; sockets for the teeth or any small hollows or cavities; singular form, alveolus.

alveolus [al•vee•oh•lus]
1. Small outpocketings of the sacks in the lungs. Gas exchange with the blood in pulmonary capillaries takes place through alveolar walls. 2. A small cell, cavity or hollow in a surface.

ambient [am•bee•unt]
Pertaining to the surrounding environment.

ambient pressure [am•bee•unt presh•ur]
The pressure of fluid (usually water plus air pressure) upon objects placed in it; usually expressed in terms of absolute pressure. (See: absolute pressure, atmospheric pressure, design pressure, gauge pressure, hydrostatic pressure, partial pressure, pressure working pressure.)

amblyopia [am•blee•oh•pee•uh]
Dimness of vision without a notable lesion of the eye.

ametropia [am•uh•trope•ee•uh]
Imperfection in the refractive functions of the eye, so that images are not brought to a proper focus on the retina; resulting in hypermetropia, myopia or astigmatism.

amidships [uh•mid•ships]
The center section of a vessel as opposed to its bow and stern; vessel's rubber position.

ammeter [am•mee•tur]
An instrument for measuring the flow of an electrical current.

ammonium nitrate [uh•mone•ee•um ny•trayt]
An ingredient in dynamite; the major ingredient in blasting agents.

amnesia [am•nee•zha]
1. Partial or total loss of memory caused by brain injury, or by shock, repression, etc. 2. Loss of memory for certain kinds of words.

amnesia auditory [am•nee•zha auditory]
Loss of memory as to word meanings.

amnesia periodic [am•nee•zha periodic]
Amnesia occurring in a period of double consciousness.

amnesia traumatic [am•nee•zha traumatic]
Amnesia caused by injury.

amnesia visual [am•nee•zha visual]
Inability to remember the appearance of objects that have been seen or to be cognisant of printed words.

ampere [am•peer]
The unit of measurement for the flow of electric current.

ampere-hour capacity [am•peer-owr kuh•pass•uh•tee]
A term used to indicate the capacity of a storage battery.

amphitrite [am•fy•trite]
A 65 foot long, 6 ton inflatable ship used as a tender in sea diving operations.

AMS
American Meteorological Society.

AN
Abbreviation for the blasting agent ammonium nitrate. (See: ammonium nitrate.)

analgesic [an•ul•jeez•ik]
A pain-relieving agent that does not cause loss of consciousness.

anatomical dead space [an•a•ta•mi•kal•ded•spays]
That area superior to the alveoli comprised of the upper airways where no gas exchange occurs to or from the blood.

anatomy [uh•nat•uh•mee]
The science of the structure of the body and the relationship of its parts to one another.

anchor [ang•kur]
A shaped implement of cast steel or heavy iron fitted with tapered flukes which engage the ground, any device which fastens a vessel to the bottom. (See: fluke.)

anchor bend [ang•kur bend]
Also called the fisherman's bend, one of the strongest hitches.

anchor buoy [ang•kur boo'ee]
A buoy marking the position of an anchor.

anchor, dead line [ang•kur, ded lyne]
In drilling, the fitting which anchors the dead line of the hoisting cable; usually fitted with a diaphragm device which indicates the loads handled by the hoisting equipment.

anemia [uh•neem•ee•uh]
A decrease in certain elements of the blood, especially red cells and hemoglobin.

anesthesia [an•us•thee•zee•uh]
The loss of feeling or sensation, particularly the sensation of pain.

aneurysm [an•yoor•iz•um]
A saclike enlargement of a blood vessel caused by a weakening of the vessel wall.

ANFO
Abbreviation for ammonium nitrate; a fuel oil mixture used as a blasting agent.

angina [an•**jyne**•uh]
Any disease characterized by severe spasmodic pain and suffocation.

angle of deviation [**ang**•gul uv de•vee•**ay**•shun]
The deviation from true vertical of a well bore hole, which may be either by accident or by design.

angle of roll [**ang**•gul uv role]
The angle between the lateral and horizontal axes of a craft.

annealed tubing [uh•**neeld toob**•ing]
Tubing soft enough to allow proper bending for fluid system installations.

annealing [uh•**neel**•ing]
Heating and cooling of pipe primarily to induce softness, to relieve internal stresses, and to obtain the optimum combination of strength and ductility.

annular seal assembly [**an**•yoo•lur seel uh•**seem**•blee]
A device connected to the top of a mudline hinge for sealing off the annular space between two casing strings. (See: casing string.)

annular space [**an**•yoo•lur spays]
The space between the drill string and the well wall, or the casing string and the well wall.

anode [**an**•ode]
A positive pole of an electrical current; metal rod or bar installed for carbon protection of steel structures in sea water.

anomalous dispersive [uh•**nahm**•uh•lus dis•**purs**•iv]
Said of waves having crests which are short compared to their length.

anoxemia [a•nok•**seem**•ya]
A reduction in the normal amount of oxygen in the blood.

anoxia [an•**ahks**•ee•uh]
The absence of oxygen. (See: hypoxia.)

anthropometry [an•throw•**pahm**•uh•tree]
The measurement of the size and shape of the human body.

aorta [ay•**ore**•tuh]
The largest artery of the body.

aperture [**ap**•ur•chor]
An opening, hole or port; in photography, the size of the circular opening controlling the amount of light passing through a lens.

API
American Petroleum Institute.

apnea [**ap**•nee•uh]
A temporary cessation of breathing.

APO
Association of Physical Oceanographers.

apparatus [ap•ur•**at**•us]
An assembly of materials or parts designed to perform a specific operation; for example, open-circuit scuba, rebreather, etc.

apparent crater dimensions [uh•**pair**•unt **kray**•tur di•**men**•shunz]
In blasting, the net excavated volume of a crater below the original ground surface.

apparent time [uh•**pair**•unt tym]
Time based upon the true position of the sun as distinguished from mean time, which is measured by a fictitious sun moving at a uniform rate.

appendages [uh•**pen**•duh•juz]
On a vessel, fittings and structures which extend beyond the outline of the hull: bilge keel, rudder, rudder post, strainers, struts, skeg, etc.

aqualung [**ah**•kwuh•lung]
A self-contained underwater breathing apparatus in which air from a cylinder is supplied to the diver at surrounding pressure; also, scuba.

arc blow [ahrk blo]
In welding, a magnetic disturbance of the arc which causes it to waver from its intended path.

arc cutting [ahrk **kut**•ing]
A group of cutting processes where the severing or removing of metals is effected by melting, using the heat of an arc between an electrode and the base metal.

Archimedes' Principle [**Ahrk**•uh•**mee**•deez **Prin**•suh•pul]
In physics, the principal that a body in fluid is buoyed upward by a force equal to the weight of the fluid it displaces.

archipelago [**ahrk**•uh•**pell**•uh•go]
A group of islands.

arch piece [ahrch pees]
On a vessel, upper curved section of the stern frame at the junction of the propeller post and the stern post.

arc length [ahrk layngth]
In welding, the distance from the end of the electrode to the point where the arc makes contact with work surface.

arc search [ahrk surch]
Underwater search of an area using semi-circular sweeps of increasing radius. (See: search pattern-underwater.)

arc voltage [ahrk **vole**•tuj]
The voltage across a welding arc.

area [air•ee•uh]
The measure of a plane or surface of a solid.

argon [**ahr**•gon]
A colorless, odorless gas which does not react chemically under standard conditions; used occasionally as a diluent gas in diving.

arm [ahrm]
An inlet; a term usually used in connection with the larger body of water of which it is a part, as an arm of the sea.

armature [**ahrm**•uh•choor]
The part of an electrical machine which includes the main current-carrying winding.

arrhythmia [uh•**rith**•me•uh]
A lack of normal rhythm, especially of the heart beat.

arteriole [ahr•**teer**•ee•ole]
The smallest artery, one that branches into the microscopic capillaries.

arthralgia [ahr•**thral**•jee•uh]
Pain in the joints of the body. (See: compression arthralgia, decompression arthralgia, hyperbaric arthralgia.)

arthritis [ar•**thry**•tis]
Inflammation of a joint or joints.

arthritis osteo [ar•**thry**•tis osteo]
Inflammation affecting the bones and joints.

artificial nourishment [**ahrt**•uh•**fish**•ul nurr•ish•munt]
The process of replenishing a beach by artificial means such as the addition of dredged material.

artificial respiration [**ahrt**•uh•**fish**•ul res•purr•**ay**•shun]
Any means by which an alternating increase and decrease in chest volume is created, while maintaining an open airway in mouth and nose passages.

asbestos [ass•**bess**•tus]
A natural fibrous mineral with great resistance to heat transfer.

ascent [uh•**sent**]
Movement in the direction of reduced pressure whether simulated or due to actual elevation in water or air. (See: buoyant ascent, emergency buoyant ascent, emergency controlled ascent, exhaling ascent, hooded ascent, swimming ascent.)

aseptic [ass•**sep**•tik]
Free from any infectious or septic material.

aseptic bone necrosis
(See: osteonecrosis.)

ASIRC
Aquatic Sciences Information Retrieval Center.

ASLO
American Society of Limnology and Oceanography.

A.S.M.E.
American Society of Mechanical Engineers.

asphyxia [ass•**fik**•see•uh]
Condition characterized by decreased oxygen and increased carbon dioxide in the body as a result of interference with respiration.

associated gas [uh•**so**•see•ay•tud gas]
Natural gas in a reservoir formation which overlies and is in contact with the crude oil in drilling.

astern [uh•**sturn**]
To the rear or abaft of an imaginary transverse line drawn at the stern of a vessel; the backward movement of a vessel; the direction the main engine is turning, as opposed to ahead.

astigmatism [uh•**stig**•muh•tiz'm]
An irregularity of the cornea or the lens of the eye, causing the image to be out of focus.

A.S.T.M
American Society for Testing Materials.

as-welded [az-**weld**•ud]
The condition of weld metal, welded joints and weldments after welding, prior to any subsequent thermal or mechanical treatment.

ataxia [uh•**taks**•ee•uh]
Lack of muscular coordination; lack of orderly motion; unsteadiness.

athwart [a•thwahrt]
Across.

atmosphere [**at**•mus•feer]
Pressure equal to normal atmospheric pressure at sea level (14.7 psi).

atmospheres absolute [**at**•mus•feerz ab•so•**loot**]
The sum of barometric and hydrostatic pressures.

atmospheric pressure [at•mus•**feer**•ik presh•ur]
Pressure exerted by the earth's atmosphere, which varies with altitude above sea level. (See: absolute pressure, ambient pressure, design pressure, gauge pressure, hydrostatic pressure, partial pressure, pressure, working pressure.)

atoll [**at**•tol]
A ring of islands encircling or nearly encircling a lagoon.

atoll reef [**at**•tol reef]
A ring-shaped coral reef, often carrying low sand islands and enclosing a body of water.

atom [**at**•um]
A unit of matter; the smallest unit of an element, consisting of a nucleus surrounded by a system of electrons equal in number to the number of nuclear protons.

atomic energy [uh•**tom**•ik **en**•ur•jee]
The energy released from an atomic nucleus in fission or fusion.

attendant
(See: tender.)

attended diving [uh•**ten**•dud **dyv**•ing]
Diving with a lifeline and a tender. (See: surface-supplied diving, tethered diving.)

audiometry [aw•dee•**ahm**•uh•tree]
The measurement of hearing.

aural [a•ral]
Pertaining to the ear. See fig.s. 2-5.

aural barotrauma [a•ral barotrauma]
Damage of one eardrum or both, caused by changes in ambient pressure.

auricle [**ore**•uh•cul]
The projecting part of the ear.

auscultation [a•skul•**tay**•shun]
Act of listening to sounds in the chest, abdomen, etc.

auscultation immediate [a•skul•**tay**•shun immediate]
When the ear is applied directly to the part.

auscultation mediate [a•skul•**tay**•shun mediate]
When practiced with the aid of an instrument, e.g. stethoscope.

autonomic [aw•toe•**nahm**•ik]
Refers to the division of the nervous system which controls automatic activities, functionally independent.

autonomic nervous system [aw•toe•**nahm**•ik **nur**•vus **sis**•tum]
That part of the nervous system not under conscious control.

autonomous diving
(See: scuba.)

autotrophic [aw•toe•**troe**•fik]
Referring to organisms able to manufacture their own food, such as green plants.

axial [ak•see•ul]
Along the axis or length of a tube, pipe, or other cylindrical item.

axial movement [ak•see•ul **moov**•munt]
Any movement along the axis of a tube.

-B-

back break [back brayk]
In blasting, rock broken beyond the limits of the last row of holes in a drilled pattern shot.

backing [**back**•ing]
Material backing up the joint during welding to facilitate obtaining a sound weld at the root; may be metal, asbestos, carbon, granulated flux, etc.

backlash [**back**•lash]
The clearance (play) between two parts, such as meshed gears.

back off [back awf]
Usually refers to the unscrewing of drill pipe from a fish in the hole. (See: fish.)

backpack [**back**•pack]
A light frame molded to conform to the back and hip contours of the diver, used to carry diving equipment.

back pressure [back **presh**•ur]
Pressure resulting from restricting the full natural flow of oil or gas.

back splice [back splys]
A method to prevent fraying or unraveling in the end of a rope.

back-step welding [back-step **well**•ding]
A welding technique where the increments of welding are deposited opposite the direction of progression.

back up man [back up man]
Member of the drilling crew who holds the tong to prevent a length of pipe from rotating while another length is attached or removed.

backwash [**back**•wahsh]
Water, piled on shore by breaking waves, which sets up an outward current; incorrectly called undertow or runout.

bacteriology [back•teer•ee•**awl**•uh•jee]
The study of microscopic organisms called bacteria.

bag type blowout preventer [bag type **bloe**•out pre•**ven**•tur]
In drilling, a protective device with a doughnut-shaped packing unit compressed by hydraulic pressure to seal around the irregular-shaped parts of the drill string.

bail [bale]
To remove water from a boat by pump or bailer.

bailer [bay•lur]
A cylindrical container fitted with a foot valve which is used to remove fluid or slurry from a hole and is run on a wire line; or, used in a well drilled by the rotary method, in order to lower the level of the mud column to reduce the hydrostatic pressure so fluid will flow into the well bore.

bails [baylz]
In drilling, the links which connect the main hoisting hook with the drill pipe elevators.

bakeout [bayk•out]
A method of speeding up the outgassing of contaminants in a vacuum system by the use of heat. (See: vacuum bakeout.)

ballast [bal•ust]
Weight in the form of water, lead, iron pigs or shot, used to change the displacement of a submersible or vessel.

ball joint [bawl joynt]
Universal joint at the bottom of a marine riser just above the blow out preventer stack, allowing for deflection.

ball up [bawl up]
When sticky material stops the bit cutters while drilling, making a round trip necessary to clean the bit. (See: round trip.)

ball weevil [bawl wee•ul]
An inexperienced oil field worker; also boll weevil.

band mask [band mask]
Full face mask affixed to the head by a network of rubber straps. (See: demand mask, full face mask, lightweight diving mask, mask, surface supplied.)

bar [bahr]
An offshore ridge or ,mound of sand, gravel or other material submerged at least at high tide, especially at the mouth of a river or estuary or lying a short distance from a beach; also a unit of measurement: 0.98692 atm, 750.06 torr (mmttg); a unit of pressure equal to 1,000,000 dynes per square centimeter, 1,000 millibars, 29.53 inches of mercury.

Baralyme [Bair•uh•lym]
Carbon dioxide-absorbent chemical.

barbiturate [bar•bichur•et]
Any salt of barbituric acid used as a sedative, or to deaden pain.

bare electrode [bair ee•leck•trod]
A filler-metal electrode used in arc welding; consists of a metal wire with no coating.

bare foot completion [bair foot kum•plee•shun]
The completion of a well in a reservoir formation which is stable and does not require a liner or perforated casing completion.

barge [bahrj]
A craft of steel of wood construction used to transport cargo over water.

barite [bair•ite]
Barium sulphate, sometimes added to drilling mud to increase its weight and provide a hydrostatic head for controlling formation pressures.

bar keel [bahr•keel]
A solid, heavy wrought iron bar of rectangular cross section used in older ships.

barnacle [bahr•nuh•kull]
A marine animal attached in the adult shell form to rocks, timbers, ship hulls, pilings, oil rigs, etc.; sharp enough to cause cuts and abrasions. (See: hazardous marine animals.)

barodontalgia [bair•oh•dahn•tahl•juh]
Acute pain in a tooth, caused by pressure.

barometer [bur•ahm•uh•tur]
An instrument for measuring atmospheric pressure.

barometric pressure [bair•uh•met•rick presh•ur]
Air or atmospheric pressure.

barotrauma [bair•oh•trahm•uh]
Physiological injury or damage to the tissues caused by unequal pressures.

barracuda [bair•uh•koo•duh]
Found in tropical and subtropical waters, a fish that grows to approximately six feet in length and has knife-like canine teeth. (See: hazardous marine animals.)

barrel [bair•ul]
The generally accepted measurement when describing the production potential of a well or when measuring mud volumes.

barrel, core
(See: core barrel.)

barrel sling [bair•ul sling]
A sling for a barrel or other heavy object, made by bringing rope ends over the top to form an overhand crossing, then down over the sides of the barrel, and finishing with a bowline.

barrel wrench [bair•ul rench]
A special friction wrench used for repairing a down hole pump. (See: down hole pump.)

barrier island [bair•ee• eye•lund]
A wave-built deposit of sand separated from the shore by a lagoon.

barrier reef [bair•ee•ur reef]
A reef which parallels land but is some distance offshore.

base charge [bays chahrj]
The main charge in a blasting cap.

base metal [bays **met**•ul]
Metal to be welded or cut.

basin [**bays**•un]
A depression of the sea floor more or less of equal dimensions; also a relatively small cavity in the bottom or shore, large enough to receive one or more vessels.

basket [**bas**•kut]
A fishing device for recovering junk from the bottom of a hole; a cylindrical tube usually fitted at its lower end with a cutting head, above which is a ring fitted with spring loaded fingers which hold the recovered fish. (See: fish, junk.)

basket, cement [**bas**•kut, see•**ment**]
A funnel shaped rubber bucket with spring type fingers to hold the upper rim against the well wall. (See: casing string.)

bathyscaph [**bath**•us•skaff]
A navigable submersible ship for deep-sea exploration having a spherical watertight cabin attached to its underside.

bathyscope [**bath**•us•kope]
A manned submarine-type research vessel.

bathysphere [**bath**•us•feer]
A tethered, strongly built diving sphere for deep-sea exploration.

battens [**bat**•nz]
Thin stripes of wood, plastic or other material set in pockets and sewed into the sail to hold or improve the set of a sail. On some racing boats the battens extend from leech to luff.

battery [**bat**•ur•ee]
Any number of complete electrical cells assembled in one housing or case.

bayou [**by**•yoo]
A waterway, generally tidal or with a slow current, and with its course generally through lowlands or swamps and connecting with other bodies of water.

B.D.C.
Bottom dead center.

beach [beech]
The zone of unconsolidated material that extends landward from the low water line to the place where there is marked change in material, or to the line of permanent vegetation.

beacon [**bee**•kun]
Underwater locating device which emits an acoustic signal; a blinking or rotating light marking navigational hazards.

beam [beem]
Imaginary line amidship at right angles to keel of vessels. Also vessel's width amidship.

bean [been]
A choke device used to control the flow of fluid or gas under pressure through a pipe line.

beance tubaire voluntaire (BTV) [**bay**•ahns **toob**•air vahl•un•**tair**]
Voluntary opening of the eustachian tubes by a maneuver during which the nose, mouth and glottis are open; performed to equalize pressure.

bearding [**beerd**•ing]
On a vessel, the line of intersection at the junction of the butts of plates and the stem of stern post.

bearing [**bay**•ring]
The direction or point of the compass in which an object is seen.

becket [**bek**•ut]
A device, such as a looped rope, hook and eye, strap, or grommet for holding or fastening ropes, spars or oars in position.

bed [bed]
The ground upon which a body of water rests.

belaying [be•**lay**•ing]
In rigging, attaching a rope to a cleat; one or two figure-eights finished with a hitch (underhand loop) pulled snug.

bell [bell]
A tethered underwater support system providing life-support services and used to transport divers. (see: observation bell, open bell, personnel transfer capsule.)

belt, weight [belt, wayt]
A belt worn by a diver to achieve neutral or negative buoyancy.

bench [bench]
A horizontal ledge along which holes are drilled vertically, commonly found in quarry blasting.

bends [bendz]
An imprecise colloquial term usually denoting decompression sickness with pain in the extremities. (See: decompression sickness.)

bentonite [**ben**•tun•yte]
A colloidal clay which swells when wet; the basis of most drilling muds. (See: mud.)

berth [burth]
A place for securing a vessel; a bed or bunk aboard a vessel; one's assigned job aboard ship.

BG
A naval architectural term for the distance in inches between the center of gravity and the

center of buoyancy; submersibles must have a positive BG to be stable.

B.H.P.
A measurement of the power developed by an engine in actual operation; brake horsepower.

bight [byte]
A slight indentation in the shore line of an open coast or bay, usually crescent shaped; also the middle or bent part of a rope, line or cable being used to form a loop.

bilge [bilj]
Lowest or almost lowest portion of a vessel inside the hull.

bilge keel [bilj keel]
Longitudinal steel plates fitted externally along the bilge strake to decrease rolling of the vessel; commonly called rolling chocks. (See: rolling chocks.)

binnacle [bin•uh•kul]
A nonmagnetic stand on which a ship's compass case is supported.

binocular vision [bin•ahk•yoo•lur viz•shun]
Vision using both eyes.

bio-diver [by•oh•dyv•ur]
Scientific diver working in the field of biology.

biota [by•oh•tuh]
The animal and plant life of a region; flora and fauna.

bird cage [burd kayj]
To flatten and spread the strands of a wire rope.

bit breaker [bit brayk•ur]
A plate which fits into the master bushing recess in a rotary table and enables drilling bits to be unscrewed from the drill string. (See: drill string, rotary table.)

bit collar [bit kahl•ur]
Heavy duty pipe which is used to connect a rock bit to the drill string.

bitter end [bit•tur end]
On a vessel, the inboard end of any line, cable, anchor chain or pendant.

bittern [bit•urn]
The liquid remaining after sea water has been concentrated by evaporation until the salt has crystallized.

bitts [bits]
Heavy castings used to lead and secure mooring or towing hawsers to a dock or ship.

blackwall hitch [blak•wahl hich]
A knot formed by looping and crossing rope as a temporary hitch for light loads.

bladder [blad•ur]
A flexible bag, usually containing a liquid.

blank liner [blank lyn•ur]
A liner which has no perforations. (See: liner.)

blast hole
(See: borehole.)

blasting agent [blast•ing ayj•unt]
Any material or mixture of mateials consisting of a combustible and an oxidizer intended for blasting, but not otherwise classified as an explosive.

bleeding [bleed•ing]
The appearance of fresh blood at the nose, ears or mouth, or from a wound; the reduction of pressure in a linear chamber by slightly opening a valve.

bleeding line [bleed•ing lyne]
A cable which, when overloaded, "bleeds" lubricant.

blind ram [blind ram]
A steel ram with rubber insert, fitted to a blow out preventer which, when closed, functions like a main valve.

block [blok]
In rigging, the combination of frame and pulley, or sheave, secured by a strap and pins and mounted with a hook and becket, which is used to gain advantage or fairlead in the make-up of lines attached to a load. (See: becket, fairlead, pulley.)

block hole [blok hole]
In blasting, a hole drilled into a boulder to allow a small charge to be placed to break the boulder.

block line [blok lyne]
The wire line which is wound onto the main drum of the drawworks and reeved over the crown block sheaves and through the traveling block for the purpose of handling the drill string or other loads. (See: crown block, drawworks, drill string, traveling block.)

blood sludging [blud sluj•ing]
Agglutination (clumping) of blood cells in intact blood vessels in diving, may occur after decompression.

bloodworm [blud•wurm]
Found under rocks or coral; having strong jaws and fangs, it can inflict a painful bite. (See: hazardous marine animals.)

blow-by [blo•by]
A leakage or loss of pressure often used with reference to leakage of compression past the piston ring between the piston and the cylinder.

blow out [blo•owt]
When a well becomes out of control due to the fluids from the formation blowing wild at the surface.

blow out plug
  (See: plug.)

blow out preventer stack [blo owt pre•ven•tur stak]
  In drilling, a system of control gates fitted at the casing head which are capable of closing around the drill pipe or casing and are designed to control a potential wild well. (See: wild well.)

blowup [blo•up]
  Uncontrolled and rapid diver ascent using a deep sea dress or variable-volume dry suit, due to positive buoyancy in conjunction with decreased water pressure.

blue mud [bloo mud]
  A common variety of deep-sea mud, having a bluish-gray color due to the presence of organic matter.

bluff bank [bluff bank]
  A bank usually located on the convex side of a river's curve which is subject to vertical plunges due to underwater erosion; hazardous to divers and surface craft.

board, head [bord, hed]
  On an oil rig, the protection board over the heads of the drillers.

BOD
  Biological Oxygen Demand.

body squeeze [bod•ee skweez]
  Squeeze caused by excessive external pressure when the diver is wearing a variable-volume dry suit with a rigid helmet, most commonly caused by falling through the water at a rapid rate, or failure of the non-return valve in the helmet exhaust system and resulting loss of air supply.

boilerhouse [boy•lur•hows]
  To make up or fake a report without actually doing the work.

boiling water reactor (BWR) [boy•ling wah•tur re•ak•tur]
  A nuclear rector that, by boiling water, produces steam directly from nuclear fission.

bollard [bal•urd]
  A strong post for holding lines fast.

boll weevil
  (See: ball weevil.)

booster [boo•stur]
  In blasting, generally a "cast primer" which boosts the detonation of a cap or cord to a level which fires blasting agents; used to increase horse power of air over compressor pressure.

bootlet [boot•let]
  Condition where a blast fails to cause total breakage of the rock, either because of insufficient explosives for the amount of material or because of incomplete detonation of the explosive.

bore [bore]
  The diameter of a hole, such as a cylinder; to enlarge a hole as distinguished from making a hole with a drill; a single high wave moving upstream at the mouth of a river, caused by incoming tide opposing river current.

borehole [bore•hole]
  In drilling, a well; in blasting, a hole drilled in rock or other material for the placement of explosives. (See: well.)

bottle [baht•ul]
  A hollow metal cylinder equipped with a narrow neck opening and retaining valve; used to contain compressed breathing gases.

bottled gas [baht•uld gas]
  Liquefied petroleum gas compressed and contained in portable cylinders.

bottom [baht•um]
  The ground under a body of water.

bottom hole differential pressure
  (See: bottom hole pressure, differential pressure.)

bottom hole pressure [baht•um hole presh•ur]
  The pressure existing at the bottom of a hole.

bottom out [baht•um•out]
  To reach the bottom.

bottom, outer [baht•um, owt•ur]
  The outer shell bottom plating of a double-bottom vessel.

bottom supported rig [baht•um suh•pore•tud rig]
  A drilling rig on a platform or structure which is supported by the ocean floor during drilling operations.

bottom time [baht•um tyme]
  The duration of elapsed time from leaving the surface to begin a dive until the completion of ascent from depth back to the surface.

bottom water [baht•um wah•tur]
  Water occurring in the formation below the oil in a well.

bounce dive [downs dyv]
  A rapid dive with a very short bottom time to minimize the time required for decompression.

bower [bow•ur]
  Anchor carried in the hawser pipe at the bow of a vessel.

bowl [bole]
  A heavy steel ring into which fit tapered slips to support a tubing string. (See: slips, tubing.)

bowl, casing [bole, kay•sing]
  A device for repairing a damaged casing string. (See: casing string.)

bowline [bo•lyn]
A knot used wherever a hitch is needed that will not slip out or jam, as in rescue work; made by forming an overhand loop, then taking the free end up through the eye, around the standing part, and back to the starting point.

boxing the compass [bahks•ing thuh kum•pus]
Naming the points and quarter points of the compass clockwise around the circle, beginning with north.

Boyle's law [Boylz law]
At a constant temperature, the volume of gas varies inversely with the pressure. (See: laws.)

brace [brays]
Diagonal transverse or longitudinal shape used to strengthen, stiffen or distribute the load between structures.

brackets [brak•uts]
Small pieces of plate, usually triangular in shape, used to join beams to frame, frame to floors, etc.

bradenhead gas [bray•dun•hed gas]
Gas produced with oil or from the casing head of an oil well; also known as casing gas.

bradycardia [bray•duh•kahrd•ee•uh]
Slowness of the heart beat, evidenced by slowing of the pulse to 60 or less per minute.

brazing [bray•zing]
A form of soldering where two metallic surfaces are joined by melting a silver-copper alloy at approximately 1200° F.

breaching [bree•ching]
The act of breaking through an obstruction.

breakers [brake•urz]
Waves broken by shore, ledge, or bar.

breaking down [brayk•ing down]
Unscrewing a drill string into "singles" when a well has been completed and the drill string is pulled out for the last time. (See: single.)

breakout [brake•owt]
To take out and prepare tools or equipment for use; the operation of unscrewing joints of pipe from the drill string. (See: drill string.)

breakwater [brake•wah•tur]
A structure built to break the force of waves.

breast hooks [brest hooks]
On a vessel, horizontal steel plates installed internally at the bow to stiffen the bow plating against panting. (See: panting.)

breathhold dive [breth•hold dyv]
A dive without breathing equipment, performed by holding the breath while underwater.

breathing air [bree•thing air]
Commercially prepared or machine-compressed air which is free of contaminants that would be injurious to a diver operating under pressure.

breathing apparatus [bree•thing ap•ur•at•us]
A device for delivering respirable breathing mixture, enabling the diver to breathe underwater; also called a breathing device.

breathing bag [bree•thing bag]
Part of the semi-closed circuit breathing apparatus used to mix gas and to assure low breathing resistance.

breathing gas [bree•thing gas]
Oxygen, or a mixture of oxygen and other gases, breathed through a supply system in diving, flying, hyperbaric chambers, and in medical treatment, or when the ambient medium is not respriable. (See: diluent gas, gas, inert gas, mixed gas, separated gas.)

breathing resistance [bree•thing re•zis•tuns]
The sum of resistance to flow within the airways and breathing apparatus.

bridge [brij]
In drilling, an obstruction in the hole due to caving formation or some similar cause such as the presence of a "fish". (See: fish.)

bridge plug [brij plug]
In drilling, a packer assembly fitted with slips and a rubber sealing sleeve which is run into a hole to isolate a down hole producing zone.

bridging [brij•ing]
The condition in which a column of explosive in a borehole is broken by either improper placement or some foreign matter plugging the hole.

bridging material [brij•ing muh•teer•ee•ul]
Fibrous material which is added to the "mud" to act as a seal. including cotton seeds, chopped hay, chopped palm, leaves, sawdust, straw, cellophane strips, torn up rags or sacking, etc. (See: mud.)

Brinell hardness [Brin•el hardd•nus]
A scale for designating the degree of hardness of a substance.

bring in [bring in]
The process of causing fluid to flow into a well from the formation, by reducing hydrostatic pressure at the reservoir face.

brisance [bree•zahns]
The shattering effect of an explosive.

bristleworm [bris•ul•wurm]
A marine animal found in the Bahamas, the Florida Keys, the Gulf of Mexico and throughout the tropical Pacific, having a row of bristles along each side which penetrate the skin and are difficult to remove. (See: hazardous marine animals.)

broach [broch]
    To veer; a vessel lying broadside to the shore as a result of wind, sea or current.

bronchi [brong•kye]
    Large tubes leading from the trachea and branching to connect to the bronchioles.

bronchiole [brong•kee•ol]
    A very small subdivision of the lung tubes; a microscopic bronchial tube leading to the alveoli. (See: alveoli.)

bull rope [bool rope]
    An endless rope used in cable tool drilling to drive the bull wheel. (See: bull wheel, cable tool drilling.)

bull wheel [bool wheel]
    Winding drum assembly used in cable tool drilling. (See: cable tool drilling.)

buoy [boo•y]
    Stationary floating object moored to the bottom with an anchor and cable.

buoyancy [boo•yun•see]
    Upward force equal to the weight of water which is displaced by an object immersed in water. (See: negative buoyancy, neutral buoyancy, positive buoyancy.)

buoyancy compensator [boo•yun•see kahm•pen•say•tur]
    A device worn and controlled by the diver to regulate buoyancy.

buoyant ascent [boo•yunt uh•sent]
    Ascent aided by an inflated flotation device. (See: ascent, emergency ascent, emergency buoyant ascent, floatation device.)

burden [bur•dun]
    In blasting, the distance from the borehole to the nearest free face at the instant the borehole charge is initiated.

bursa [bur•suh]
    A fluid-filled sac or space in the body, located in areas where friction may develop between moving parts, for example, near joints, under muscles and over bony projections.

bushing [boosh•ing]
    Steel inserts fitted into a rotary table to accommodate the kelly drive bushing. (See: kelly bushing, rotary table.)

butane [byoo•tayn]
    A petroleum hydrocarbon compound which has a boiling point of about 32 degrees F., used as engine fuel; loosely referred to as Liquefied Petroleum Gas and often combined with Propane.

butt weld [but weld]
    A weld made in the joint between two pieces of metal approximately in the same plane.

-C-

C-4
    A military high explosive.

cable tool bit [kay•bul tool bit]
    A chisel type bit used in cable tool drilling. (See: cable tool drilling.)

cable tool drilling [kay•bul tool dril•ing]
    Drilling a hole using a chisel-type bit suspended on a wire line.

caisson [kay•sahn]
    A water-tight pressure chamber used for underwater construction.

caisson disease [kay•sahn diz•eez]
    (See: decompression sickness.)

calcareous algae [kal•sair•ee•us al•gee]
    Marine plants which form a hard external covering of calcium compounds.

calf line [caff lyne]
    Wire line used in cable tool drilling to lower casing into the hole.

calf wheel [caff wheel]
    The hoisting drum on a cable tool rig which handles the calf line. (See: cable tool drilling, calf line.)

calking; caulking [kal•king]
    Forcing filler material into the seams of the planks in a boat's deck or sides, to make them watertight.

calliper log [kal•uh•pu log]
    An electric log which records on film the variations of diameter of a bore hole from total depth to the surface.

calm [cahm]
    A wind of less than one knot or one mile per hour.

calm belt [cahm belt]
    A belt of latitude in which the winds are generally light and variable.

calorie [kal•ur•ee]
    A unit of heat, the amount required to raise the temperature of 1 gram of water 1 degree Centigrade; The kilocalorie used in nutrition and metabolic studies, is the amount of heat necessary to raise 1 kilogram of water 1 degree Centigrade).

calorimeter [kal•ur•im•uh•tur]
    An instrument to measure the amount of heat given off by a substance when burned.

camber [kam•bur]
The transverse curvature of the deck of a vessel or other structure, sloping downward from the center toward the sides.

canal [kuh•nal]
An artificial watercourse cut through a land area.

capacity [kuh•pass•uh•tee]
The ability to receive, hold or absorb; the maximum amount that can be contained.

capacity plate [kap•as•it•ee playt]
Must be in full view of the operator's station. Gives maximum weight capacity and horsepower rating.

cap rock [kap rahk]
An impermeable layer of rock which overlays an oil or gas reservoir and prevents movement of fluids.

carbon [kar•bun]
A common non-metallic element which is an excellent conductor of electricity.

carbon-arc cutting [kar•bun-ahrk kut•ing]
An arc-cutting process where the severing of metals is effected by melting with the heat of an arc between a carbon electrode and the base metal.

carbon dioxide [kar•bun dy•ahks•yd]
CO_2, a colorless, odorless and tasteless gas produced by the body's metabolism, which is harmful when breathed in excessive amounts.

carbon dioxide excess
(See: hypercapnia.)

carbon monoxide [kar•bun mun•ahks•yd]
CO, a colorless, odorless and tasteless gas produced by partial combustion; cumulative and leading to asphyxiation when breathed.

carbon monoxide poisoning [kar•bun mun•ahks•yd poy•sun•ing]
Insufficient oxygen reaching the tissues, caused by carbon monoxide combining with hemoglobin in the blood and preventing the blood from carrying oxygen.

cardia [car•dya]
The cardiac orifice of the stomach, the point where it is entered by the esophagus, being to the left and in the vicinity of the heart.

cardiac [kar•dee•ak]
Pertaining to the heart.

cardiac arrest [kar•dee•ak uh•rest]
Discontinuation of the heartbeat.

cardiopulmonary [car•dyo•pul•ma•neri]
Of the heart and lungs as a unified body system.

cardiovascular [car•dyo•vas•kyr•ler]
Of the heart and blood vessels as a unified body system.

carotid [kur•aht•ud]
Relating to the principal artery extending up through the neck to the head.

carotid sinus reflex [kur•aht•ud sy•nus re•fleks]
Condition caused by pressure at the point in the neck at which the carotid artery divides, resulting in slowing of the heartbeat, dilation of the arteries, and possible fainting.

carrick bend [kar•rik bend]
A knot used for joining together large ropes; easy to untie after being subjected to strain.

case-harden [kase-har•dun]
To harden the surface of steel.

casing [kase•ing]
Steel pipe used to line a well while drilling the hole.

casing bowl [kase•ing bole]
A device for repairing a damaged casing string. (See: casing string.)

casing clamp [kas•ing klamp]
A clamp which fits around the casing being run in or pulled out of a hole.

casing collar [kas•ing kahl•ur]
A collar screwed to a casing joint for connecting the next joint to be run. (See: casing string.)

casing cutter [kas•ing kut•ur]
A device which is run on a drill string and which has cutters controlled by fluid pressure, used for milling through a casing string.

casing line [kas•ing lyne]
Steel line used on a cable tool rig for running a casing string, otherwise known as a calf line. (See: cable tool drilling, casing string.)

casing perforator [kas•ing pur•fur•ay•shun]
A device for making perforations in a casing string opposite an oil zone to allow oil to flow into the casing. (See: casing string.)

casing pressure [kas•ing presh•ur]
Gas pressure built up between a casing string and a tubing string. (See: casing string.)

casing protector [kas•ing pro•tek•shun]
A rubber sleeve fitted to the drill string to reduce wear in the casing and drill pipe joints. (See: drill string.)

casing pump [kas•ing pump]
A down hole pump fitted in the casing to pump a non-flowing well; may be powered by an electric motor or by sucker rods run by a pumping jack installed over the well head. (See: pumping jack, sucker rods.)

casing rack [kas•ing rak]
In drilling, a rack usually made of steel pipes and located outside the derrick floor on which casing lengths are stacked before running into the well.

casing ramp [kas•ing ramp]
A steel or wooden ramp from the casing rack to the derrick floor to facilitate pulling casing lengths into the derrick. (See: casing rack, derrick.)

casing shoe [kas•ing shoo]
Heavy steel tube fitted to the lower end of a casing string to protect it when it is run into the well. (See: casing string.)

casing spear [kay•sing speer]
A fishing tool which can be set inside a string of casing to recover a dropped string or other object. (See: casing string, fishing tool.)

casing string [kay•sing string]
The term used for the steel tube which lines a well, after it has been drilled, made up of section of pipe 20 ft. to 30 ft. (6.1 m to 9.1 m) in length and screwed together; a deep well, 15,000 ft. to 30,000 ft. (4,572 m to 9,144 m), may have as many as five strings of casing cemented in position.

casing tester [kay•sing test•ur]
A packing device used to locate leaks in a casing string; set in the casing with fluid pressure applied to ascertain where a leak occurs. (See: casing string, packer.)

casing tong [kay•sing tahng]
A heavy duty adjustable wrench used to tighten casing joints when running a casing string. (See: casing string.)

catamaran [kat•uh•muh•ran]
A twin-hulled boat.

catfish [kat•fish]
A fish of which some species have a stiff, venomous spine in the front part of the dorsal and pectoral fins. (See: hazardous marine animals.)

cathead [kat•hed]
A bollard, or post, on the drawworks of an offshore rig's cathead shaft used for handling a rope to pull pipe or casing tongs when making up or breaking out lengths of drill pipe or casing. (See: drawworks.)

cathode [kath•ode]
The negative pole of an electric current.

cat line [kat lyne]
A rope or combination of a rope and wire line operated by the cathead and used for lifting equipment on the derrick floor.

cat's paw [kat's paw]
A way to attach the middle of a rope to a hook that will not slip and needs no constant strain in order to hold.

catwalk [kat•wahk]
A ramp connecting the drilling rig floor to the casing rack which provides a means of pulling drill pipe or casing joints onto the rig floor.

causeway [kawz•way]
A raised road across wet or marshy ground or water.

caving [kay•ving]
In drilling, the situation where formation from the well wall caves into a hole.

cavitation [kav•uh•tay•shun]
The formation of bubbles due to a localized partial vacuum in a liquid; in the ocean, the result of the passage through water of a swiftly moving object; in the human body, caused by ultrasonic energy producing reductions in the fluid pressure.

cavity [kav•uh•tee]
In drilling, enlargement of the hole due to caving or wash out of a soft formation, in extreme cases plugged back with a cement plug and redrilled. (See: cement plugs.)

cell [sell]
A mass of protoplasm in the body, containing a nucleus.

cellar [sell•ur]
The excavation made before the drilling of a well which provides space for the installation of the surface well head equipment.

celsius [sell•se•us]
(See: temperature-celcius.)

cement head [see•ment hed]
Removable head fitted to the landing joint of a casing string to facilitate a cement job (See: casing string, cement job.)

cement hopper [see•ment hop•ur]
Funnel shaped container for dry cement, fitted at its base with a nozzle through which water is injected at high pressure to form a cement slurry; used for cementing a string of casing or setting a cement plug. (See: casing string, cement plugs, slurry.)

cement job [see•ment jahb]
The operation of cementing a casing string in the hole or setting cement plugs. (See: casing string, cement plugs.)

cement plugs [see•ment plugz]
A column of cement placed in a well bore; a few feet in length or some hundreds of feet; may be placed to seal off porous formation zones which allow the circulating mud to flow into the formation, to isolate porous formations which

could contaminate fresh water reservoirs with salt water, etc. (See: dry hole.)

cement squeeze [see•**ment** skweez]
In drilling, the forcing of cement slurry into a formation with high pressure pumps. (See: slurry.)

center of gravity [**sen**•tur uv **grav**•uh•tee]
The point of an object at which its entire weight appears to be concentrated.

centigrad (C) temperature [**sen**•tuh•grayd tem•pur•uh•choor]
Thermometric scale on which the interval between the freezing point and the boiling point of water is divided into 100 degrees with 0 degrees representing the freezing point and 100 degrees the boiling point. (See: temperature.)

centimeter [**sen**•tuh•mee•tur]
A unit of measurement, one hundredth part of a meter.

centralizer [**sen**•truh•**lyz**•ur]
In drilling, a fitting which is placed on a length of casing to hold it centrally in the hole in order to ensure a uniform sleeve of cement around the casing joint.

centrifugal force [sen•**trif**•yoo•gul fors]
A force which tends to move a body away from its center of rotation.

cephalic [se•**fa**•lik]
Combining form meaning head or skull; a., of the head, skull or cranium.

CERC
Coastal Engineering Research Center.

cerebellum [sair•uh•**bell**•um]
The part of the hindbrain that lies below the occipital part of the cerebrum on each side, concerned with the coordination of movement. (See: occipital.)

cerebrovascular [sair•uh•bro•**vas**•kyoo•lur]
Pertaining to the blood vessels of the brain.

cerebrum [sair•**ee**•brum]
The largest part of the brain located in the upper portion of the cranium, consisting of two cerebral hemispheres divided into lobes.

cerumen [suh•**roo**•mun]
Earwax.

cetacean [sec•**tay**•shun]
A marine mammal of the order *Cetacea*, which includes the whales, dolphins and porpoises.

CFFF
(See: critical flicker fusion frequency.)

CFM
(See: cubic feet per minute.)

chafing gear [**chayf**•ing geer]
In rigging, material such as canvas, wood or soft metal installed on wire or fiber rope to minimize the effects of rubbing and wearing; in diving, an overgarment worn on the body to protect a diving suit.

chamber [**chaym**•bur]
A vessel designed to withstand differential pressures. (See: altitude chamber, compression chamber, deck decompression chamber, double-lock chamber, hyperbaric chamber, monoplace chamber, multiplace chamber, single-lock chamber, submersible decompression chamber.)

chamber attendant [**chaym**•bur uh•**ten**•dunt]
A person who attends another inside a chamber.

chamfer [**cham**•fur]
The angle of a joint formed by cutting a bevel into the faces of two adjoining wood surfaces.

channel [**chan**•ul]
The deeper part of a river, harbor or strait.

channelling [**chan**•ul•ing]
In drilling, a condition where cement around a casing string is not uniform and allows fluid or gas to escape towards the surface. (See: casing string.)

charge [charj]
The explosives load in a hole; also, to load; to pass an electrical current through a battery to restore it to activity.

Charles' law [**Charlz** law]
At a constant pressure the volume of an ideal gas varies directly with the absolute temperature. (See: laws.)

chart [chart]
A map of a body of water that contains piloting information.

cheater [**chee**•tur]
A length of pipe which is slipped onto the handle of a wrench to give additional leverage.

chemical oceanography [**kem**•uh•kul oh•shun•**ahg**•ruff•ee]
The study of the chemical composition of the dissolved solids and gases, material in suspension, and acidity of ocean waters and their relationship to the atmosphere and the ocean bottom.

chert [churt]
A rock formation harder than flint; composed of non-crystalline silica, it is the most difficult rock to drill.

chert clause [churt klahz]
A clause in a drilling contract which stipulates that normal contract rates do not apply if chert

formation is encountered while drilling. (See: chert.)

chine [chine]
The intersection of sides and bottom of flat or V-bottom boats.

chip [chip]
To cut with a chisel.

choke [chok]
A removable steel orifice which may be fitted to a well flow line to restrict the flow of fluid. (See: flow line.)

choke and kill lines [chok and kill lynz]
Two lines from the side outlets in a blow out preventer stack, equipped with fail-safe or hydraulically operated valves. (See: blow out preventer stack.)

choker [chok•ur]
A short, flexible sling, rope or wire having two spliced eyes, used in rigging for lifting pipe, cylinders, etc.

chokes [choks]
Colloquial term for the pulmonary manifestations of decompression sickness. (See: decompression sickness.)

choking [chok•ing]
Running a rope around pipe once, then again, and fastening into the standing part with a pin.

choppy sea [shop•ee see]
Describing short, rough irregular wave motion on a sea surface.

Christmas tree [cris•mus tree]
The total assembly of fittings and valves on a final casing to control the rate of oil production.

CIM
Committee on International Geophysics.

circuit [sur•kut]
The path of electrical current, fluids or gases.

circular search [sur•kyoo•lur surch]
Underwater search of an area using concentric circles of increasing radius around a fixed point. (See: search patterns-underwater.)

circulating fluid
(See: mud.)

circulating head [sur•kyoo•lay•ting hed]
In drilling, a swivelling attachment for a string of drill pipe or casing to permit the pumping of circulating mud or fluid into the pipe, at the same time allowing the pipe to be rotated, raised and lowered.

circulatory system [su•kyoo•luh•tor•ee sis•tum]
All the arteries and veins through which blood is pumped through the body by the heart.

cirrocumulus [sere•o•kyoom•yoo•lus]
High clouds composed of small white flakes or small globular masses, arranged in groups or lines or in ripples resembling sand on the seashore.

cirrostratus [sere•o•strat•us]
Thin, white, high clouds covering the sky and giving it a milky appearance, or presenting a formation like a web.

cirrus [sere•us]
Detached high clouds, generally white in color and often of a silky appearance.

clamp connection [klamp kun•ek•shun]
Connection consisting of two flat face hubs and either a metal or "O" ring sealing gasket, held in alignment by clamp segments bolted together.

clay [klay]
Fine sediment with particle size smaller than approximately 0.00008 inch (0.004 millimeter); sometimes classed as mud.

clean out [kleen out]
Repair or cleaning operation in a well bore.

clearance diver [kleer•uns dyv•ur]
Explosive ordinance disposal diver (Royal Navy).

cleat [kleet]
A piece of wood or metal with projecting ends to which lines are made fast.

clinker [klin•kur]
A method of planking in which the lower edge of each strake overlaps the upper edge of the strake next below. (Also called lapstrake).

closed center [klozd sen•tur]
Hydraulic tool system in which oil flows only when power is being used.

closed circuit gas system [klozd sur•kut gas sis•tum]
A life-support system or breathing apparatus in which the gas is recycled, carbon dioxide removed, and oxygen periodically added, thus minimizing gas loss. (See: rebreather.)

closed circuit hot water suit [klozd sur•kut haht wah•tur soot]
A dry suit and special set of underwear through which heated water is circulated; pumped from a heater through a series of loops in the underwear, and back to the heat source; heater may be carried by the diver or positioned on the surface.

closed circuit scuba [klozd sur•kut skoo•buh]
A self contained underwater breathing apparatus (S.C.U.B.A.) in which the breathing gas is recirculated through purifying and oxygen replenishing systems, oxygen replenishment is controlled by oxygen sensors; no exhaled gas lost into the surrounding water. (See: scuba, semi-closed circuit scuba.)

closed in pressure [klozd in **presh**•ur]
The pressure at the well head when all production valves are closed.

close in [klos in]
A well which is capable of producing oil or gas but which is temporarily closed in at the well head.

clove hitch [klov hich]
One of the most widely used knots which passes around an object in only one direction, putting very little strain on the rope; for fastening rope to an upright or for making a line fast.

clove hitch over bar [klov hich o•vur bahr]
Like a clove hitch, but used if the bar is closed, or an upright is closed at both ends or too high to toss loops over.

CO
(See: carbon monoxide.)

CO2
(See: carbon dioxide.)

CO2 scrubber unit [**skrub**•ur yoo•nut]
Used to limit carbon dioxide concentrations in the SWC or DDC to a safe operating level; generally, granular soda sorb is used as a CO_2 high potency absorbent. (See: SWC, DDC..)

coaming [**kom**•ing]
The vertical surface fitted around the periphery of an opening on a vessel.

coast [kost]
The general region of indefinite width that extends from the sea inland to the first major change in terrain features.

coastal area [kost•ul air•7ee•uh]
The land and sea area bordering the shoreline.

coastal currents [kost•ul kur•unts]
Movements of water which generally parallel the shoreline, caused by tide or wind.

cochlea [kok•lee•uh]
That part of the inner ear which contains the organ of hearing and is sometimes affected by decompression sickness. (See: decompression sickness.)

code alpha flag [kod al•fuh flag]
A blue and white swallowtail international signal flag flown by ships when divers are in the water.

coefficient [ko•ee•fish•unt]
A number expressing the ratio of change under certain specified conditions such as temperature, length, volume, etc.

coefficient of friction [ko•ee•fish•unt uv frik•shun]
Ratio between the forces which act when one surface moves on another surface.

coefficient of thermal expansion [ko•ee•fish•unt uv thur•mul ek•span•shun]
The fractional change in length of a material per degree of temperature change as compared to the length at the reference temperature.

cofferdam [kahf•ru•kam]
A watertight structure temporarily installed on a submerged vessel in order to pump out the water and raise the vessel.

coffin jack [kahf•un jack]
Lever-operated lift-pull rigging device used for exerting lateral pull or balancing awkward loads.

coiling [koyl•ing]
Forming rope or hose into loops one atop the other; in construction, formed by sheet pilling, not neccessarily water-tight, used in bridge foundations, piers, etc.

collar [kahl•ur]
On a vessel, a plate double-fitted around a pipe at its penetration through a bulkhead or deck in order to form a watertight joint.

collar, bit [kahl•ur, bit]
In drilling, heavy duty pipe which is used to connect a rock bit to the drill string.

collar, drill
(See: drill collar.)

collar, float
(See: float collar.)

color, underwater
(See: day vision, night vision, perception of color underwater.)

color vision [kul•ur viz•shun]
The ability to see different hues as red, green, blue, etc.

column of explosive [kahl•um uv ek•splo•suv]
Explosive in a column form, such as in a well-tamped borehole.

comber [kom•ur]
A deep water wave whose crest is pushed forward by a strong wind.

combination tool [kahm•buh•nay•shun tool]
In drilling, a tool with coarse right-hand male threads on one end used for landing and retrieving the wear bushing, and hydraulic packing on the other end for pressure testing casing head housing and preventers.

combustion [kum•bus•chun]
The process of burning.

come-along [kum-uh•long]
A lever-operated lift-pull rigging device.

come in [kum in]
A situation where fluid or gas enters the well from the formation.

come out of the hole [kum owt uv thuh hol]
In drilling, the action of pulling the drill string out of the hole.

commercial production [kum•ur•shul pro•duk•shun]
Production capacity which will show a financial reward from a drilling operation.

common cap [kam•en cap]
A nonelectric blasting cap.

compass [**kum**•pus]
A device for determining geographical direction, usually consisting of a magnetic needle mounted horizontally or suspended so as to align with the magnetic field of the air.

complementary colors. [kahm•pluh•**men**•tur•ee **kul**•urz]
Pairs of colors that, when mixed together, give the appearance of white light.

completion [kum•**plee**•shun]
Refers to the installation of permanent production equipment at a well site for the production of oil or gas.

composite material [kahm•**pahz**•ut muh•**teer**•ee•ulz]
Structural materials of metal alloys or plastics with strengthening agents in the form of filaments, foils or flakes of strong material.

compound [**kahm**•pownd]
A substance made of two or more elements.

compressed air [kum•**prest air**]
Air under pressure; may be used as a breathing mixture if free from contaminants.

compressed air demand unit [kum•**prest air de•mand yoo**•nut]
A breathing device using compressed air that is delivered to the diver through a regulator, as he demands it by inhalation. (See: regulator.)

compressed air illness [kum•**prest** air il•nus]
An obsolete term for decompression sickness. (See: decompression sickness.)

compressed air narcosis
(See: nitrogen narcosis.)

compression [kum•**press**•un]
That part of a dive involving an increase in pressure upon the diver, either due to the admission of compressed gas to a chamber or to descent in the water.

compression arthralgia [kum•**presh**•un ahr•**thrall**•juh]
Pain in the joints during comrpession, particularly during rapid compression to pressures greater than 10 atmospheres. (See: arthralgia, decompression arthralgia, hyperbaric arthralgia.)

compression chamber [kum•**presh**•un **chaym**•bur]
A chamber used for compression.

compression stage [kum•**presh**•un stayj]
One of the steps taken to pressurize air.

compressive force [kum•**pres**•uv fors]
The squeezing together of material.

compressor [kum•**press**•ur]
A machine that raises air or gas to a pressure above one atmosphere.

concentricity [kahn•sen•**tris**•uh•tee]
Two or more circles with a common center; in circular seals, the concentricity of the mating members is critical to effective sealing.

condensate [**kahn**•den•sayt]
Hydrocarbons, in the gaseous state under reservoir conditions, which become liquid either as they rise up the well hole or at the surface due to reduced pressure conditions.

condensation [kahn•den•**say**•shun]
The physical process by which a vapor becomes a liquid or solid.

condenser discharge [kun•**den**•sur dis•charj]
A blasting machine that uses electric power to charge a series of condensers; activation of the firing switch releases the energy stored in the condensers and initiates the caps.

conductance [kun•**duk**•tuns]
The ability of a material to conduct an electric current.

conduction [kun•**duk**•shun]
The transfer of energy within and through a conductor by means of internal particle of molecular activity, and without any net external motion.

conduction impairment [kun•**duk**•shun im•**pair**•munt]
A hearing decrement caused by damage to the ear drum or auditory ossicles.

conductor [kun•**duk**•tur]
In drilling, a large diameter pipe which extends from beneath the rotary table to the starting point of the well; provides a means of returning the circulating fluid to the mud screen on its return from the well bore. (See: rotary table.)

conductor [kun•**duk**•tur]
A material through which electricity will flow with slight resistance.

conductor pipe [kun•**duk**•tur pyp]
The first string of pipe set in a well, usually 100-300 feet long.

cone bit [kon bit]
A rock bit with cone-shaped cutters mounted on roller bearings.

cone shell [kon shel]
A shell animal of which there are more than 500 species throughout the world; every one producing a venom peculiar to its species which may affect some animals but not others; six species are considered deadly to humans. (See: hazardous marine animals.)

confinement [kun•fyn•munt]
The enclosing of an explosive in a solid material.

confused sea [kun•fyoozd see]
A disturbed water surface without a single direction of wave travel.

conjunctivitis [kun•junk•uh•vyt•us]
Inflammation of the conjunctiva (mucus membrane) of the eye.

connecting wire [kun•ek•ting wyr]
Any wire used in a blasting circuit to extend the length of a leg wire or leading wire.

connection [kun•ek•shun]
The joining of two lengths of pipe.

connector [kun•ek•tur]
In blasting, a device used to connect two parts of a detonating cord circuit; may or may not incorporate a delay element.

constant volume dry suit [kahn•stunt vahl•yoom dry soot]
A dry suit designed to be partially inflated to prevent squeeze and to provide insulation against cold.

continental shelf [kahn•tuh•nen•tul shelf]
A zone adjacent to a continent or around an island extending from the low water line to the depth (usually 200 to 250 meters) at which there is a marked increase in slope.

control console [kun•trol kahn•sol]
A panel of displays and controls used to manage a diving system.

control tower [kun•trol tow•ur]
Center on a pipe lay barge from which the anchors are controlled, allowing the barge to move ahead as sections of pipe are completed.

control van [kun•trol van]
The place where control and monitoring of a dive system are maintained by instruments and equipment by the rack operator, life support technician, and dive supervisor, and where auxiliary and support systems are channelled to the diving bell (SWC) and decompression facility (DDC).

convection [kun•vek•shun]
TRansmission of heat or electricity by the mass movement of heated or electric particles, as in air, gas or liquid currents.

convulsion [kun•vul•shun]
A violent involuntary contraction of voluntary muscles usually accompanied by loss of consciousness.

coral [kor•ul]
A marine organism whose sharp, calcerous edges can cause wounds which are generally superficial but very slow to heal; secondary infection from coral wounds is common. (See: hazardous marine animals.)

coral reef [kor•ul reef]
A ridge or mass of limestone built up of material deposited around a framework of the skeletal remains of mollusks, colonial coral and massive calcareous algae.

core [kor]
That area within a layer of water where temperature, salinity, velocity, etc., reach extreme values; a soild bar of the formation being drilled which is recovered by using a core barrel; a vertical, cylindrical sample of bottom sediments that allows a geologist to determine the nature and stratification of the bottom. (See: core barrel.)

core barrel [kor bair•ul]
A tubular device with a bit on the end, used to recover a solid bar of the formation being drilled.

core bit [kor bit]
An annular type bit which screws to the lower end of a core barrel and cuts a cylindrical bar of the formation, which is then retained in the core barrel by the core catcher. (See: core catcher.)

core catcher [kor kach•ur]
A spring ring, or a fitting with spring loaded fingers, located at the lower end of a core barrel to provide the means of retaining a core in the barrel.

corer [kor•ur]
A metal or plastic tube that can be driven into the bottom sediments.

coring [kor•ing]
The process of recovering cores from the wall of a hole already drilled, with a hydraulic or gun type device which forces small core retainers into the wall and obtains samples for examination.

corium [kor•ee•um]
The deeper part of the skin found below the epidermis; the dermis or true skin, containing blood vessels, nerves and connective tissue.

cornea [kor•nee•uh]
The transparent front part of the eyeball.

coronary [kor•uh•nair•ee]
Refers to structures that encircle a part or organ in a crownlike manner; for example, the coronary arteries encircling the base of the heart.

cor pulmonale [kor **pull**•mun•ayl]
Heart disease secondary to disease of the lungs or of their blood vessels.

corrosion [kur•roz•shun]
Eating away or deterioration due to interaction of two materials; most familiar example is the rusting of carbon steel.

corrosion [kur•roz•shun]
The destruction of a metal or alloy by chemical or electrochemical reaction with the environment.

corrosion fatigue [kur•roz•shun fuh•**teeg**]
When a metallic structure subjected to a corrosive environment, and repeated or alternating stresses, fails due to the development of a crack.

counter [**kown**•tur]
The section of a vessel which extends abaft of the sternpost and overhands the aperture and rudder. (See: abaft.)

counterdiffusion [kownt•ur•duh•**fyooz**•shun]
The movement of two inert gases in opposing directions through a semipermeable membrane.

couple [**kup**•ul]
Two equal forces acting in opposite directions along parallel lines, tending to produce rotation.

cove [kov]
A small, sheltered recess in a shore or coast.

cover bubbles
(See: silent bubbles.)

covered electrode [kuv•urd e•**lek**•trod]
A filler-metal electrode used in arc welding; consists of a metal core wire with a thick covering which provides protection for the molten metal and stabilizes the arc.

cowls [kowls]
Hooded openings used for ventilation.

crack a valve [krak uh valv]
To open a valve slightly to allow a very small flow of fluid.

crater [**kray**•tur]
A depression at the end of a weld.

cratering [**kray**•tur•ing]
The use of explosives in boreholes without adjacent free faces to produce a crater-shaped excavation.

creep strength [kreep strength]
The rate of continuous deformation of pipe under stress at a specified temperature.

crest [krest]
The maximum height of a wave.

crest of wave [krest uv wayv]
The highest part of a wave.

crimpers [**krim**•purz]
In demolition, a tool used for crimping blasting caps to a safety fuse.

critical flicker fusion frequency (CFFF)
[krit•uh•kul **flik**•ur fyooz•shun **free**•kwen•see]
The frequency at which a flickering visual stimulus appears to become continuous; used to measure neurological changes; commonly CFF without the final letter.

cross sea [krahs see]
A series of waves or swells crossing another wave system.

crown block [krown blahk]
The sheave assembly at the top of a derrick or mast which accommodates the hoisting line from the drawworks drum to the travelling block. (See: drawworks, travelling block.)

crown knot/back splice [krown naht/bak splys]
A splice which forms a smooth rope end by weaving end strands back down into the rope.

crucible cast steel [kroo•sub•ul kast steel]
Low tensile wire, not frequently used in rigging.

crude oil [krood oil]
Oil in its crude form direct from the formation being drilled.

cryogenics [kry•o•**jen**•iks]
Refers to the study, production or utilization of low temperatures.

CSIGY
Special Committee for International Geophysical Year.

CTFM
Continuous Transmission Frequency Modulation; a type of sonar that sends out a continuous sonic beam that is reflected off hard objects.

cubic feet per minute (CFM) [**kyoo**•bik feet pur **min**•ut]
The total volume of air drawn into a cylinder before compression.

cumulonimbus [kyoo•myoo•low•**nim**•bus]
A huge cloud whose summits rise in the form of mountains or towers.

cumulus [**kyoo**•myoo•lus]
A dense cloud with vertical development, having a horizontal base and dome-shaped upper surface.

current [**kur**•unt]
A horizontal movement of the water.

CURVE [kurv]
Controlled Underwater Research Vehicle; an unmanned, tethered vehicle for salvage and recovery to 7,000 feet.

cushion [**koosh**•un]
A horizontal movement of water, classified as tidal or nontidal; tidal currents are cuased by forces of the sun and moon and generally rise and fall at regular intervals accompanied by movement in bodies of water; nontidal currents include the permanent currents in the general circulatory systems of the sea as well as temporary currents arising from weather conditions.

cushion chamber [**koosh**•un **chaym**•bur]
A small tank that reduces the surge from piston action.

CUSS
Continental, Union, Shell and Superior Oil Companies' barge and drill rib.

cutaneous [kyoo•**tay**•nee•us]
Pertaining to the skin

cutaneous reflex[kyoo•**tay**•nee•us reflex]
Common gooseflesh.

cutaneous respiration[kyoo•**tay**•nee•us respiration]
The transpiration of gas through the skin.

cut/burnoff ratio [kut/**burn**•ahf **ray**•sho]
In burning or cutting with electrodes, the linear inches of metal cut per inch of electrode consumed.

cutoff [**kut**•ahf]
In demolition, the cutting of a time fuse or detonating cord line by another or part of the same piece of burning time fuse, or by exploding detonating cord so that some or all of the charges do not detonate.

cut oil [kut oyl]
Oil that contains water; also known as wet oil.

cutting nozzle
(See: cutting tip.)

cuttings [**kut**•ingz]
In drilling, the chippings from the formation which return to the surface in the drilling mud and are separated out by the vibrating screen. (See: vibrating screen.)

cutting tip [**kut**•ing tip]
That part of an oxygen-cutting torch from which the gases issue.

cutting torch [**kut**•ing torch]
A device used in oxygen cutting for controlling the gases used for preheating and the oxygen used for cutting the metal.

CV
(See: control van.)

Cv
Flow co-efficient; the number of gallons per minute of water that will flow through a device in the open position with a one p.s.i. pressure differential; a measurement of valve flow capacity.

CWEB cap [kap]
Copper wire electric blasting cap.

cyanosis [sigh•uh•**no**•sus]
Blueness of the skin due to insufficient oxygenation of the blood.

cycle fatigue life [**sy**•kul fuh•**teeg** lyf]
A specific value of usable service for a system or component based upon varied combinations of pressurizations and the number of times the material has been stressed.

cyclodial waves [sy•**klo**•dee•ul wayvz]
Refers to the shape of inshore waves that are short and shoppy, and forceful when produced by strong winds.

cylinder [**sil**•un•dur]
In diving, a compressed breathing gas container. (See: bottle.)

cytoplasm [**sy**•to•plaz•'m]
That part of a cell outside the nucleus and within the cell membrane, the protoplasm of a cell with the exception of that of the nucleus cell.

-D-

Dalton's law [**dahl**•tunz law]
The partial pressure of a given quantity of gas is the pressure it would exert if it alone occupied the same volume; the total pressure of a mixture of gases is the sum of the partial pressures of the components of the mixture. (See: laws.)

damping [**dam**•ping]
Dissipation of energy with time or distance.

danger buoy [**daynj**•ur **boo**•y]
A buoy marking an isolated danger to navigation, such as a rock, shoal or sunken wreck.

dark water [dahrk **wah**•tur]
When underwater visibility is reduced to a minimum by material in suspension or by lack of natural light.

dart [dahrt]
Special fluid pressure diverting device used to plug off some fluid passages and open others.

datum [**day**•tum]
Any numerical or geometrical quantity which may serve as a reference for other quantities; plural: data.

davit [da•vut]
A small crane for hoisting.

DAWS
An atmospheric diving system (ADS); diver alternative work system.

day tour [day toor]
The shift period worked by a drilling crew from 0800 hours to 1600 hours.

day vision [day viz•zhun]
Normal vision which includes color perception. (See: night vision, perception of color underwater.)

DC
Direct current; electric current which flows only in one direction; in welding, an arc welding process where the power supply at the arc is direct current.

DCEN
(See: straight polarity.)

DCEP
(See: reversed polarity.)

DDC
(See: deck decompression chamber.)

dead air space [ded air spays]
Space in diving equipment and in the human respiratory system that receives minimum ventilation.

dead center [ded sen•tur]
The extreme upper or lower position of crankshaft throw at which the piston is not moving in either direction.

deadline [del•lyn]
The block line which is anchored to the dead line anchor and extends from the floor to the crown block. (See: anchor-deadline, crown block.)

deadline anchor
(See: anchor-deadline.)

dead rise [ded ryz]
On a vessel, the amount of vertical rise of the bottom from the keel to the turn of the bilge, also called the rise of floor.

debilitation [dee•bil•i•tay•shun]
The act of weakening; the state of being weakened.

debris [duh•bree]
Wreckage or junk, the result of destruction or discard.

decanting [de•kant•ing]
Colloquially used by caisson workers to indicate surface decompression.

decibel [des•uh•bul]
A unit for measuring the relative loudness of sound.

deck beam [dek beem]
A horizontal transverse shape connecting the port and starboard shell frames of a vessel; the deck plating is secured on top of the deck beams.

deck decompression chamber [dek de•kum•presh•un chaym•bur]
A hyperbaric chamber which is an integral part of a deep diving system, located on a surface platform from which diving is coducted.

deck girder [dek gurd•ur]
On a vessel, a horizontal structural, attached beneath the deck beams to distribute the load on deck to the stanchions.

deck modules [dek mah•joolz]
Steel boxes containing equipment and machinery ready for assembly on the deck of a production platform at sea.

decks [deks]
Working platforms supported by the jacket of an offshore drilling structure. (See: jacket.)

deck stringer plate [dek streeng•ur playt]
On a vessel, the heavier outboard strake of the main deck plating.

decompression [de•kum•presh•un]
Releasing from pressure or compression;following a specific decompression table or procedure during ascent; ascending in the water or experiencing decreasing pressure in the chamber.

decompression accident [de•kum•presh•un ak•suh•dent]
An occurrence of decompression sickness; colloquially, a hit.

decompression arthralgia [de•kum•presh•un ahr•thral•juh]
Pain in the joints during decompression. (See: arthralgia, compression arthralgia, decompression, hyperbaric arthralgia.)

decompression chamber [de•kum•presh•un chaym•bur]
An enclosed space used to gradually decrease pressure to which a diver is exposed, from ambient underwater pressure back to 1 atmosphere.

decompression dive [de•kum•presh•un dyv]
Any dive deep enough or long enough to require controlled decompression following its completion.

decompression meter [de•kum•presh•un mee•tur]
A device which automatically computes decompression requirements based on depth and time of exposure; more precisely termed decompression computer.

decompression schedule [de•kum•presh•un sked•jool]
A set of depth-time relationships and instructions for controlling pressure reduction.

decompression sickness [de•kum•**presh**•un **sik**•nus]
A condition caused by the formulation of inert gas bubbles in the tissues and circulatory system as a result of releasing pressure too rapidly. (See: bends, caisson's disease, diver's disease.)

decompression table [de•kum•**presh**•un **tay**•bul]
A tabulation of decompression schedules.

deep sea diving suit [deep see **dyv**•ing soot]
A dry diving suit with helmet, weights, boots and umbilical; also called hard-hat, heavy gear, deep sea dress.

deep-sea dress
(See: suits - diving.)

deep scattering layer [deep **skat**•uring **lay**•ur]
The stratified population of organisms in most ocean waters which scatter sound.

DEER
Directional Explosive Echo Ranging.

deflagration [de•fluh•**gray**•shun]
The rapid burning or combustion resulting from medium-order explosive detonation.

deflecting tool [de•**flek**•ting tool]
A wedge or other tool used for deflecting a hole from vertical.

deflection [de•**flek**•shun]
Deviation of a hole from true vertical.

degassing [de•**gas**•ing]
In drilling, the removal of gas from the formation oil by the use of separators or a similar plant at the surface.

dehydration [de•hy•**dray**•shun]
A condition due to excessive water loss from the body or its parts.

delay blasting [de•**lay blast**•ing]
Any blasting circuit which utilizes delay elements to obtain a desired time sequence for the detonation of a series of two or more charges.

delay element [de•**lay el**•uh•munt]
That portion of a blasting cap or connector which causes a delay between the instant of initiation and the time of detonation.

delta [**del**•ta]
An area of alluvial deposit, usually triangular in outline, near the mouth of a river.

demand mask [de•**mand** mask]
A diving mask having a demand regulator which activates the gas supply by the negative pressure associated with inhalation. (See: regulator.)

demand regulator
(See: regulator.)

demand system [de•**mand sis**•tum]
Diver life support equipment in which gas flows only during diver's inhalation and exhalation.

demolition assembly [**dem**•uh•**lish**•un uh•**sem**•blee]
A military designation for a group of charges packaged for combined or individual use.

density [**den**•suh•tee]
The ratio of the mass of any object to the volume of the object; in oceanography, equivalent to specific gravity.

density of loading [**den**•suh•tee uv **lode**•ing]
(See: loading density.)

depth [depth]
The vertical distance from a specified sea level to the sea floor.

depth gauge [depth gayj]
A pressure-sensitive meter used to determine depth.

depth of burial [depth uv **bair**•ee•ul]
The depth of the center of an explosive below the surface of the material to be excavated.

depth of fusion [depth uv **fyoo**•zhun]
In welding, the distance from the surface of the base metal to the point in the joints where fusion ceases.

depth recorder [depth re•**kord**•ur]
An instrument used to obtain a pictorial record of the ocean bottom.

dermatitis [**dur**•muh•**ty**•tus]
Inflammation of the skin.

derrick [**dair**•ik]
A tower-like structure built over the spot selected as the site for a well to be drilled.

derrick barges [**dair**•ik **barj**•uz]
Large barges having a crane used for lifting heavy equipment onto an offshore platform. (See: production platform.)

derrick man
(See: drilling crew.)

desanders [de•**san**•durz]
In drilling, a series of centrifuges used to remove sand particles from the circulating fluid on its return from the well and after it has passed over the vibrating screen. (See: vibrating screen.)

design pressure [de•**zyn presh**•ur]
A pressure rating of a component established by physical characteristics and stress analysis.

desilter [de•**sil**•tur]
In drilling, a series of centrifuges used to remove very fine particles from the circulating fluid on its return from the well and after it has passed over the vibrating screen and through the desander. (See: desander, vibrating screen.)

DESO
Double end shut-off.

detonating cord [det•uh•nay•ting kord]
A plastic-covered core of high-velocity explosive in cord form, used to transmit a detonation from one point to another.

detonation [det•uh•**nay**•shun]
The rapid change of an explosive from a solid or liquid form to a gaseous state.

detonation pressure [det•uh•**nay**•shun presh•ur]
The pressure of the detonation shock wave formed by an explosion.

detonation velocity [det•uh•**nay**•shun vuh•**lahs**•uh•tee]
The rate at which the detonation wave travels through an explosive.

detonator [det•uh•nay•tur]
Caps or detonating cord used in blasting.

devil's claw [dev•ulz klaw]
A hook-shaped clamp, forked to engage a link of anchor chain and hold the anchor and chain while the windlass is disengaged. (See: windlass.)

dewpoint [dyoo•point]
The temperature at which air becomes saturated and produces dew.

diabetic coma [dy•uh•bet•ik ko•muh]
An involved medical condition which, over-simplified, may be said to be brought about by too much sugar in the blood.

diagonal lashing [dy•ag•uh•nul lash•ing]
In rigging, used to lash together two spars that do not touch where they cross.

diamond hitch [dy•mund hich]
A rigging hitch having the advantage of becoming tighter from a pull on any section of the line.

diaphragm [dy•uh•fram]
A large muscle separating the chest from the abdomen; when breathing, the diaphragm pushes the intestines down to create more potential volume, thus decreasing the pressure so air from outside enters to equalize the pressure.

diastole [dy•uh•stole]
The period of relaxed dilatation of the heart muscle, especially of the ventricles; adjective: diastolic.

die collar [dy kahl•ur]
A fishing tool used to recover drill pipe lost in a hole; capable of cutting threads and screwed onto the top of a fish usually by a string of drill pipe which is threaded with left hand threads. (See: fish, fishing tool.)

diesel engine [dee•sul en•jun]
Named after its developer, Dr. Rudolph Diesel, an engine that ignites the fuel in the cylinder from the heat generated by compression.

differential pressure [dif•ur•en•chul presh•ur]
The difference between the absolute pressures of two locations.

differential pressure, bottom hole [dif•ur•en•chul presh•ur, baht•um hol]
In drilling, the difference between the pressure existing at the bottom of the hole due to the fluid column in the hole, and the flowing bottom hole pressure of the formation fluids.

diffraction [di•frak•shun]
The process which allows sound waves to bend around obstacles in their path.

diffusion [di•fyoo•zhun]
The process in which particles of liquids, gases or solids intermingle as the result of spontaneous movement caused by thermal agitation and, in dissolved substances, move from a region of higher to lower concentration. (See: perfusion.)

diffusion dead space [di•fyoo•zhun•ded•spays]
the fraction of gas in the lung that does not diffuse due to damage to the intra-pulmonary diffusion capability.

digestive system [di•jest•uv sis•tum]
The organs of the body that accomplish the assimilation of food.

dilation [dy•lay•shun]
Enlargement of the pupil of the eye.

diluent gas [di•loo•unt gas]
Inert gas used in breathing mixtures to dilute oxygen to physiologically acceptable limits.

dip meter [dip me•tur]
A device for measuring the angle of dip of a formation; run on an electric cable and the information recorded on film by the recording unit at the surface.

directional drilling [dur•ek•shun•ul dril•ing]
The controlled changing of direction of a hole from true vertical.

directional gyro [dur•ek•shun•ul jy•ro]
Also known as a free gyro, a type of compass with a drift of several degrees per hour, as well as the rotation of the earth; relatively inaccurate.

dished plates [disht playts]
On a vessel, describing the shape of the flat plate keel when it is slightly flanged upward where it joins the garboard strakes. (See: flat plate keel, garboard strake.)

dislocation waves [dis•lo•kay•shun wayvz]
Inaccurately called tidal waves; caused by underwater landslide, earthquake, or volcanic eruption; also called seismic waves.

displacement [dis•plays•munt]
The weight of water displaced by a body floating in it, this weight being equal to the weight of the body.

displacement hull [dis•plays•ment hul]
Type of hull that plows through the water even when more power is added.

dissolved gas [duh•**zahlvd** gas]
Natural gas which is in solution with crude oil in a reservoir; also, gas dissolved into the body tissue of a diver.(See: gas - natural.)

diurnal [dy•**ur**•nul]
Describing the daily rise and fall of tide; daytime, as opposed to nighttime.

dive [dyv]
An exposure to increased pressure whether underwater or in a hyperbaric chamber. (See: air dive, breath hold dive, decompression dive, excursion dive, mixed gas dive, no decompression dive, repetitive dive, saturation dive.)

dive at altitude [dyv at al•tuh•tood]
A dive conducted at any significant altitude above sea level. (See: altitude corrections.)

diver's palsy [**dyv**•urz **pahl**•zee]
Paralysis assiciated with serious decompression sichness. (See: decompression sickness.)

diverter [duh•**vur**•tur]
In drilling, a wedge-shaped piece in the vertical run of the underwater Christmas tree for directing objects coming up the tubing into a side outlet.

diving bell
(See: bell.)

diving gas
(See: breathing gas.)

diving physics
(See: physics of diving.)

diving physiology
(See: physiology of diving.)

diving stage [**dyv**•ing stayj]
A suspended platform on which the diver can be lowered into or raised from the water.

diving suit
(See: suits - diving.)

diving system [**dyv**•ing **sis**•tum]
A system composed of three basic subsystems which can be used in various combinations: (1) a surface support ship or platform; (2) a deck decompression chamber used to decompress divers on the surface; (3) a tethered capsule used to transport divers from the surface to the underwater work site.

diving trim [**dyv**•ing trim]
Refers to a submarine balanced so that flooding of ballast, safety and buoyancy tanks will cause it to submerge evenly.

DOB
(See: depth of burial.)

documented vessel [dok•u•men•ted ves•ul]
Vessel registered with the U.S. Coast Guard.

dog house [dahg hows]
Drillers' office on the derrick floor which houses the lazy bench and knowledge box. (See: lazy bench, knowledge box.)

dog leg [dahg leg]
In drilling, a bend in the hole.

dolphin [**dahl**•fun]
A cluster of numerous piles driven adjacent to each other and bound together with wire rope, clamps, and through bolts; used to fend and warp vessels while docking. (See: warp.)

dome [dom]
A geological structure resembling a dome which, if it has a cap rock, may contain oil or gas. (See: cap rock.)

Donald Duck effect [**Dahn**•uld Duk uh•fect]
Changes in the quality of the voice caused by breathing light gases, such as helium. (See: helium.)

dope [dop]
A lubricant of the consistency of medium thick grease, used on drill pipe and casing threads when making up a string of pipes; also, the mastic coating applied to bare pipe after welding together.

dope station [dop **stay**•shun]
The final work station at the stern of a pipe lay barge, from which pipe is pushed into the water. (See: lay barge.)

Doppler
(See: silent bubbles.)

Doppler detector [**dahp**•lur de•**tek**•tur]
In diving, a device employing the Doppler effect to detect moving bubbles in the circulation; also called Doppler flow meter and Doppler monitor.

Doppler effect [**dahp**•lur uh•**fekt**]
A physical principle based upon changes in the frequency of sound reflected from moving objects.

dorsal [**dor**•sul]
Toward or pertaining to the back, or upper, surface.

double [**dub**•ul]
Two joints of drill pipe screwed together to form a stand approximately 60 ft. (18.3 m.) in length. (See: drill pipe, stand.)

double blackwall [**dub**•ul **blak**•wahl]
A rigging hitch somewhat safer than the single blackwall, but considered temporary. (See: single blackwall.)

double board [dub•ul bord]
In drilling, a platform erected in the derrick to allow the derrick man to handle doubles. (See: double.)

double bottom [dub•ul baht•um]
Describing a vessel fitted with bottom tanks extending from the bottom plating approximately 4 feet high to the inner bottom plating or tank top. (See: tank top.)

double box [dub•ul bahks]
A connector, screwed double female with fast tapered threads, to accommodate two drill pipes pins. (See: pin.)

double carrick bend [dub•ul kair•ik ̦bend]
A knot with the same properties as the single carrick, except that it is begun with an underhand loop in the left-hand rope instead of a bight, with the result that there are two crossovers instead of one; used on large hawsers for towing ships.

double lock chamber [dub•ul lahk chaym•bur]
A chamber wtih two compartments that can be pressurized independently.

double Matthew Walker knot [dub•ul math•hyoo wahk•ur naht]
A knot differing from the single Matthew Walker knot in that the ends are carried through a third bight, forming three interlocked overhand knots.

double pin [dub•ul pin]
A connector with fast tapered double male threads to accommodate two drill pipe boxes. (See: tool joint.)

doubler [dub•lur]
On a vessel, a steel plate of small dimensions used to reinforce openings in the hull for additional strength.

doughnut [doe•nut]
In drilling, a ring of wedges fitted with slips that supports a string of drill pipe, casing, or tubing. (See: slips.)

down hole pump [down hol pump]
A pump which is installed in a non-flowing well below the oil level, and operated by a pumping jack or a down hole electric motor. (See: pumping jack.)

draft [draft]
The depth to which a vessel is submerged.

drag [drag]
Said of a vessel which is trimmed by the stern.

drag bit [drag bit]
A blade type cutting bit.

drain holes [drayn holz]
Small holes drilled in the way of the bottom of longitudinals and floors to facilitate the draining of liquids when pumping.

drawworks [draw•wurks]
The main winch, mounted on the derrick floor of a drilling rig, which handles the power for raising and lowering drill pipe and casing loads, and for rotating the drill pipe.

drill collar [dril kahl•ur]
In drilling, heavy sections of pipe in the drill string above the rock bit, providing weight on the bit and stabilizing the drill string. (See: drill string.)

driller
(See: drilling crew.)

drill gauge [dril gayj]
The diameter of a drill bit.

drilling [dril•ing]
The operation of boring a hole in the earth's crust for the production of hydrocarbons, steam or water; or to obtain geological information by examination of the formation cuttings.

drilling, cable tool [dril•ing, kay•bul tool]
The method of drilling a hole using a chisel-type bit suspended on a wire line, with pulverized rock removed by a bailer or sand pump. (See: bailer)

drilling crew [dril•ing kroo]
All the men working on a rig at one time, alternating to provide 24-hour operation: drilling superintendent, in charge of the drilling operation; tool pusher, responsible to the superintendent for day-to-day operations and for the availability of equipment, tools, materials and services; driller, responsible for his crew and the running of the rig during his 8- or 12-hour tour; sometimes a trainee driller; derrick man, who is responsible for the handling and racking of drill pipe stands; roughneck, who works on the derrick floor handling the placement of slips to support the drill string; roustabout, who handles the loading and unloading of equipment and assists in operations.

drilling, diamond [dril•ing, dy•mund]
Diamond drilling rigs are commonly used for mineral investigation when cores of the formation are required for analysis; rotary system is used but the bits are set with industrial diamonds and rotary speeds are much higher than those used in oil well drilling; also used for directional drilling of oil wells.

drilling in [dril•in in]
Term used when a well is drilled into the producing formation.

drilling log
(See: log-drilling.)

drilling mud
(See: mud.)

drilling out [dril•ing owt]
Term used for drilling residue cement at the bottom of a casing string after a cement job. (See: casing string, cement job.)

drilling, percussion [dril•ing, pur•kush•un]
One form of percussion drilling is the cable tool method; percussion hammers are also used with the rotary system in situations where compressed air circulation is possible when there is no formation fluid to flow into the hole. (See: drilling-cable tool.)

drilling platform [dril•ing plat•form]
A structure or ship from which offshore drilling operations are conducted.

drilling, rotary [dril•ing, roe•tur•ee]
System of oil well drilling where a rock bit is rotated by a string of drill pipe extending from the surface to the bottom of the hole; cuttings from the hole removed by circulating mud, water or air through the drill pipe, and returning them to surface in the space between the drill pipe and the well wall. (See: drill pipe, mud, rock bit.)

drilling spool [dril•ing spool]
A spacer fitted into the wellhead; may act as an adaptor for connecting two items with unlike flanges, i.e., a blow out preventer stack to a casing string. (See: blow out preventer stack, casing string.)

drilling superintendent
(See: drilling crew.)

drill pipe [dril pyp]
High grade pipe which is screwed together to make up the drill string. (See: drill string.)

drill ship [dril ship]
A Self-propelled mono hulled vessel with a drilling rig which can be moved from place to place.

drill stem test [dril stem test]
In drilling, a method of testing the potential production from a reservoir formation.

drill string [dril string]
In drilling, a column of drill pipe, made up of singles and drill collars, which extends from the surface to the bottom of the hole.

drive shoe [dryv shoo]
A short length of heavy pipe run on the lower end of a casing string to be forced into a hole. (See: casing string.)

drowning [drown•ing]
Suffocation or strangulation in water or other liquid.

dry battery [dry bat•ur•ee]
A complete battery unit which does not contain liquid electrolyte; also, dry cell.

dry boat [dry bot]
A submersible, dry inside, that operates at one-atmosphere by use of a pressure hull.

dry cell [dry sell]
A primary cell having an electrolyte in the form of moist paste.

dry hole [dry hol]
A non-producing well, also known as a duster.

dry rot [dry rot]
A fungus decay which causes wood to become soft and to fall apart.

dry submersible [dry sub•mur•suh•bul]
A submersible in which the occupants are maintained in a dry environment at near atmospheric conditions. (See: lock-out submersible, self-propelled submersible, submersible, and wet submersible.)

dry suit [dry soot]
Protective diving garment which is completely sealed to prevent water entry.

dry suit squeeze [dry soot skweez]
A squeeze consisting of pinching of the skin in the folds of a dry suit, caused by insufficient pressure inside the suit during descent.

DSL
Deep Scattering Layer; a stratified popultion of organisms in the ocean which reflect or scatter sound.

DSRVG
Deep Submergence Review Vehicle Group; created by the U.S. Navy in 1963.

dual completion [doo•ul kum•plee•shun]
Said of a well which will produce from two separate reservoir formations at different levels, and has two strings of production tubing to isolate each producing formation from the other.

ductility [duk•til•uh•tee]
The property which allows deformation under tension without rupture.

dump [dump]
To expel gas into the water.

dump system [dump sis•tum]
A system built into a chamber which transports exhaled gas out of the chamber to prevent oxygen buildup; also, overboard dump system. (See: chamber.)

duplex pump [doo•pleks pump]
A two cylinder, double acting pump with interchangeable liners and pistons; used for handling

the circulating mud or fluid when drilling a well. (See: mud.)

durometer [dur•**ahm**•uh•tur]
An instrument for measuring the hardness of rubber; measures the resistance of the penetration of an indentor point into the surface of rubber.

duster
(See: dry hole.)

dutchman [**duch**•mun]
The part of a stud or screw which remains in place after twisting off.

Dutchman's log [**duch**•munz lahg]
A buoyant object thrown overboard to determine the speed of a vessel.

dynamic seal [dy•**nam**•ik seel]
A seal in pipe required to prevent leakage past parts which are in relative motion.

dynamo [**dy**•nuh•mo]
A generator of electricity.

dysbaric osteonecrosis [dis•**bair**•ik ahs•tec•oh•nek•**ro**•sus]
Changes in the structure of bone in which the radiographic density of the affected bone is increased by sclerosis; found in caisson workers and divers, associated with inadequate decompression; also aseptic bone necrosis and avascular bone necrosis.

dysbarism [dis•**bair**•iz•um]
An imprecise term denoting any pathological condition caused by a change pressure; includes but is not synonymous with decompression sickness. (See: decompression sickness.)

dyspnea [disp•nee•uh]
Shortness of breath out of proportion to physical exertion.

-E-

ead
(See: equivalent air depth.)

eagre
(See: bore.)

ear drum
(See: tympanic membrane.)

ear squeeze [eer•skweez]
A symptom complex resulting from pressure imbalance, causing symptoms ranging from pain to hemorrhage and/or rupture of the tympanic membrane of the ear.

ebb current [ebb•**kur**•unt]
The movement of tidal current away from shore or down a tidal stream; a tide that is flowing out or causing a lower water level.

echocardiography [ek•o•kahr•dee•ah•grof•ee]
A method for detecting abnormalities of the heart using high-frequency sound impulses.

ecology [ek•**ahl**•uh•jee]
The natural environment of the earth in which organisms can live in natural relationships between themselves and the environment.

ECU
(See: environmental control unit.)

eddy [**ed**•ee]
A circular movement of water, in a comparatively limited area, formed on the side of a main current; may be created at a point where the mainstream passes a projection or meets an opposite current.

edema [uh•**deem**•uh]
The presence of abnormallu large amounts of fluid in the extravascular spaces of the body; swelling.

edge water [edj•**wah**•ter]
Water in a formation on the outer rim of an oil reservoir which, in certain circumstances, provides water drive to produce the field. (See: water drive.)

eel grass [eel•gras]
Long, thin, green strands which grow along the coast in rocky areas.

effusion [e•**fyoo**•shun]
The escape of fluid into a space or part; also, the fluid that has escaped.

ejecta [e•**jek**•tuh]
In blasting, a material thrown out of the limits of the crater formed by a cratering shot.

elastic limit [e•**las**•tik **lim**•ut]
The greatest stress which a material can stand and still return to its original size or shape upon removal of the load.

elastic work [ee•las•tik werk]
That work performed in the act of breathing to overcome the elastic resistance of the lung and pleural cavity.

elastomer [e•**las**•tuh•mur]
A general term for elastic, rubber-like substances.

electric logging [e•**lek**•trik lahg•ing]
The method of surveying a bore hole by means of running special tools on an electric cable.

electric ray [e•**lek**•trik ray]
Torpedo ray that grows from one to six feet long and weighs up to 200 pounds; found on both the

Atlantic and Pacific coasts as well as other parts of the world; slow moving and not difficult to avoid, but the diver who is not alert can get a shock of as much as 220 volts from a large ray. (See: hazardous marine animals.)

electroacoustical transducers [e•lek•tro•uh•**koos**•tuh•cul trans•**doo**•surz]
Genetic term for hydrophones, microphones, telephone receivers and loudspeakers; capable of changing sound or audio waves to electrical impulses, or vice versa.

electrocardiogram [e•lek•tro•**kahr**•dee•uh•gram]
The tracing of the electric current produced by heart muscle activity; the record produced by an electrocardiograph.

electrocardiograph [e•lek•tro•**kahr**•dee•uh•graf]
An instrument used for making records of the heart's electric currents.

electrode [e•**lek**•trod]
Usually refers to the insulated center rod of a spark plug; also sometimes used to refer to the rods attached to the shell of the spark plug; a solid electric conductor used in welding and burning.

electrode holder [e•**lek**•trod **hol**•dur]
In welding, a device used for holding the electrode and conducting current to it.

electrode lead [e•**lek**•trod lead]
The electrical conductor between the source of arc welding current and the electrode holder.

electroencephalogram [e•lek•tro•en•**sef**•uh•luh•gram]
A graphic record of the electrical activity of the brain.

electroencephalograph [e•lek•tro•en•**sef**•uh•luh•graf]
An instrument for making records of the brain's electric currents.

electrolysis [e•lek•**trahl**•uh•sus]
The process of chemical decomposition of an electrolyte by the action of an electric current; decomposition of metals in sea water.

electrolyte [e•**lek**•tro•lyt]
Any substance which, in solution or fused, exists as electrically charged ions that make the liquid capable of conducting a current.

electromagnet [e•lek•tro•**mag**•nut]
A coil of insulated wire wound around an iron rod, magnetizing the rod and causing it to attract any other iron in the vicinity, provided an electrical current is passed through the wire.

electron [e•**lek**•trahn]
One of the three basic particles of atoms which has a negative charge. (See: proton.)

electron-beam welding [e•**lek**•trahn-beem **wel**•ding]
A welding process where coalescence is produced by the heat obtained from a concentrated beam composed primarily of high velocity electrons.

electronic flash [e•lek•**trahn**•ik flash]
In photography a flash of very short duration produced by passing an electrical discharge through a closed tube containing an inert gas (usually xenon); also, strobe flash.

electronystagmogram [ee•lek•troh•ny•**stag**•moh•gram]
A tracing showing changes in eye movements (e.g. nystagmus).

element [**el**•uh•munt]
A fundamental and irreducible constituent of a composite entity.

elevator [**el**•uh•vay•tur]
In drilling, a lifting device with hinged doors and a fast-release latch which fits around the drill pipe or casing to lift or lower it. (See: drill pipe, casing.)

elevator links [**el**•uh•vay•tur links]
Long steel links which connect the elevators to the main hook. (See: elevator.)

embolism, air or gas [**em**•buh•liz•um, air or gas]
Gas bubbles in the arterial system caused by gas or air passing into the pulmonary veins after rupture of the alveolar vaculature. (See: air embolism, gas embolism.)

embolus [**em**•bo•lus]
A foreign or abnormal object carried by the blood stream into a smaller vessel, causing its obstruction.

emergency ascent [e•**mur**•jun•see uh•sent]
Unplanned ascent to the surface under stressful conditions. (See: blowup.)

emergency bouyant ascent [e•**mur**•jun•see **booy**•unt uh•**sent**]
Rapid ascent to the surface caused by dropping the weight belt or inflating the flotation device; the diver continuously exhales in order to avoid pulmonary barotrauma.

emergency controlled ascent [e•**mur**•jun•see kun•**trold** uh•**sent**]
A little-used term meaning ascent to the surface, using breathing apparatus, at a rate which ignores standard ascent rates or decompression stops.

emphysema [em•fuh•**see**•muh]
Swelling or inflation due to the abnormal presence of gas in body tissues.

emphysema, interstitial [em•fuh•**see**•muh, in•tur•**stee**•shul]
The thinning and loss of elasticity in a space in body tissue or structure.

emphysema, mediastinal [em•fuh•**see**•muh, mee•dee•**ass**•tu•nul]
Presence of air in tissues in the vicinity of the heart, lungs, and the large blood vessels in the middle of the chest.

emphysema, subcutaneous [em•fuh•**see**•muh, sub•kyoo•**tayn**•ee•us]
Swelling or inflation due to abnormal presence of air in tissues just under the skin; usually appears in or near the neck.

end knots [end nahts]
Used to prevent slipping; may be tied in either the end or standing part of the rope to check it from sliding through a block, hole, or part of another knot.

endocardium [en•do•**kahr**•dee•um]
The membrane which lines the heart chambers and assists in forming the heart valves.

endocrine [**en**•do•krin]
Secreting to the inside, into tissue fluid or blood.

endolymph [**en**•do•limf]
The straw-colored fluid within the semicircular canal and structures of the inner ear.

environment [en•**vyrn**•munt]
The sum of all the external conditions which may affect an organism, community, material or energy.

environmental control unit (ECU) [en•vyrn•ment•ul kun•**trol** yoo•nut]
Diver support system; three main functions are carbon dioxide control, humidity control and temperature control.

environmental effects [en•**vyrn**•ment•ul e•fekts]
In blasting, those effects on the environment caused by an explosion, including but not limited to ground motion, water shock and air blast.

EOD
Explosive Ordnance Disposal.

epicardium [ep•uh•**kahrd**•ee•um]
The membrane that forms the outer layer of the heart wall and is continuous with the lining of the sac that encloses the heart.

epicenter [ep•uh•**sen**•tur]
The term used in oceanography, wave mechanics and other appropriate fields to denote the focal point of great waves.

epidermis [ep•uh•**durm**•us]
The outer epithelial layer of the skin, which contains no blood vessels.

epidermophytosis [ep•uh•**dur**•mo•fy•**to**•sus]
A fungous infection of the skin, especially of the toes and soles of the feet; also, athlete's foot.

epiglottis [ep•uh•**gleht**•us]
In the throat, a lid acting as a valve to esophagus tubes.

epistaxis [ep•uh•**stak**•sus]
Nosebleed; nasal hemorrage.

epithelium [ep•uh•**theel**•ee•um]
The tissue that: forms the outer part (epidermis) of the skin; lines hollow organs and passages that lead to the outside of the body; makes up the active part of many glands.

equilibrium [e•kwil•**ib**•ree•um]
In thermodynamics, any state of a system which would not change if the system were isolated.

equivalent air depth [e•**kwiv**•uh•lunt air depth]
The air breathing depth which has a nitrogen partial pressure equivalent to that at the diving depth.

equivalent bottom time [e•**kwiv**•uh•lunt **baht**•um tym]
A hypothetical period of time taken to represent residual gas elimination time, and which is added to the bottom time of one dive to determine the decompression obligation for comparable dives.

erg [urg]
A measurement representing one unit of work.

ergometer [ur•**gahm**•uh•tur]
An apparatus for measuring muscular work.

erosion [e•**ro**•zhun]
Wearing away the surface of a material by the action of a moving stream of fluid.

erosion of explosive [e•**ro**•zhun uv eks•**plo**•siv]
Removal of parts of an explosive charge by moving water, such as currents or surge.

ERV
(See: expiratory reserve volume.)

erythema [air•uh•**thee**•muh]
Skin redness usually due to congestion of the blood in the capillaries.

esophageal [uh•**sahf**•uh•**jee**•ul]
Relating to the gullet. (See: esophasus.)

esophagus [uh•**sahf**•uh•gus]
The gullet; a tubular passage extending from the pharynx to the stomach.

estuary [**es**•choo•air•ee]
The place at which tide meets river current; a narrow arm of the sea meeting the mouth of a river; a tidal bay.

etiology [et•ee•**ahl**•uh•jee]
The study of the causes of disease, including theories of origin and organisms that may be involved in causation.

eucapnia [yoo•**cap**•nee•a]
The condition in which the carbon dioxide of the blood is normal.

euphoria [yoo•**for**•ee•a]
1. a feeling of wellbeing, 2. an abnormal feeling of buoyant vigor and health. Also written: euphory.

eupnea [**yoop**•nee•a]
Normal repiration (opposed to dyspnea). Also written: eupnoes.

eustachian tube [yoo•**stay**•shun toob]
The canal connecting the middle ear and the throat; permits the equilibration of pressure between the external and middle ears.

excursion [eks•**kur**•zhun]
Movement of a diver either vertically or horizontally from the work platform, bell, chamber or habitat at saturation depth.

excursion dive [eks•**kur**•zhun dyv]
Movement of a diver either upward or downward from saturation depth; the permissible safe distance and time of the excursion dive depend on the saturation depth.

exhale [**eks**•hayl]
To breathe out. (See: expiration.)

exhaling ascent [eks•**hayl**•ing uh•**sent**]
Ascent in which the diver exhales all the way to the surface without breathing apparatus of any kind; also, free ascent.

exoskeleton [eks•o•**skel**•uh•tun]
A hard structure developed on the outside of a body, as the shell of a crustacean.

Experimental diving unit [Eks•peer•uh•**men**•tul dyv•ing yoo•nut]
U.S. Navy diving research center, Washington, D.C.; also, EDU.

expiration [eks•pur•**ay**•shun]
The act of breathing out or emitting air from the lungs; also, exhaling.

expiratory reserve volume [eks•**pyr**•uh•tor•ee re•zurv **vahl**•yoom]
Maximum amount of air that can be breathed out after normal exhalation.

exploitation well [eks•ploy•**tay**•shun well]
A well drilled to explore the potential of a field. (See: field.)

explosion [eks•**plo**•zhun]
A violent bursting effect as a result of great mechanical pressure.

explosion pressure [eks•**plo**•zhun **presh**•ur]
The pressure from the hot gases formed by an explosion.

explosive [eks•**plo**•siv]
A chemical substance that rapidly changes into a gas, creating heat and pressure.

explosive efficiency [eks•**plo**•siv e•**fish**•un•see]
The amount of energy released by a detonating explosive, compared to the amount of energy it is capable of releasing under ideal conditions.

explosive train [eks•**plo**•siv trayn]
The series of explosives that is required to convert the initiating impulse into the detonation of the main charges; consists of one or more of each of the following detonator, booster and main charges.

exposure latitude [eks•**po**•zhur **lat**•uh•tood]
In photography, the margin of departure from the correct exposure that is permissible without seriously affecting the quality of the final photograph.

external auditory canal [eks•**turn**•ul **aw**•duh•tor•ee kuh•**nal**]
The canal leading from the outer ear to the eardrum.

external charge [eks•**turn**•ul chahrj]
A charge placed external to, and usually in intimate contact with, material to be blasted.

external ear squeeze [eks•**turn**•ul ear skweez]
Squeeze caused by the sealing of the space between the external ear and the eardrum during compression; can be caused by tightly fitting hood, bathing cap, or ear plugs.

externa otitis [eks•**turn**•ah oh•**ty**•fus]
A superficial infection of the auditory canal; a common occurance in habitat living, wet pot and open-sea diving; usually caused by a mold or bacterium. (See: media obtitis, obitis.)

extraneous electricity [eks•**tray**•nee•us e•lek•**tris**•uh•tee]
Any unwanted electrical energy which may enter blasting circuits from any source.

eye bolt [aye bolt]
A bolt with looped head or an opening in the head.

eye of the storm [aye uv thu storm]
The center of a tropical cyclone, marked by relatively light winds, confused seas, rising temperature, lowered relative humidity, and often by clear skies.

eye splice [aye splys]
A splice used to form a loop in the end of rope or wire.

eye squeeze [aye skweez]
Squeeze of the eyes caused by using nonpressure-compensated goggles.

-F-

face mask
(See: mask.)

face of weld [fays uv weld]
The exposed surface of a weld made by arc or gas welding, on the side from which the welding was done.

face plate [fays playt]
Glass or plastic window in a diving helmet, constructed to provide an air space between the eyes and the water and to permit both eyes to see in the same plane; the skirt makes contour contact with the face, preserving air space; pressure may be equalized by breathing into the mask.

face plate squeeze [fays playt skweez]
Pressure building up in the mask on descent; also, mask squeeze.

face squeeze [fays skweez]
Squeeze of the face caused by failure to compensate for increased ambient pressure.

fahrenheit
(See: temperature — Fahrenheit.)

fail safe valve [fayl•sayf•valv]
A valve held open by remotely maintained hydraulic pressure, which operates in a safe mode when failure occurs.

fairlead [fair•leed]
In rigging, refers to fittings or devices used in maintaining the direction of a line onto or off from a sheave or drum.

falls [fahlz]
In rigging, the rope which makes up the tackle through the sheaves of a block. (See: block, sheave, tackle.)

fast line [fast lyn]
In drilling, the line which spools onto the main drum of the drawworks so-called because it runs faster than the lines spooled in the traveling blocks. (See: drawworks, travelling block.)

fathom [fath•um]
The term for the unit of measurement of depth in the ocean, for countries using the English system of units; equal to six feet (1.83 meters).

fathometer [fath•ahm•uh•tur]
A device used to determine water depth by means of echoes reflecting off the bottom.

fatigue [fuh•teeg]
Weakening or deterioration of metal or other material occurring under load, especially under repeated or continued loading.

fault [fawlt]
Geological term for a break in the earth's subsurface formation.

fauna [faw•nuh]
The animal life of a region.

feed off [feed awf]
In drilling, running the drill string continuously while drilling without using the drawworks brake. (See: drill string, drawworks.)

ferrules [fair•oolz]
Specially designed components used in tube fittings to grip and seal on the outer surface of tubing.

fetch [fetch]
The length of fetch is distance over which a wind blows across water and develops waves; the greater the distance, the greater the possibility of the development of large waves.

Fick's law [fiks law]
A law which describes the way in which diffusion occurs in fluids, depending upon: the concentration gradient, measured over a specified time; the area over which diffusion is taking place; the ambient temperature; the type of molecule; the interaction between the molecules of solvent and solute.

field [feeld]
An area consisting of a single reservoir or multiple reservoirs, all grouped on or related to the same geological structural features or conditions; usually applies when oil has been discovered in sufficient quantities to justify a profitable production program.

figure-eight knot [fig•yur-ayt naht]
A knot often used at the end of a rope forming a lariat loop.

filling the hole [fil•ing thuh hol]
Pumping mud into a well to replace the volume of the drill pipe being pulled out when round tripping; pumping mud to keep the hole full. (See: drill pipe, mud, round trip.)

film pack [film pak]
A container holding a number of flat photographis films which are exposed singly.

film transport [film trans•port]
The mechanism by which film is advanced in a camera frame by frame.

filter cake [fil•tur kayk]
In drilling, the material remaining on a filter paper when the mud properties are tested with a filter press. (See: mud.)

finger [fing•ur]

In drilling, a pipe or rack fastened to the derrick above the floor for the purpose of racking stands of drill pipe when round tripping. (See: derrick, drill pipe, round trip, stand.)

finish [fin•ish]

The texture or quality of a surface.

fins [finz]

Device attached to the feet of a diver to increase area and thus power, speed and control in the water, also called swim fins.

fire [fyr]

In blasting, to detonate a blast.

fish [fish]

In drilling, any tool, part of a drilling string, etc., which is lost in a hole and necessitates a fishing job before normal operations can be resumed. (See: drill string, fishing hook, fishing jar, fishing magnet, fishing tap, fishing tools.)

fisherman's knot [fish•ur•munz naht]

A knot used for joining two fine lines.

fishing hook [fish•ing hook]

In drilling, a fishing tool used for pulling the top of a fish into the center of the hole to allow it to be secured by a recovery tool. (See: fish.)

fishing jar [fish•ing jahr]

In drilling, a fishing tool used to exert an upward blow to a stuck pipe. (See: fish.)

fishing magnet [fish•ing mag•nut]

In drilling, a magnetized tool used to recover small steel items from a hole. (See: fish.)

fishing tap [fish•ing tap]

In drilling, a long tapered tap used to screw into the top of a fish; often run in conjunction with a set of fishing jars. (See: fish, fishing jar.)

fishing tools [fish•ing toolz]

Any of several devices for recovering a fish. (See: fish.)

fishtail bit [fish•tayl bit]

In drilling, a blade-type bit suitable for drilling soft formations.

fit [fit]

An imprecise term denoting convulsions. (See: convulsions.)

fixed bottom stations [fikst baht•um stay•shunz]

Underwater work sites that are maintained at 1 atmosphere of pressure, dependent upon land- or sea-based support equipment. For example, an underwater welding chamber;

fjarlie bottle [fahr•lee baht•ul]

A series of metal tubular bottles mounted outside a submersible that allow water to be sampled by remote control valves.

flaccid [flak•sud]

Weak, lax and soft.

flag

(See: signal.)

flange [flanj]

The projecting rim, collar or edge on an object for keeping it in place.

flare [flair]

A pyrotechnic device used for light or signalling.

flashback [flash•bak]

In welding or burning, a recession of the flame into or back of the mixing chamber of the torch.

flash point [flash point]

The temperature at which, when heated, an oil will flash and burn.

flat plate keel [flat playt keel]

On a vessel, a fabricated steel keel built up from three members: the dished keel and the keelson and the rider plate.

flat position [flat po•zish•un]

The position of welding where welding is performed from the upper side of the joint and the face of the weld is horizontal; also, downhand welding.

flatus [flat•us]

Gas, usually air, in the stomach or bowel.

flexible tubing [fleks•uh•bul toob•ing]

A pliable tube, of elastomer, plastic, or convoluted metal, which can return to its original shape after being bent.

float [flot]

A marking device that floats on the surface of the water.

floatation device

(See: flotation device.)

float collar [flot kahl•ur]

In drilling, a short length of casing screwed to the lower end of a casing string having a non-return valve which provides a means of floating a casing string into the hole; relieves the hoisting equipment of excessive loads. (See: casing string.)

floating dry dock [flot•ing dry dahk]

A U-shaped dock which can be lowered by flooding, to accommodate the keel of a ship, then pumped out, raising the ship so hull repairs may be made.

floating rig [flot•ing rig]

A ship or other structure fitted with drilling equipment capable of drilling in deep water; usually self-propelled for moving from one site to another; also called a floater.

float shoe [flot shoo]

In drilling, a casing shoe fitted with a non-return

valve which operates similarly to a float collar. (See: casing shoe, float collar.)

flood tide [flud tyd]
Incoming tide.

flora [**flor**•uh]
The plant life of a region.

flotation device [flo•**tay**•shun de•vys]
An inflatable vest used to assist ascent or to provide positive bouyancy; used for fine bouyancy control while submerged; alternate spelling, flotation.

flotsam [**flaht**•sum]
Wreckage of a ship or its cargo found floating on the sea.

flow [flo]
Movement of a fluid.

flow bean [flo been]
A choke or adjustable choke used to restrict the flow of fluid or gas from a production well. (See: choke.)

flowing well [**flo**•ing wel]
A well which produces oil or gas without any artificial lifting equipment.

flow line [flo lyn]
The return pipe from a well head, through which mud or fluid passes to the mud screens; also, a pipe through which a well produces oil or gas. (See: mud, vibrating screen.)

flow string [flo string]
In drilling, the final tubing or casing set into a production well.

flow tank [flo tank]
A storage tank into which a producing well discharges oil.

flow test [flo test]
Controlled production from a well to establish reservoir conditions.

flow-through casing hangar [flo•throo **kay**•sing **hang**•ur]
In drilling, a hanger with a large fluid by-pass area machined on the outside. (See: casing.)

fluid [**floo**•ud]
A substance having particles which easily move and change their relative position; both liquids and gases are fluids.

fluid level [**floo**•ud **lev**•ul]
In a well which is not a flowing well, the level to which fluid rises in the bore. (See: bore, flowing well.)

fluid system [**floo**•ud **sis**•tum]
A continuous arrangement of piping or tubing for the transfer of gases or liquids from one location to another; may include piping, tubing,

valves gauges, meters, storage tanks, pumps, etc.

fluke [flook]
The tapered prong of an anchor which holds the ground.

flush joint casing [flush joint **kay**•sing]
In drilling, casing joints which have a uniform outside diameter, as opposed to collar casing where the connecting collars have a larger outside diameter than that of the casing joints.

flux [fluks]
A fusible material or gas used to dissolve or prevent the formation of oxides, nitrides or other undesirable inclusions formed in welding.

focal length [**fo**•kul layngth]
In photography, the distance between the optical center of a lens and the sensitive emulsion when the lens is focused at infinity.

foot valve [foot valv]
A clapper valve installed on the lower end of a vertical pipe.

force [fors]
Pull or push tending to produce motion in the direction of the force.

forced expiration reserve volume [**for**•sd eks•py•**ray**•shun ree•**serv** vol•yoom]
The rate of flow of air per second that can be forcefully expired after the end of the normal tidal volume.

forced expiratory volume [**for**•sd eks•**py**•ra•tor•ee **vol**•yoom]
The volume (of the forced vital capacity) which can be forcibly exhaled in one second (of importance in submarine escape).

forced wave [forst wayv]
A wave generated and maintained by a continuous force.

force of G [fors uv jee]
Downward force equal to the weight of an object.

forces at rest [**fors**•uz at rest]
Two equal forces working in opposite directions.

fore [for]
Used to distinguish the forward part of a boat or things forward of amidships. It is the opposite of aft or after.

forefoot [**for**•foot]
On a vessel, that part of the lower end of the stem which is connected to the keel.

formation
(See: geology.)

formation pressure [for•**may**•shun **presh**•ur]
The pressure at the bottom of a well when it is closed in at the well head.

formation tester [for•**may**•shun **test**•ur]
In drilling, a packer assembly set into the open hole or in a casing above the producing formation; allows fluid from the formation to flow freely into the test string and to the surface where it can be measured. (See casing.)

fouling [**fowl**•ing]
The assemblage of marine organisms that attach to and grow upon underwater objects; the snarling or catching of an air line or umbilical in wreckage or underwater structures.

fourble [**for**•bul]
In drilling, four joints of pipe screwed together to form a stand. (See: fourble board, stand.)

fourble board [**for**•bul bord]
In drilling, a board or platform located above the floor of a derrick for handling drill pipe stands being run in or pulled out of a wall. (See: derrick, stand.)

fracture [**frak**•choor]
The breaking of rock without movement of the broken pieces.

fracturing, formation [**frak**•choor•ing, for•**may**•shun]
In drilling, a technique by which the formation is cracked and the fissures are propped open by pumping walnut shells, glass balls or similar propping agents into the formation.

fragmentation [frag•men•**tay**•shun]
The extent to which rock is broken into small pieces when blasted.

frames [fraymz]
On a vessel, vertical structural shapes, extending from the floors to the point where the deck stringer plate joins the sheer strake. (See: sheer strake, stringer.)

free air [free air]
Air discharge from a compressor at 1 atmosphere per minute; computed in cubic feet per minute.

free air space [free air spays]
Air space trapped in an underwater structure.

freeboard [**free**•bord]
On a vessel, the distance between the surface of the water and the main deck.

free communication [free kum•yoo•nuh•**kay**•shun]
On a vessel, water that is allowed to come in and go out to the open sea through a hole or damage.

free diving [free **dyv**•ing]
Diving without tether, umbilical or marking device; also breathhold diving. (See: breathhold.)

free face [free fays]
Any surface of material to be blasted that is exposed to a medium of much lesser density, such as air or rock.

free flow system [free flo **sis**•tum]
Continuous flow life-support system with flow rate independent of breathing.

freeing ports [**free**•ing ports]
On a vessel, openings in the lower ends of bulwarks at the deck, to allow for quick drainage of water, thus freeing the deck of the weight of the seas.

free point indicator [free point in•duh•**kay**•tur]
In drilling, an instrument which is run into a stuck drill pipe string on an electric cable, to record the point at which the string is stuck. (See: drill string.)

free surface [free **sur**•fus]
Water trapped in a compartment and allowed to move fore, aft and athwartship (sidewise).

free wave [free wayv]
A wave that continues to exist after the generating force has ceased.

French bowline [french **bo**•lyn]
A double bowline knot providing two nonslip loops; the loops can be of different sizes; excellent for rescue work or for working over the side of a ship.

Frenzel maneuver [**fren**•zul muh•**noo**•vur]
A maneuver to equalize pressure in the middle ear with ambient pressure against the outer surface of the eardrum; with the nose compressed shut, the mouth open, and the glottis closed, the tongue is moved upward and backward, resulting in increased pressure which forces air through the eustachian tubes.

friction socket [**frik**•shun **sahk**•ut]
In drilling, an infrequently used fishing tool for recovering drill pipe which has been lost in the hole; a tube which can be forced over a fish to recover pipe which is not firmly stuck in the well. (See: fish, fishing tools.)

frost up [frahst up]
The icing up of equipment due to the expansion of gas when it passes from high pressure to lower pressure through a partially closed valve or other small space.

frozen sheave [**fro**•zun sheev]
In rigging, a problem that occurs when a sheave will not turn because wire rope is sawing down the length of groove, or as a result of a bent shaft or other irregularity.

fulcrum [**full**•krum]
The support on which a lever turns in moving a body.

full face mask [full fays mask]
A diving mask, either supplied with breathing gas on demand or continuously and independent of respiration, which covers the eyes, nose and mouth of the diver.

full hole [full hol]
In drilling, a borehole drilled to full diameter.

full hole tool joint [full hol tool joint]
In drilling, a threaded connector used for joining joints of drill pipe, having the same bore as the pipe. (See: drill pipe.)

fulminate of mercury [ful•mun•ayt uv **mur**•kree]
A high explosive used in blasting caps.

fumes [fyoomz]
Toxic gases.

functional residual capacity [**funk**•shun•ul ree•zid•yul ka•**pas**•i•tee]
The volume of gas remaining in the lung after a normal expiration. The sum of EVR and RV (about 2300 ml.).

fundamental frequency [fun•duh•**ment**•ul **fre**•kwen•see]
The lowest natural frequency of an oscillating system.

fungus [**fung**•gus]
A group of simple plants that contain no chlorophyll, feed on living or dead plants or animals; plural: fungi.

-G-

gall [gahl]
Pickup and tearing of metal caused by high friction and force.

galvanic action [gal•**van**•ik ak•shun]
In blasting, the process in which dissimilar metals in close proximity to each other create an electric voltage and current flow between them, especially prevalent in the presence of salt water, may cause sufficient electric voltage to initiate an electric blasting cap.

galvanize [gal•vun•ayz]
To coat with a molten alloy of lead and tin to prevent rusting.

galvanometer [gal•vun•**ahm**•uh•tur]
A device containing a silver chloride cell which is used to measure resistance in an electric blasting circuit.

ganglion [**gang**•glee•un]
A small knotlike mass; in the nervous system, a collection of nerve cells.

gang plank [gang plangk]
A board or ramp used as a moveable footway between a vessel and a boarding structure such as a pier.

gangrene [**gang**•green]
Death of a mass of tissue, accompanied by bacterial invasion and putrefaction; usually due to blood vessel obstruction.

garboard strake [**gar**•burd strayk]
On a vessel, the first longitudinal strake of plating secured to the dished keel; usually heavier plate than the adjacent bottom plating and identified as an A strake. (See: dished plates, strake.)

gas [gas]
A fluid which tends to expand without limit; in diving, any respirable mixture breathed by the diver. (See: breathing gas, diluent gas, insert gas, mixed gas, separated gas.)

gas console [gas **kahn**•sol]
A station for monitoring and controlling the flow of breathing gas to a diver; also, gas rack.

gas cut mud [gas kut mud]
In drilling, mud in circulation containing gas which has seeped into the column from a gas reservoir. (See: mud.)

gas cutter [gas **kut**•ur]
(See: oxygen cutting.)

gas drive [gas dryv]
In drilling, pressure exerted by the formation or injected gas to cause or assist a production flow.

gas exchange
(See: diffusion, inert gas elimination, inert gas uptake, perfusion.)

gas in gut [gas in gut]
The presence of gas in the large bowel.

gas laws [gas lawz]
Mathematical descriptions of the relations of pressure, temperature and volume under ideal conditions. (See: laws.)

gas lift [gas lift]
In drilling, gas run into a well through a pipe or tubing in order to lighten the fluid column and induce a production flow from the reservoir.

gas metal-arc cutting [gas **meh**•tul-ark **kut**•ing]
Method of metal-arc cutting where the severing of metals is effected by melting with an arc between a continuous metal electrode and the work.

gas metal-arc welding [gas **meh**•tul-ark **wel**•ding]
An arc-welding process where coalescence is

produced by heating with an electric arc between continuous filler metal electrode and
the work.

gas, natural [gas, **nach**•ur•ul]
Unprocessed gas from a gas reservoir.

gas nucleation [gas noo•klee•**ay**•shun]
The process of forming gas nuclei. (See: gas
nuclei.)

gas nuclei [gas **noo**•klee•aye]
Necessary for bubble formation in pure liquids;
also called microbubbles.

gas oil ratio [gas oil **ray**•sho]
The number of cubic feet of gas produced from a
barrel of oil at atmospheric pressure.

gas pocket [gas **pah**•kut]
Any cavity caused by entrapped gas.

gas rack
(See: gas console.)

gas shielded arc welding [gas **sheel**•dud ark **weld**•
ing]
(See: MIG welding, TIG welding.)

gas, stripped [gas, stript]
Processed natural gas with the condensate removed passing high pressure gas through separators and reducing the pressure by stages; the
gas cools due to expansion, and the condensate
produced can be drawn off from the bottom of
the separator.

gas supply hose
(See: hose.)

gas switching [gas **swich**•ing]
Changing the composition of breathing gas.

gastric [**gast**•rik]
Of, in or near the stomach. See fig. 7.

gastritis [gas•**try**•tus]
Inflammation of the stomach, usually of the lining mucosa.

gastroenteritis [gas•tro•en•**try**•tus]
Inflammation of the stomach and intestines.

gas tungsten-arc welding [gas **tung**•stun-ark
weld•ing]
An arc-welding process where coalescence is
produced by heating with an arc between a
single tungsten electrode and the work.

gas washout
(See: inert gas elimination)

gas well [gas wel]
A well which produces natural gas.

gauge pressure [gayj **presh**•ur]
The difference between absolute pressure and
atmospheric pressure. (See: absolute pressure,
ambient pressure, atmospheric pressure, design

pressure, hydrostatic pressure, partial pressure,
pressure, working pressure.)

gel [jel]
In drilling, the ability of mud to hold solids in
suspension when normal circulation by pumping is suspended. (See: mud.)

general gas law [**jen**•rul gas law]
Boyle's and Charles' laws combined. (See:
Boyle's Law, Charles' Law.)

general squeeze [**jen**•rul skweez]
Injury that occurs because of closed air spaces
in the body that are not equalized to ambient
pressure. (See: squeeze.)

generator [**jen**•ur•ay•tur]
A device consisting of an armature, field coils
and other parts which, when rotated, will generate electricity.

geological oceanography [jee•uh•**lah**•juh•kul
o•shun•**ah**•gru•fee]
The study of the floors and margins of the
oceans.

geolograph [jee•**ahl**•uh•graf]
An instrument which records the speed of penetration of the bit during drilling operations; the
penetration rate being affected by type and
hardness of the formation, type of rockbit used,
type of mud in circulation, weight applied to the
bit by the drill collar string, speed of rotation of
the bit, expertise of the driller, capacity of the
slush pumps to handle the circulating fluid.

geology [jee•**ahl**•uh•jee]
The study of the origin, history and structure
of the earth.

geophysics [jee•oh•**fiz**•iks]
The study of the physical characteristics and
properties of Earth.

giant clam [**jy**•unt klam]
Common in the reefs of Pacific tropical waters,
may be four feet across and weigh several hundred pounds; it grip can be released by cutting
the two muscles which hold the clam's valves
together. (See: hazardous marine animals.)

gill [gil]
A platelike or filamentous outgrowth; the respiratory organ of aquatic animals.

gill, artificial [gil, art•uh•**fish**•ul]
A device for obtaining oxygen from water by
diffusion.

girth [gurth]
In drilling, a horizontal brace between the main
legs of a derrick; also called a girt.

girth hitch [gurth hich]
A means of attaching a leather strap or rope to a
metal ring.

glaucoma [glah•ko•muh]
A disease of the eye caused by intense intra-ocular pressure due to an excess of fluid within the eye.

global sea [glo•bul see]
The concept of all of the sea-waters of the earth being parts of one global ocean.

glossopharyngeal [glahs•uh•fur•in•jee•ul]
Referring to the tongue and pharynx.

goggles [gah•gulz]
Protective glasses in a flexible frame, worn by swimmers.

gone to water [gahn to wah•tur]
Said of a well producing edge water as production from the field affects the gas and oil water levels; the well must be closed down and production taken from other wells closer to the center of the field. (See: edge water.)

goose neck [goos nek]
In drilling, the connecting bend between the rotary swivel and the kelly hose. (See: hose-rotary, swivel.)

gradient [gray•dee•unt]
The degree of change of one quantity with respect to another; for example, the degree of temperature change with respect to ocean depth.

Graham's law [gray•umz law]
The rates of diffusion of two gases are inversely proportional to the square roots of their densities; fairly accurate in gases, but only approximately so in liquids. (See: laws.)

grain [grayn]
A unit of weight: 15.4 grains equal 1 gram.

gravel packed completion [gra•vul pakt kum•plee•shun]
In drilling, when a reservoir formation is made up of loose sand which tends to fall into the hole, packing the annular space between the well wall and the liner with gravel; acts as a filter to prevent the sand from entering the well with the fluid.

graveyard tour [grayv•yahrd toor]
The drilling shift which normally begins at midnight and ends at 0800 hours.

green sky [green sky]
A greenish tinge to part of the sky, supposed by seamen to herald wind or rain.

grief stem
(See: kelly.)

groin [groin]
A structure projecting from shore designed to break the current, check erosion, and build out the shore by causing a deposit of new material.

grommet sling [grawm•ut sling]
In rigging, a sling formed by hand from a single strand.

groove weld [groov weld]
A weld made in the groove between two members to be joined; the position of welding where the axis of the weld is horizontal and the face of the weld is vertical.

gross tonnage [gros tun•uj]
A volumetric measurement of the internal capacity of a vessel.

ground [grownd]
Electrical connection to earth.

grounding [grown•ding]
A vessel's bottom touching ground voluntarily or involuntarily.

ground motion [grownd mo•shun]
The motion of the ground caused by the detonation of one or more explosive charges.

ground swell [grownd swel]
Large and usually smoothly swelling waves.

ground tackle [grownd tak•ul]
On a vessel, the combination of anchor and cable.

grouper [groop•ur]
A fish, some species of which are twelve feet long and weigh more than 700 pounds; found around rocks, caverns and submarine structures such as offshore oil rigs; not considered vicious, but can be unintentially dangerous because of their size and curiosity. (See: hazardous marine animals.

gudgeon [guh•jun]
A metal pivot at the end of a shaft or axle, around which a pivot or other device turns; on a vesel, the socket for the pintles of a rudder. (See: pintles.).

guide base [gyd bays]
In offshore drilling, a structural frame permanently attached to the conductor pipe on the ocean floor.

guide line [gyd lyn]
In rigging, a line attached to an unsteady load to prevent it from swinging when being hoisted or lowered.

guide posts [gyd posts]
In drilling, the upright members on the guide base into which guide lines are anchored.

guide shoe [gyd shoo]
In drilling, a short section of thick wall pipe screwed to the bottom end of a casing string to protect the casing when running into the hole. (See: casing string.)

guide structure [gyd **struk•**chur]
In drilling, a fabricated structure around a unit such as a blow out preventer stack, with members that encircle two or more guide cables. (See: blow out preventer stack.)

gun perforator [gun **pur•**fur•ay•tur]
In drilling, a device for perforating casing at a point opposite a reservoir formation, to permit the production of fluid from the formation into the flow string. (See: casing, flow string.)

gunwale bar [**gun•**'ul bahr]
On a vessel, a structural shape, usually angle bar used to tie together the deck stringer plate and the sheet strake. (See: deck stringer plate, sheet strake.)

gusher [**gush•**ur]
A flowing well; possibly not under control; also called a blow out.

gust [gust]
A sudden brief outburst of wind.

guy [gy]
In rigging, a rope or cable attached to steady a load.

gyro compass [**jy•**ro **kum•**pus]
A gyroscopically-driven compass that shows a true north orientation rather than magnetic north.

-H-

habitat [**hab•**uh•tat]
A seafloor structure, either movable or fixed, in which divers can live for extended periods and from which they make excursion dives. (See: excursion dive.)

half hitch [haf hich]
In rigging, a hitch that is the beginning of other hitches; when doubled, useful by itself as a temporary attaching knot.

half tide level [haf tyd **lev•**ul]
A plane midway between mean high water and mean low water; also known as mean tide level.

half time [haf tym]
In diving, the time required for a tissue to absorb or eliminate one-half the equilibrium amount of inert gas.

handling system [**hand•**ling **sis•**tum]
A system used to pick up, launch and recover a submersible work chamber in a safe and smooth operation while maintaining safety and comfort for the personnel inside. (See: submersible work chamber.)

hand signals
(See: signals.)

hangfire [**hang•**fyr]
A nonelectric firing circuit that has not detonated at the expected time but still is burning.

hard hat [hahrd hat]
Common term for diving helmet, also, protective hat worn by riggers, etc.

hardness [**hard•**nus]
Resistance to the deformation of a material by indentation, penetration, scratching or bending.

hard tank [hard tank]
A tank designed to withstand maximum submergence pressure, used to hold water or oil that is pumped out into a rubber bladder to alter displacement.

hardwire phone [**hard•**wyr fon]
A communication link used at the surface between a support ship and a submersible during launching.

harness assembly [**har•**nus uh•**sem•**blee]
The combination of straps used to attach diving equipment to the diver.

haversack [**hav•**ur•sak]
A military explosive package in the form of a canvas haversack, usually containing 20 pounds of explosives in demolition blocks.

hawser [**haw•**zur]
A hemp or manila rope of large circumference, or wire rope of large diameter, used for mooring or towing.

hazardous marine animals
(See: barnacle, barracuda, bristleworm, catfish, cone shell, coral, electric ray, giant clam, grouper, jellyfish, killer whale, lionfish, moray eel, octopus, Portuguese man-of-war, pufferfish, rabbitfish, sawfish, sea anemone, sea bass, sea lion, sea snake, sea urchin, scorpionfish, shark, shellfish-poisonous, spiny dogfish, stinging coral, stingray, stonefish, surgeonfish, triggerfish, weeverfish, zebrafish.)

H.C.
High compression.

headache block [**hed•**ayk blahk]
In rigging, the travel block of the main load; also headache ball.

headache post [**hed•**ayk post]
In drilling, a post on the floor of a cable tool rig which prevents the walking beam from falling when the pitman is disconnected from the driving crank. (See: cable tool drilling, pitman, walking beam.)

head board
(See: board-head.)

heart stoppage [hart **stap**•uj]
(See: cardiac arrest.)

heat affected zone [heet uh•**fek**•tud zon]
That portion of base metal which has not been melted, but which has been altered by the heat of welding or cutting.

heat conduction [heet kun•**duk**•shun]
The transfer of heat from one part of a body to another, or from one body to another.

heat loss
(See: hypothermia.)

heat sink [heet sink]
A method used to dissipate heat.

heaving shale [**heev**•ving shayl]
In drilling, a shale formation which falls into the hole.

heavy gear
(See: suits — diving.)

height criterion [hyt kry•**teer**•ee•un]
A measure of the impact sensitivity of an explosive.

heliox [**hee**•lee•ahks]
A breathing mixture of helium and oxygen used at depth because it has little narcotic effect; also, oxyhelium.

heliox diving [**hee**•lee•ahks **dyv**•ing]
Mixed gas diving using oxygen with helium as an inert diluent.

helium [**hee**•lee•um]
A colorless, odorless gas used as a replacement for nitrogen in the gas mixture for deep-sea divers; breathing helium-oxygen mixtures causes temporary speech distortion which hinders communication. (See: Donald Duck effect.)

helium speech unscrambler [**hee**•lee•um speech un•**skram**•blur]
A device designed to render intelligible the words spoken in a hyperbaric helium environment.

helmet [**hel**•mut]
A device worn over the head of a diver, designed to furnish breathing gas, allow visibility through viewports, enable two-way communication, and be compatible with dry suit and wet suit.

hematoma [hee•muh•**to**•muh]
A tumor or swelling filled with blood.

hemiplegia [hee•muh•plee•juh]
Paralysis of one side of the body.

hemo- [**hee**•mo]
Combining form denoting a relationship to blood.

hemoconcentration [hee•mo•kahn•sun•**tray**•shun]
Relative increase in the amount of red blood cells per unit volume.

hemodilution [hee•mo•duh•**loosh**•un]
Relative decrease in the number of red blood cells per unit volume.

hemoglobin [**hee**•mo•glo•bun]
The oxygen-carrying colored compound in the red blood cells.

hemorrhage [**hem**•ur•uj]
Any discharge of blood from the blood vessels.

Henry's law [**hen**•reez law]
At a constant temperature the amount of a gas which dissolves in a liquid with which it is in contact is proportional to the partial pressure of that gas. (See: laws.)

hepatitis [hep•uh•**tyt**•us]
Inflammation of the liver.

hernia [**hur**•nee•a]
The protrusion or projection of an organ or a part of an organ through a tear or other abnormal opening in the wall of the containing cavity.

hertz [hurts]
A unit of frequency equal to one cycle per second; abbreviation, Hz.

high carbon steel [hy **kar**•bun steel]
Steel containing .45 percent or more carbon.

high explosive [hy eks•**plo**•suv]
An explosive material to which the explosive reaction or detonation propagates at a velocity faster than the speed of sound.

high line [hy lyn]
In drilling, the combination of a rope and wire line which is used for pulling pipe and equipment from outside the derrick onto the derrick floor. (See: derrick.)

high pressure nervous syndrome [hy **presh**•ur **nur**•vus **sin**•drom]
Neurological and physiological dysfunction resulting from hyperbaric exposure or from compression or hydrostatic pressure; may include tremor, somnolence, heart rhythm changes, visual disturbances, nausea, dizziness and convulsions; also, HPNS.

high pressure oxygen
(See: hyperbaric oxygenation.)

high tension [hy **ten**•shun]
In electricity, refers to the secondary or induced high voltage electrical current; includes the wiring from the cap of the ignition distributor to the coil and to each of the spark plugs.

high water [hy **wah**•tur]
The maximum height reached by a rising tide,

may be due to periodic tidal forces alone or augmented by weather conditions.

hit [hit]
Common term for decompression sickness. (See: decompression sickness.)

hogging [**hahg**•ing]
The tendency of a vessel to arch amidships, or lower at both ends and simultaneously rise amidships, as a result of loading or working in seas; the practice of hauling a patch to a ship's side using lines which extend below the patch and beneath the hull.

hole, crooked [hol, **krook**•ud]
In drilling, a well bore which is unintentionally deviated.

hole, dry [hol, dry]
A non-productive well; also, a duster.

homing device
(See: beacon.)

hooded ascent [**hood**•ud uh•**sent**]
Bouyant ascent during which the diver breathes from an air-containing hood.

hook [hook]
In drilling, a heavy duty hook of 500 tons or more capacity which is suspended from the travelling block to handle the drill pipe and casing loads when drilling, running in or pulling out. (See: pullout, run in, travelling block.)

hookah diving [**hoo**•kuh **dyv**•ing]
A diving apparatus consisting of a demand regulator worn by the diver, and a hose connected to a compressed air supply at the surface.

hook, wall [hook, wahl]
In drilling, a fishing tool used for pulling the top of a fish into the center of the hole to permit the use of a fishing device to recover the fish. (See: fish, fishing tools.)

horse head [hors hed]
In drilling, the fitting of a pumping jack at the end of a walking beam, to which the sucker rods and an elevator are attached. (See: on the pump, pumping jack, walking beam.)

hose [hoz]
Flexible pipe for conveying fluid or gas.

hose charge [hoz charj]
A flexible linear charge consisting of a core of explosive surrounded by an outer skin or hose.

hose, rotary [hoz **ro**•tur•ee]
In drilling, high pressure rubber or steel hose which connects the stand pipe to the rotary swivel for conveying circulating mud to the drill string. (See: drill string, mud, stand pipe.)

hot water open circuit suit [haht **wah**•tur **oh**•pun **sur**•kut soot]
A wet suit modified by a system of tubes, designed to allow hot water to be distributed evenly over the body; after use, the hot water is dumped into the surrounding environment.

hot water suit [haht **wah**•tur soot]
A loose-fitting wet suit through which hot water is circulated to maintain thermal equilibrium in extreme cold water exposure.

hot water system [haht **wah**•tur **sis**•tum]
Provides hot water to support divers and to keep them reasonably comfortable for extended bottom time in relatively cold water.

HP
Horsepower, the energy required to lift 550 pounds one foot in one second.

HPNS
(See: high pressure nervous syndrome.)

HTGCR
High temperature gas cooled reactor.

hurricane [**hur**•uh•kayn]
A storm originating over water, consisting of wind rotating counterclockwise at a tremendous velocity; develops in a low-pressure center and usually is accompanied by abnormally high tides.

hydraulic [hy•**draw**•lik]
Moved or worked by fluid pressure.

hydraulic connector [hy•**draw**•lik kuh•**nek**•tur]
A device for making a remotely operated high pressure connection between various components of underwater equipment.

hydraulic rams [hy•**draw**•lik ramz]
Used to move the "U" boom in and out on a ball handling system.

hydraulic reservoir [hy•**draw**•lik **rez**•ur•voor]
Used to store, cool and supply a suction head for a hydraulic pump.

hydraulic tubing [hy•**draw**•lik **toob**•ing]
Annealed tubing that is used in fluid systems; also pressure tubing.

hydrocarbon [**hy**•dro•kar•bun]
A compound made up of molecules of hydrogen and carbon.

hydrogen [**hy**•dro•jun]
A colorless, odorless, tasteless, nontoxic gas; explosive when mixed with air in certain proportions; as a breathing gas, is less narcotic than nitrogen, has thermal properties and distorts the voice similar to helium.

hydrogen embrittlement [**hy**•dro•jun em•**brit**•ul•munt]
Embrittlement caused by entrance of hydrogen into a metal.

hydrometer [hy•**drahm**•uh•tur]
An instrument used to determine the density or specific gravity of a liquid.

hydrophone [hy•dro•fon]
A type of transducer that receives sonar energy from the water and converts it to electrical energy for sonars and underwater communication.

hydrosphere [hy•**drus**•feer]
The aqueous vapor of the atmosphere; commonly used to denote oceans, seas, lakes and streams.

hydrostatic [hy•dro•**stat**•ik]
Of or relating to liquids at rest or to the pressures they exert or transmit.

hydrostatic pressure [hy•dro•**stat**•ik **presh**•ur]
The pressure of a column of water acting upon a body immersed in the water, equal in all directions at a specific depth.

hygroscopic [hy•gro•**skahp**•ik]
Referring to the ability to absorb water.

hyperbaric [hy•pur•**bair**•ik]
1. of or having a pressure or specific gravity greater than that within the body tissues of fluids, 2. designating or of a pressurized (usually oxygenated) chamber, used in diving or treatment of various diseases and conditions.

hyperbaric arthralgia [hy•pur•**bair**•ik ahr•**thral**•juh]
A general term describing ecompression arthralgia; sometimes described by divers as "no joint juice." (See: arthralgia, compression arthralgia, decompression arthralgia.)

hyperbaric chamber [hy•pur•**bair**•ik **chaym**•bur]
A chamber designed to withstand high internal pressure; used in hyperbaric experimentation, diving simulations, and medical treatment.

hyperbaric facility [hy•pur•**bair**•ik fuh•**sil**•uh•tee]
The entire group of systems and subsystems used to support a high pressure chamber or chambers; may include a wet pot or compartment to simulate an actual underwater environment. (See: chamber, wet pot.)

hyperbaric oxygenation [hy•pur•**bair**•ik akhs•uh•jun•**ay**•shun]
The inhalation of oxygen at pressures above one atmosphere.

hypercapnia [hy•pur•**kap**•nee•uh]
An excess of carbon dioxide in the body's tissues; elevated carbon dioxide levels may occur in a habitat or other closed space, in a diving suit, or in breathing equipment; also, hypercarbia.

hypercarbia
(See: hypercapnia.)

hyperglycemia [hy•pur•gly•**see**•mee•uh]
An abnormal increase in the amount of sugar (glucose) in the blood.

hyperoxia [hy•pur•**akhs**•ee•uh]
An excess of oxygen in the body tissues produced by breathing a mixture in which the inspired oxygen pressure is greater than its partial pressure in air.

hyperoxic [hy•pur•**ahks**•ik]
Relating to raised partial pressures of oxygen.

hyperpnea [hy•pur•**pnee**•a]
An increased respiratory rate or breathing which is deeper than that seen in resting subjects. A certain degree of hyperpnea is normal after exercise.

hypertension [hy•pur•**ten**•shun]
High blood pressure.

hyperthermia [hy•pur•**thur**•mee•uh]
The elevation of body temperature above normal; in diving, may occur in hyperbaric chambers as a result of environmental exposure to heat or failure of the body's thermoregulatory system.

hyperventilation [hy•pur•ven•tuh•**lay**•shun]
Increase in rate and/or volume of respiration above normal; may lead to hypocapnia; also called overbreathing.

hypocapnia [hy•po•**kap**•nee•uh]
A physiological state in which the systemic arterial carbon dioxide pressure is low; symptoms may include finger tingling, muscle spasms, dizziness, loss of consciousness; commonly caused by hyperventilation (overbreathing).

hypotension [hy•po•**ten**•shun]
Lower than normal blood pressure.

hypothermia [hy•po•**thurm**•ee•uh]
Reduction of body temperature as a result of environmental exposure to cold or failure of the body's thermoregulatory system; some hypothermia accompanies most dives; unless a diver is suitably protected, it may result in reduced performance; if exposure is prolonged or extreme, it can be fatal.

hypoxemia [hy•pok•**see**•mya]
insufficient oxygenation of the blood.

hypoxia [hy•**pahks**•ee•uh]
Tissue oxygen pressure below normal; may be produced by breathing mixtures deficient in oxygen, by disease states, or by gases such as carbon dioxide.

-I-

ICEI
Internal Combustion Engine Institute, Inc.

I.D.
Abbreviation for inside diameter.

ideal gas [ay•deel gas]
A term denoting a gas which would exactly obey the gas laws.

ideal gas law [ay•deel gas law]
A law that defines the relationships among pressure, temperature, volume and quantities of substance of any ideal gas. (See: laws.)

igloo [ig•loo]
Pressurized space above the wet pot in some hyperbaric facilities, used either as a dry work area or preparation area before entry to the wet pot. (See: hyperbaric facility, wet pot.)

IGY
International Geophysical Year.

I.H.P.
Indicated horsepower; a measurement of the pressure of the explosion within the cylinder of an engine, expressed in pounds per square inch.

impression block [im•presh•un blahk]
In drilling, a tube filled with lead or wax which is run into the hole to obtain an impression of the top of a fish in order to plan its recovery. (See: fish.

improved flow steel [im•proovd flo steel]
Highest strength and most wear-resistant of standard grades of rope wire.

inert gas [in•urt gas]
The transfer of inert gas (nitrogen, helium, etc.) under the influence of a pressure gradient from the tissues to the blood to the lungs, from which it is exhaled; also called gas washout.

inert gas elimination [in•urt gas e•lim•uh•nay•shun]
The transfer of inert gas (nitrogen, helium, etc.) under the influence of a pressure gradient from the tissues to the blood to the lungs, from which it is exhaled; also called gas washout.

inert gas narcosis [in•urt gas nahr•ko•sus]
Narcosis produced by inert gases. (See: inert gas, narcosis, nitrogen narcosis.)

inert gas uptake [in•urt gas up•tayk]
Absorption of inert gas by the tissues of the body under the influence of a pressure gradient; the rate of uptake depends on the duration of the exposure, the partial pressure, and the nature of the gas.

inertia [in•nursh•uh]
A physical law which tends to keep a motionless body at rest, or a moving body in motion.

inflatable flotation device
(See: flotation device.)

inguinal [in•gwin•ul]
Pertaining to the region of the groin.
Hernia in the inguinal region.

inhalation [in•hul•ay•shun]
The process of bringing air into the lungs.

inhibitor [in•hib•uh•tur]
In drilling, an additive to reduce corrosion in the casing when pumping acid to increase the flow of hydrocarbons from a limestone formation. (See: acid treatment.)

initiation [in•ish•ee•ay•shun]
In demolition, the act of detonating a high explosive by means of a mechanical detonator or other device.

initiator [in•ish•ee•ay•tur]
An intermediate charge used to initiate the main charge when blasting.

injection well [in•jek•shun wel]
In drilling, a well used for injecting gas, oil or water into the reservoir formation; gas injection helps to maintain the field pressure and provides a way of disposing of surplus gas.

inlet [in•let]
A narrow strip of water running inland or between two islands.

inner core barrel [in•nur kor bair•ul]
In drilling, the innermost barrel of a double or triple core barrel which retains the core cut from a formation (See: core.)

insensitive [in•sen•suh•tiv]
Said of an explosive not easily detonated.

in situ [in sit•too]
A physiological term meaning in the natural or normal place or position; confined to the site of origin without invasion of neighboring tissues.

inspiration [in•spur•ay•shun]
The act of breathing air into the lungs.

inspiratory capacity [in•spir•a•tor•ee ka•pas•i•tee]
The volume by which the lung can be increased by a maximum inspiratory effort following a normal expiration.

inspiratory reserve volume [in•spyr•uh•tor•ee re•zurv vahl•yoom]
The maximum amount of air that can be breathed in after normal inspiration.

insulin shock [in•suh•lun shahk]
Circulatory insufficiency resulting from overdose of insulin which causes reduction of blood sugar.

intensify [in•ten•suh•fy]
To increase or concentrate, such as to increase the voltage of an electrical current.

intercooler [in•tur•kool•ur]
A device for lowering temperature of compressed air between compression stages. (See: compression.)

interface [in•tur•fays]
A surface separating two media; also the surface of the sea.

internal charge [in•turn•ul chahrj]
A charge placed inside the material to be blasted, usually by means of boreholes that penetrate into the material.

internal combustion [in•turn•ul kum•bus•chun]
The burning of a fuel within an enclosed space.

intervention dive
(See: bounce dive.)

intrapleural pressure [in•truh•ploor•ul presh•ur]
Pressure within the space between the chest wall and the lungs (pleural space).

IOMS
International Organization on Marine Sciences.

ISA
Instrument Society of America.

ischemia [is•kee•me•uh]
A lack of sufficient blood to a part of the body usually due to the obstruction of an artery.

I.S.O.
International Standards Organization.

isobaric [ay•so•bair•ik]
Relating to process taking place without change of ambient pressure.

-J-

jacket [jak•ut]
The lower section of an offshore drilling platform, mostly below water level and fastened into the sea bed by pilings.

jackstay search [jak•stay surch]
Underwater search of an area by two or more divers, using a series of overlapping rectangular patterns defined by straight pre-positioned lines on the sea floor or a ship's hull. (See: search patterns underwater.)

jackup [jak•up]
An offshore drilling rig with a floating hull, similar to a ship but with retractable legs which can be lowered to the sea bed to elevate the hull structure above wave level.

jammed [jamd]
Said of rope which has jumped the head sheave and is wedged between sheave and housing of the machine.

jar [jahr]
A fishing tool which may be matched to the top of a fish and used for striking heavy upward blows; also run above the bit in a cable tool string to provide a means of striking an upward blow to the bit. (See: fishing jar.)

jaundice [jawn•dus]
A yellowish discoloration of the skin which may be due to the presence of bile in the blood.

jellyfish [jel•ee•fish]
A marine animal, some species of which constitute potential danger to the driver, such as the sea wasp, one of the most venomous marine animals known, less dangerous but very painful are the stings of the sea nettle and the sea blubber. (See: hazardous marine animals.)

jetsam [jet•sum]
Cargo or equipment thrown overboard to lighten the load of a ship in distress. (See: flotsam, jettison.)

jet sled [jet sled]
A device on a jet (or dredge) barge which is towed over the bottom and used to blast a pipeline ditch into the ocean bottom with high-pressure water jets, then to recover the loosened mud or sand.

jettison [jet•uh•sun]
Throwing objects overboard, especially to lighten a craft in distress.

jetty [jet•ee]
A structure, for example, a pier, extended into a sea, lake or river to influence the current or tide in order to protect a harbor.

J.I.C
Joint Industry Conference.

jip line [jip lyn]
In rigging, a single load line; also called a whip line.

joggling [jahg•ling]
The offsetting of the edge of a plate or structure by knuckling to allow a fair outline in way of lapped joints.

joint, safety [joynt, sayf•tee]
(See: safety joint.)

jugular [jug•yoo•lur]
Referring to the veins of the neck which drain the areas supplied by the carotid arteries.

jump [jump]
A dive.

jumping the line [jump•ing thuh lyn]
The practice of a tug boat using full power, suddenly coming up taut on a slack tow hawser.

junk [junk]
In drilling, roller bearings, bit cutters, or anything else that may fall into the bottom of a hole.

jury rig [joo•ree rig]
Any temporary or makeshift device, rig or piece of equipment.

juxtra-articular osteonecrosis [juk•struh-ahr•tik•yoo•lur ahs•tee•oh•nek•kro•sus]
Osteonecrosis occurring near the joint articulation, usually hip or shoulder; may lead to collapse of the joint, together with pain and dysfunction. (See: dysbaric osteonecrosis, medullary osteonecrosis.)

j-valve [jay valv]
A spring loaded valve which begins to close when scuba cylinder pressure approaches a predetermined level. (See: scuba.)

-K-

keel [keel]
The principal structural member of a vessel, running fore and aft on the center line and forming the backbone of the vessel to which the frames are attached.

kelly [kel•ee]
In drilling, a square or hexagonal pipe is screwed to the top of the drill string and attached to the swivel, which can be raised or lowered while being rotated by the rotary table. (See: drill string, rotary table, swivel.)

kelly bushing [kel•ee boosh•ing]
In drilling, a driving assembly which transmits rotary motion to the kelly from the rotary table and also permits the kelly to be raised or lowered. (See: kelly, rotary table.)

kelly cock [kel•ee kahk]
In drilling, a cock placed between the top of the kelly and the swivel; in an emergency, enables the closing off of the flow of fluid from the well through the drilling string. (See: drill string, kelly, swivel.)

kelp [kelp]
Various varieties of large brown sea weeds.

Kelvin temperature [kel•vun tem•pur•uh•choor]
A thermometric scale on which the unit of measurement equals the centigrade degree. (See: temperature.)

kerf [kurf]
The space from which metal has been removed by a cutting process.

key seat [kee seet]
In drilling, a groove in the well wall which may cause difficulty in pulling out of the hole because of the bit or tools on the bottom of the drill string catching in it.

killer whale [kil•ur whayl]
Found in all seas and oceans from the Bering Straits to beyond the Arctic Circle; characterized by a blunt snout, high black dorsal fin, white patch behind and black above the eye with contrasting white underparts. (See: hazardous marine animals.)

killing a well [kil•ing uh wel]
Controlling a wild well, or mudding off a completed well to maintain the pressure of the reservoir. (See: mud off, wild well.)

kilowatt [kil•uh•waht]
A measure of electrical energy consisting of 1,000 watts; equal to one and one-third horsepower.

kinetic energy [kuh•net•'ik en•ur•jee]
Energy associated with motion.

kinking [kink•ing]
Referring to the problem occurring when rope has been allowed to run loose and develops a twist.

kluge line [klooj lyn]
Auxiliary gas line used in conjunction with a pneumofathometer for diver depth measurement.

knot [naht]
Velocity unit of one nautical mile (6,080.20 feet) per hour; equivalent to 1.689 feet per second; to convert feet per second into knots, multiply by 0.592.

knowledge box [nah•lij box]
The desk in the dog house or driller's office on the floor of a drilling rig. (See: dog house)

knuckle [nuk•'ul]
On a vessel, a change in direction of plating, framing or hull structure, usually within a short radius.

knuckle joint [nuk•'ul joynt]
A directional drilling tool controlled by hydraulic pressure of the circulating mud; a means of setting the bit or tools at an angle in the hole.

KWH
Kilowatt hours; the amount of watts used per hour; in thousands.

-L-

laced blocks [layst blahks]
Improper method of making up a set of falls, having the tendency to tilt, causing excessive wear on sheaves and load line. (See: falls, reeved blocks.)

lagoon [luh•goon]
A shallow body of water, usually with a shallow restricted outlet to the sea.

land breeze [land breez]
A breeze from the direction of the land.

land casing [land kay•sing]
The situation when a casing string is hung in its final position. (See: casing string.)

landing joint [land•ing joynt]
The top joint of a casing string, removed after cement slurry has been pumped into the well and has set. (See: casing string, slurry.)

landlocked [land•lahkt]
An area of water enclosed, or nearly enclosed, by land.

landward [land•wurd or land•urd]
In the direction of or being toward the land.

lap joint [lap joynt]
A joint between two overlapping construction members.

lap strake
(See clinker)

lariat loop [lair•ee•et loop]
An overhand knot with the free end brought back and given a stopper knot such as a figure eight or double Matthew Walker; must be pulled or hammered very snug; can be used as running knot.

laryngospasm [lar•in•joh•spasm]
Reflex closure of the airway.

larynx [lair•inks]
The voice box; covered by two membranes, the vocal cords.

laser [lay•zur]
Light amplification by stimulated emission of radiation.

latch on [lach ahn]
In drilling, to attach the elevators to the drill string. (See: drill string, elevator.)

laws [lawz]
(See: Boyle's law, Charles' law, Dalton's law, Fick's law, general gas law, Graham's law, Henry's law, ideal gas law, Martini's law, Pascal's law.)

lay [lay]
The direction strands are twisted in rope.

lay barge [lay bahrj]
A barge equipped to handle the laying of underwater pipelines.

lazy bench [lay•zee bench]
In drilling, a long wooden seat in the dog house on the derrick floor level. (See: derrick, dog house.)

L.C.
Low compression.

lead tong [leed tahng]
A pipe wrench which hangs in the derrick and is operated by a wire line from the cathead to make up or break out joints of pipe from the drilling string. (See: cathead, derrick, drilling string.)

lead wire [leed wyr]
In demolition, the main blasting line; also, shooting cable.

league [leeg]
A nautical measurement unit; in the U.S., approximately 3 miles, either statute or nautical.

leak rate [leek rayt]
The rate of flow of a fluid volume per unit of time at a differential pressure.

LEDC
(See: low-energy detonating cord.)

lee [lee]
A sheltered place or side; that side of a ship farthest from the point from which the wind blows.

leeward [lee•wurd or loo•'urd]
Pertaining to or in the direction of the lee side; opposed to windward.

leeward tide [lee•wurd (or loo•'urd) tyd]
A tide running in the same direction in which the wind is blowing.

leeway [lee•way]
A drifting to the leeward caused by wind or tide.

left lang lay [left lang lay]
Wire rope where strands and wire both are twisted to the left.

left regular lay [left reg•yoo•lur lay]
Wire rope where the strands twist to the left, and wires in the strands twist to right.

leg wires [layg wyrz]
In demolition, wires, often of different colors, leading from the top end of an electric blasting cap into a circuit.

lesion [lee•zhun]
A wound or local injury.

lifeline [lyf•lyn]
A line between the diver and tender, used to signal and supply the diver, to assist in normal ascent, and retrieve the diver in an emergency; usually part of the umbilical.

life support system [lyf suh•**port** sis•tum]
A system designed to produce a controlled environment for chamber occupants; may include capability to supply metabolic oxygen, control temperature and humidity, and remove carbon dioxide.

lift to seal [lift too seel]
A mechanical action by which leak-tight seals are effected without torque.

light breeze [lyt breez]
A wind of four to six knots.

lightening holes [lyt•tun•ing holz]
Large holes cut or punched in a floor, or a deep web frame, in order to reduce its weight without sacrificing strength.

lightweight diving mask [lyt•wayt **dyv**•ing mask]
A full face cover through which surface-supplied breathing gases are delivered to a diver; gases may flow freely through the mask or may be delivered through an oronasal demand assembly. (See: mask.)

limber holes [**lim**•bur holz]
On a vessel, small holes cut or drilled in the lower ends of floors and longitudinals to permit the passage of water for drainage.

limiting orifice [**lim**•uh•ting **or**•uh•fus]
A hole or opening, usually of calculated size, through which the passage of a liquid or gas may be restricted within specified limits, as determined by pressure drop across the opening to control the rate of flow.

limnology [lim•**nahl**•uh•jee]
The physics and chemistry of fresh water bodies and the ecology of the organisms living in them.

line charge [lyn charj]
A charge with its length much greater than its diameter that, when detonated, acts as if the explosive energy comes from a line rather than from a point.

line pulls
(See: signals.)

liner [**lyn**•ur]
In drilling, a string of casing which is run into the production area of a well to prevent sand or debris from flowing into the well; usually hung with a liner hanger set in the lower section of the last casing string in the hole. (See: casing string, liner hanger.)

liner hanger [**lyn**•ur **hang**•ur]
In drilling, an assembly fitted with slips and packers, used for the hanging of a liner in the lower section of the casing string of a producing well. (See: casing string, packer, slips.)

lionfish [**ly**•un•fish]
A member of a group of scorpionfishes, the lionfish is brightly colored and does not camouflage itself and makes little effort to avoid humans; the venom is very potent. (See: hazardous marine animals.)

lipoid pneumonia [**lip**•oyd nuh•**mon**•yuh]
Infection caused by the pressure of non-absorbent fat in the lungs.

liquid [**lik**•wud]
Any substance which assumes the shape of the vessel in which it is placed without changing volume.

liquid breathing [**lik**•wud **breeth**•ing]
An experimental technique involving flushing the lungs with a highly oxygenated liquid from which the subject derives enough oxygen to sustain life; so far unable to provide for adequate elimination of carbon dioxide.

littoral [**lit**•ur•ul]
The zone between high and low water marks.

live boating [lyv•**bot**•ing]
Diving from a vessel which is underway.

live oil [lyv oyl]
Oil containing gas.

LMFBR
Liquid metal fast breeder reactor; a nuclear reactor that produces more nuclear fuel than it burns up.

LNG
Liquified natural gas; a process by which gas is manufactured and stored at cryogenic temperatures. (See: cryogenics.)

loaded [**lod**•ud]
Said of a compressor at rest with pressurized air in the cylinder.

loading density [**lod**•ing **den**•suh•tee]
The density of an explosive in a hole after tamping.

load train [lod trayn]
Combination of fitting components that generate the seal force.

lock [lahk]
A pressurized compartment; or a compartment used to transfer personnel or supplies between two pressure levels, for example: air lock, man lock, medical lock and service lock.

lockout [**lahk**•owt]
The release (locking out) of divers from an underwater bell, chamber or submersible.

lock out capability [lahk•owt kay•puh•**bil**•uh•tee]
Said of a vehicle, usually maintained at a dry 1 atmosphere pressure, having a chamber that can be pressurized to the ambient underwater pressure to allow a lockout; can be used to decompress the divers back to 1 atmosphere pressure. (See: lockout.)

lock out submersible [lahk owt sub•**mur**•suh•bul]
A submersible that has a compartment maintained at 1 atmosphere pressure for the pilot or observer, and a compartment that can be pressurized to ambient pressure so the diver can enter and exit (lock out) to perform underwater work. (See: submersible.)

loess [les]
An unstratified deposit ranging in grain size from clay to fine-grain sand, deposited by wind action.

log, blast [lawg, blast]
In demolition, the record of shots showing significant details of blasts.

log, drilling [lawg, dril•ing]
The record of the drilling operations recorded by the driller on each tour. (See: tour.)

log, electric [lawg, e•**lek**•trik]
In drilling an extremely accurate means of logging, i.e., recording depth to within a few inches; information is obtained by running special tools into the well on an electric cable and recording, on film at the surface, the effects of an electric current to determine the differential resistance of various formations.

logging, mud [**lawg**•ing, mud]
A method of continuous examination of the mud which is being circulated in a well; record gives pump delivery details, mud weight figures, mud properties, and oil or gas content. (See: mud, well.)

log line [lawg lyn]
A graduated line used to measure the speed of a vessel through the water or to measure the velicity of the current from a vessel at anchor.

log, well [lawg, wel]
A record of geological formation encountered during drilling, and technical details of the operation.

longshore currents [**lahng**•shor **kur**•unts]
Movement of water close to and parallel with the shoreline.

long splice [lahng splys]
A splice used for pulley work; permits spliced ropes to be run through sheave blocks without jamming.

Lorrain Smith effect [lur•**ayn** smith e•fekt]
The pulmonary toxic effect of high pressure

oxygen in small animals, first observed by the physiologist for which it is named.

lose returns [looz re•turnz]
In drilling, a splice used for pulley work; permits spliced ropes to be run through sheave blocks without jamming.

low carbon steel [lo **kahr**•bun steel]
Steel containing .20 percent or less carbon; also mild steel.

low energy detonating cord [lo **en**•ur•jee det•uh•nay•ting kord]
Low-energy detonating cord used to initiate nonelectric caps at the bottom of boreholes.

lower high water [lo•ur hy **wah**•tur]
The lower of the two high waters of any tidal day.

lower low water [lo•ur lo **wah**•tur]
The lower of the two low waters of any tidal day.

low explosive [lo eks•**plo**•siv]
An explosive material in which the explosive reaction propagates at a velocity less than or equal to the speed of sound in the material.

low water [lo wah•tur]
The minimum level reached by a falling tide; the height may be solely the result of periodic tidal forces, or may be further affected by weather conditions.

L.P.G.
Liquified petroleum gas, made usable as a fuel for internal combustion engines by compressing volatile petroleum gases to liquid form; must be kept under pressure or at low temperature in order to remain in liquid form.

lubricator [**loob**•ruh•**kay**•tur]
In drilling a special cylindrical container fitted with valves which facilitate the running of wire line tools into a well under pressure, or the injection of mud or other fluids into the well under similar pressure conditions. (See: mud.)

luffing [**luf**•ing]
In rigging, attaching additional sets of falls to the lead line of the first set, to provide greater pulling power.

lungs [lungz]
Two sponge-like breathing organs consisting of approximately 750 million alveoli.

lymph [limpf]
A slightly yellow watery fluid found in the lymphatic vessels; any clear watery fluid resembling true lymph.

-M-

macaroni [mak•uh•ro•nee]
Small diameter drill pipe of 2-3/8 inch or 2-7/8 inch (60 mm or 73 mm) outside diameter.

machine oxygen cutting [muh•**sheen ahks**•uh•jun **kut**•ing]
Oxygen cutting with equipment which performs the cutting operation under the constant observation and control of an operator.

magnet, fishing [**mag**•nut, **fish**•ing]
In drilling, a permanent magnet run on the end of a drilling string to recover small steel junk which may be present in the hole. (See: junk.)

magneto [mag•**nee**•to]
An electrical device which generates current when rotated by an outside source of power; used for the generation of either low tension or high tension current.

main deck [mayn dek]
The principal strength deck in a vessel and the upper flange of the hull girder; also called the weather deck.

make it up another wrinkle [mayk it up uh•**nuth**•ur ring•kul]
To tighten a connection one more turn.

making a connection [**mayk**•ing uh kuh•**nek**•shun]
In drilling, the operation of adding a single joint of drill pipe to the drill string after the kelly has been drilled down its full length. (See: drill string, kelly.)

making a trip [**mayk**•ing uh trip]
In drilling, the operation of pulling the drill pipe out of the hole, changing the bit or tools, and re-running the pipe to the bottom.

man harness knot [man **hahr**•nus naht]
A knot to make a loop in the middle of a rope that is being used for hauling.

manifold [**man**•uh•fold]
A pipe with multiple openings, used to connect various cylinders to one inlet or outlet.

manifold spool [**man**•uh•fold spool]
In drilling, the top section of the underwater Christmas tree which provides access into the tree for extension tubing strings; used during completion or repair work. (See: Christmas tree, completion.)

manometer [muh•**nahm**•uh•tur]
An instrument for measuring the pressure of gases and vapors both above and below atmospheric pressure.

manual oxygen cutting [**man**•uoo•ul **ahks**•uh•jun **kut**•ing]
Oxygen cutting where the entire cutting operation is performed and controlled by hand.

margin plank [**mahr**•jun plangk]
The notched, wooden deck plank or covering board extending around the outboard edge of the main deck of a vessel, to which the deck planks are fitted.

margin plate [**mahr**•jun playt]
On a vessel, the outboard diagonal plate which connects the inner bottom plating to the shell plating at the turn of the bilge.

marine biology [muh•**reen** by•**ahl**•uh•jee]
The study of the plants and animals living in the sea.

marine completion [muh•**reen** kum•**plee**•shun]
Completion of an oil or gas well in a marine environment with a Christmas tree, either on the ocean floor or above the water. (See: Christmas tree, completion.)

marine diving technician [muh•**reen dyv**•ing tek•**nish**•un]
A diver with a high degree of technical skills.

marine ecology [muh•**reen** e•**kahl**•uh•jee]
The science of the interrelations of marine organisms and their environment, and the interrelations among the organisms themselves.

mariner's measure [**mair**•uh•nurz **may**•zhur]
6 ft. = 1 fathom; 100 fathoms = 1 cable; 10 cables = 1 mile; 6080 feet = 1 mile; 3 miles = 1 league.

marl [mahrl]
A general term for calcareous clay or calcareous loam; elsewhere but in the U.S. compact impure lime stones also are called marls.

marling [**mahr**•ling]
A simple hitch, formed by a series of overhand knots, used by seamen to lash hammocks or other gear.

marsh funnel [marsh **fun**•ul]
A funnel shaped instrument used for determining the viscosity of the circulating fluid in a well. (See: viscosity.)

Martini's law [mahr•**teen**•eez law]
A humorous "gas law" invented to help explain nitrogen narcosis: that the mental effect of each 50 feet of descent, breathing air, is approximately equivalent to that of one American-style dry martini.

mask [mask]
Diving equipment worn over the face to provide an air pocket for better vision; also may have a breathing valve. (See: band mask, demand mask, full face mask, lightweight diving mask, oronasal mask.)

mask squeeze
(See: face plate squeeze.)

mast [mast]
In drilling, the steel structure erected over a well to handle the lifting and lowering operations of a drill string or casing string. (See: casing string, drill string.)

master bushings [mast•ur boosh•ingz]
In drilling, heavy steel inserts which fit into the rotary table to support the weight of the drill string by means of removable tapered slips. (See: drill string, rotary table, slips.)

master gate [mas•tur gayt]
The main valve fitted to a wellhead of a production well.

masthead knot [mast•hed naht]
A useful knot originally used to place a strap around a temporary masthead to which other straps could be made fast.

matter [mat•ur]
Any entity displaying gravitation and inertia when at rest as well as when in motion.

maximal breathing capacity [maks•uh•mul breeth•ing kuh•pas•uh•tee]
The greatest respiratory minute volume which a person can produce during a short period of extremely forceful breathing. (See: minute volume)

maximum expiratory flow rate [mak•si•mum ek•spy•ra•toh•ree flho rayt]
The rate of flow of expirate at maximum voluntary effort on the part of the subject.

maximum inspiratory flow rate [mak•si•mum in•spy•ra•toh•ree floh rayt]
The rate of flow of inspirate at maximum voluntary effort on the part of the subject.

M.C.F.H.
Micron cubic feet per hour; a leak rate.

measure in [may•zhur in]
In drilling, to measure the drill pipe with a steel tape when running into the hole to check the true depth of the hole. (See: drill string.)

measure out [may•zhur owt]
To measure the drill pipe with a steel tape when pulling out of the hole to check the true depth of the hole. (See: drill string.)

mechanical tubing [muh•kan•uh•kul toob•ing]
Tubing for fabricating parts such as racks, scaffolding, etc., but not to be used in fluid work.

media otitis [mee•dee•uh oh•tyt•us]
Inflammation or infection of the middle ear; in diving, often used to describe a condition in which the middle ear fills with fluid. (See: externa otitis, otitis, squeeze.)

mediastinal emphysema [mee•dee•ass•tun•ul em•fuh•see•muh]
The presence of air in the mediastinum, which is the area around the heart which separates the lungs, large blood vessels and trachea. (See: emphysema.)

medical lock [med•uh•kul lahk]
Located in the inner lock in the deck decompression chamber (DDC) to facilitate the transfer of medical supplies, food or other articles between occupants of the DDC and the topside support crew. (See: deck decompression chamber.)

medullary osteonecrosis [med•joo•lair•ee ahs•tee•oh•neh•kro•sus]
Osteonecrosis occurring in the shaft of the bone; usually symptomless and unaffected by X-ray. (See: dysbaric osteonecrosis, juxta-articular osteonecrosis.)

melting time [melt•ing tym]
The weight or length of an electrode melted in a given length of time. (See: electrode.)

mesoscaph [mez•oh•skaf]
The same as a bathyscaph except for depth of operation. (See: bathyscaph.)

messenger [mes•un•jur]
In rigging, a convenient line of small diameter used to pass a line of larger diameter.

metabolism [muh•tab•uh•liz•um]
The physical and chemical changes or processes by which living substance is maintained and energy produced. Adj.: metabolic.

metal arc cutting [met•'ul ahrk kut•ing]
An arc-cutting process where the severing of metals is effected by melting with the heat of an arc between a metal electrode and the base metal.

metal to glass transition [met• ul too glas tran•zish•un]
A means of joining metal to glass.

meteorology [mee•tee•ur•ahl•uh•jee]
The study dealing with the phenomena of the atmosphere.

meter [meet•ur]
The basic unit of the metric system; equal to 1,670,763.71 wavelengths of orange-red radiation.

MEWA
Motor and Equipment Wholesalers Association.

micrometer [my•**krahm**•uh•tur]
A measuring instrument for either external or internal measurement in thousandths (sometimes tenths of thousandths) of inches.

microphone [**myk**•ruh•fon]
An electroacoustic transducer that responds to sound waves and delivers essentially equivalent electric waves.

middle ear squeeze [mid•'ul eer skweez]
Squeeze caused by the inability to equalize the pressure in the middle ear through the Eustachian tube as the external pressure builds up against the eardrum; results in bleeding between the tympanic membrane and the middle ear spaces. (See: squeeze.)

M.I.G.
Metal inert gas; a form of welding used to weld non-ferrous metals such as aluminum.

MIG welding [MIG **weld**•ing]
An arc welding process where coalescence is produced by heating with an electric arc between a filler metal electrode and the work.

MIL
Military specification.

mild plow steel [myld plow steel]
Rope wire of little tensile strength or abrasion resistance.

miller's knot [**mil**•urz naht]
A knot similar to the clove hitch. (See: clove hitch.)

millimeter [**mil**•uh•mee•tur]
The metric equivalent of .039370 of an inch, one inch being the equivalent of 25.4 mm.

millisecond caps [**mil**•uh•sek•und kaps]
In demolition, delay electric caps which have a built-in delay element; also, MS caps.

millisecond connectors [**mil**•uh•sek•und kun•**ek**•turz]
In blasting, detonating cord connectors which have a built-in delay element; also, MS connectors.

minute volume [**mi**•nut **vol**•yoom]
The total volume of air passing in and out of the lungs in one minute.

mirror finish [**meer**•ur **fin**•ish]
A bright, polished surface.

misfire [mis•**fyr**]
In blasting, a charge, or part of a charge, that has failed to fire as planned; misfires considered extremely dangerous until the cause of the misfire has been determined.

mixed gas [mikst gas]
A breathing medium consisting of oxygen and one or more inert gases, synthetically mixed.

(See: gas, breathing gas, diluent gas, inert gas, separated gas.)

mixed gas dive [mikst gas dyv]
A dive using a mixture of gases as a breathing medium; the ratio of diluent gas to oxygen is changed to keep the partial pressure of oxygen at or near the normal 1-atmosphere level.

moderate breeze [**mah**•dur•ut breez]
A wind of 11 to 16 knots (13 to 18 miles per hour.

moderate gale [**mah**•dur•ut gayl]
A wind of 28 to 33 knots (32 to 38 miles) per hour.

modulation [mah•joo•**lay**•shun]
Refers to variation in the value of some sound parameter characterizing a periodic oscillation; best known are: amplitude modulation (AM) and frequency modulation (FM).

modules [**mah**•joolz]
Large containers in which are housed the various units of drilling equipment such as power packs, pumping sets, control equipment, sewage plant, etc., for installation on a production platform. (See: production platform.)

mohole [**mo**•hol]
A word coined to refer to a project which attempts to drill, at sea, through the crust of the earth.

molecule [**mahl**•uh•kyool]
A stable grouping of atomic nuclei and electrons bound together by electrostatic and electromagnetic forces.

monkey board [**mung**•kee bord]
In drilling the platform used by the derrick man above the derrick floor to handle stacking of the stands when pulling out or running in the drill string. (See: derrick, drilling crew, drill string, pulling out, running in, stand.)

monkey tail [**mung**•kee tayl]
In rigging, wooden four-by-four or other item used to prevent a travel block or turnbuckle from twisting.

monochrome [**mahn**•uh•krom]
One color; refers to black and white photography.

monoplace chamber [**mahn**•oh•plays **chaym**•bur]
A portable one-person hyperbaric chamber used for therapy in a hospital setting and for transport. (See: altitude chamber, chamber, compression chamber, deck decompression chamber, double lock chamber, hyperbaric chamber, multiplace chamber, single-lock chamber, submersible chamber.)

mooring [**moo**•ring]
Commonly, the anchor, chain, buoy, pennant,

etc., by which a boat is pernamently anchored in one location.

moray eel [mor•ay eel]
A snake-like marine animal with powerful jaws and strong, sharp teeth capable of inflicting severe lacerations; seldom attack without provocation, but may act aggressively to defend their territory. (See: hazardous marine animals.)

motor [mo•tur]
Used in connection with an electric motor and not when referring to an engine.

mouse hole [mows hol]
In drilling, a shallow hole drilled near the rotary table to accommodate a single joint of drill pipe; allows for the addition of single joints of drill pipe to the drilling string without having to set back the kelly into the rathole when making a connection. (See: drill string, kelly, making a connection, rathole, rotary table.)

mousing [mows•ing]
In rigging, wiring the throat of a hook to prevent the choker from jumping out, or the block from slipping off. (See: block, choker, hook.)

mouthpiece [mowth•pees]
A relatively watertight channel for the flow of breathing gas between the life-support system and the diver; consists of a flange which fits between the lips and teeth and two bits, one on either side of the mouthpiece opening, which serve to hold the teeth comfortably apart; held in place by slight pressure of the lips and teeth.

M.S.
Military standard or military specification; also mil spec.

muck pile [muk pyl]
The rock, broken by an explosive, that remains within the limits of the excavation.

mucus [myoo•kus]
The watery secretion of the mucous membranes, that moistens and protects them

mud [mud]
Fluid used for circulating in a well during a drilling operation, containing chemicals and additives to provide correct specific gravity, viscosity, fluid loss, gelling capability, etc.; type of formation pressure, and other conditions dictate the exact mixture. (See: gel, mud-cake.)

mud box [mud bahks]
In drilling, the tank or container from which the circulating pump sucks mud to deliver it to the well.

mud cake [mud kayk]
In drilling, a deposit of solids from the drilling mud which builds up on the wall of a well; possibly keeping the bit from being pulled out of the hole. (See: bit, mud.)

mud ditch [mud dich]
In drilling, a ditch or flume through which mud returns from the vibrator screen to the circulating pump suction tank. (See: mud, vibrating screen.)

mud, gas cut [mud, gas kut]
In drilling, circulating mud containing gas, causing the hydrostatic pressure of a column of mud to be below normal, leading to possible blow out; small quantities of gas can be removed by gunning but in extreme cases the mud is replaced. (See: mud, mud gun.)

mud gun [mud gun]
A stand pipe fitted with a swivelling jet pipe which is used for agitating fluid in a tank for the purpose of thoroughly mixing the ingredients of a drilling mud. (See: mud.)

mud hog [mud hahg]
In drilling, a slush pump for circulating the mud in a well bore. (See: duplex pump, mud.)

mud logging
(See: logging-mud.)

mud mixing plant [mud muks•ing plant]
A combination of pumps, piping manifold, hoppers guns and tanks used in mixing drilling mud. (See: cement hopper, mud, mud gun.)

mud off [mud awf]
The procedure used to kill a well or to prevent the formation fluids from entering the well bore. (See: killing a well.)

mud pit [mud pit]
In drilling, the pit or tank into whch return fluid from the well discharges; also used for storing reserve mud.

multiplace chamber [mul•tuh•p'l chaym•bur]
A pressure chamber designed to be used by more than one person at a time; usually a double lock chamber. (See: chamber, altitude chamber, compression chamber, deck compression chamber, double-lock chamber, hyperbaric chamber, monoplace chamber, single-lock chamber, submersible decompression chamber.)

muscle voluntary [mus•'ul vahl•un•tair•ee]
A bundle of contractile fibers which produce movement in the body.

M value [em val•yoo]
The maximum valve of the partial pressure of dissolved gas which can be tolerated in a specific compartment of the human body and still permit a diver to ascend safely to the next stop.

myalgia [my•al•jee•uh]
Muscle pain or aching.

myocardium [my•oh•kahrd•ee•um]
The muscular substance of the heart.

myopia [my•**oh**•pee•uh]
A vision deficiency in which light rays forcus in front of the retina,corrected by concave lens; near sightedness.

-N-

narcosis [nahr•**ko**•sus]
A state of altered mental function ranging from mild impairment of judgment or euphoria (false sense of well-being), to complete loss of consciousness; resembles alcoholic intoxication; produced by exposure to increased partial pressure of nitrogen and certain other gases. (See: inert gas narcosis, Martini's law, nitrogen narcosis.)

nasal passages [**nay**•zul **pas**•uh•juz]
Openings where air enters the body as it is breathed in; nose hairs collect dust, moist walls filter the air, and the air is warmed as it moves through the passages.

natural gas
(See: gas-natural.)

nausea [**naw**•zhuh]
An unpleasant sensation, vaguely referred to the stomach, often culminating in vomiting.

nautical mile [**naw**•tik•ul myl]
A unit of distance designed to equal approximately 1 minute of arc of latitude; according to the National Bureau of Standards, its length is 6,080.20 feet, or approximately 1.15 times as long as the statute mile of 5,280 feet; also known as a geographical mile.

NAVOCEANO
Naval Oceanographic Office; located in Washington, D.C., engaged in deep ocean survey.

NCN
(See: nitro-carbo-nitrate.)

neap tide [neep tyd]
A tide which occurs near the first and third quarters of the moon; low because of the sun and moon pulling at right angles to each other; also called nipped tide or scanty tide.

nearshore zone [neer•**shor** zon]
Zone extending seaward from the shore to an indefinite distance beyond the surf zone.

necrosis [hek•**roh**•sis]
The death or decay of tissue in a part of the body, as bone; it is the result of loss of blood supply, burning or other severe injuries.

negative buoyancy [neg•uh•tiv **booy**•yun•see]
State in which the weight of the submerged body is greater than the weight of the displaced liquid, causing the body to sink.

negative pole [**neg**•uh•tiv pol]
The point to which an electrical current returns after passing through the circuit.

negative-pressure breathing [NPB]
Breathing from a mask, helmet, or the like, where the pressure of the gaseous mixture being breathed is less than the ambient pressure thus requiring an additional conscious effort to inhale.

neon [**nee**•ahn]
A colorless, odorless gas found in air (1 part in about 65,000 parts of ordinary air); has been used as a breathing gas for divers because it has minimal narcotic effect.

neoprene [**nee**•uh•preen]
An oil-resistant synthetic rubber; because of its insulation properties, it is used for diver wet suits.

nervous system [**nur**•vus **sis**•tum]
Brain, spinal cord, and nerves of the body.

net tonnage [net **tun**•uj]
A volumetric measurement of the internal capacity of a vessel; the mesurement excludes the crew quarters and machinery spaces.

neuralgia [nyoor•**al**•juh]
An aching or spasmodic pain along the course of nerves.

neuritis [nyoor•**eye**•tus]
Inflammation of a nerve, usually accompanied by pain, tenderness, and possibly loss of sensation.

neuromuscular [noo•roh•**mus**•kyoo•ar]
Intermediate in nature between nerve and muscle; pertaining both to nerve and muscle, as neuromuscular cells.

neuron [**nyoor**•ahn]
The nerve cell body plus its processes; the structural unit of nerve tissue.

neutral buoyancy [noo•trul **booy**•un•see]
The state in which the weight of the body is equal to the weight of the displaced liquid, so the body remains suspened in the liquid. (See: buoyancy, negative buoyancy, positive buoyancy.)

N.G.
(See: nitroglycerin.)

niggle [**nig**•'ul]
Mild, transient and poorly localized symptoms of decompression sickness not requiring treatment.

night vision [nyt **vi**•zhun]
The natural adaptation to darkness as a diver descends; includes no color perception; when a diver remains on the bottom for a period of time, it will seem as if the light has increased.

nitramon [**ny**•truh•mahn]
A high explosive.

nitro-carbo-nitrate [**ny**•tro-**kahr**-bo-**ny**•trayt]
A nonexplosive substance used as a blasting agent.

nitrogen [**ny**•truh•jun]
A colorless, odorless, tasteless, nontoxic inert gas found in great abundance in the atmosphere; nitrogen is commonly used as a diluent with oxygen in diving gas mixtures; when breathed under pressure, has narcotic effect. (See: narcosis, nitrogen narcosis.)

nitrogen narcosis [**ny**•truh•jun nahr•**ko**•sus]
Narcotic effect resulting from breathing the nitrogen in compressed air at depths greater than approximately 100 feet; also called air narcosis and "rapture of the deep". (See: inert gas narcosis, rapture of the deep.)

nitroglycerin [ny•tro•**glis**•ur•un]
A highly explosive oil; a sensitizing and energy ingredient in most dynamites.

nitrox [**ny**•trahks]
A breathing mixture containing nitrogen and oxygen in various proportions; used in diving when the oxygen partial pressure must be reduced because of the depth of the dive and the danger of oxygen poisoning.

no-decompression dive [no-de•kum•**presh**•un dyv]
A dive from which a diver can return directly to the surface at a controlled rate without stopping at shallower depths to allow inert gas to be eliminated from the body; also called a no-stop dive.

no-decompression limits [no-de•kum•**presh**•un lim•uts]
Specified times at given depths from which no decompression stops are required on return to the surface; also referred to as a no-stop curve and no-stop limits.

non-ferrous metals [nahn-**fair**•us met•'ulz]
Metals which contain no iron or very little iron and are therefore not subject to rusting.

non-return valve
(See: valve — non-return.)

nontidal current [nahn•**tyd**•ul **kur**•unt]
Current that is due to causes other than tidal forces; classed as nontidals are the Gulf Stream, the Japan current, Labrador, and equatorial currents which are part of general ocean circula-

tion; also river discharges and temporary currents set up by winds.

normoxie [nor•**mahk**•see•uh]
Tissue oxygen pressure with levels of oxygen equivalent to normal partial pressures of oxygen found in air at one atmosphere.

normoxic [nor•**mahk**•sik]
Relating to normal partial pressures of oxygen equivalent to those found in air at one atmosphere.

Norske Veritas [**norsk**•ee vair•uh•tahs]
Shipping classification society of Norway, instituted in 1864.

nose plate [noz playt]
On a vessel, the vertical rounded plate fitted around the forward face of the stem which joins the forward edges of the port and starboard strakes. (See: strake.)

no-stop
(See: no-decompression limits.)

no-stop curve
(See: no-decompression limits.)

NSPA
National Standard Parts Association.

nucleation
(See: gas nucleation.)

nucleus [**nyoo**•klee•us]
A small spherical body within a cell; in chemistry, the central part of an atom.

nun buoy [nun bu•oee]
A conical red buoy bearing an even number and marking the starboard side of a channel from seaward.

nystagmus [ny•**stag**•mus]
An involuntary, rapid, movement of the eyeball.

-O-

oakum [oh•kum]
Rope strands of hemp or jute impregnated with pine tar.

observation bell [ahb•zur•**vay**•shun bell]
A tethered one-atmosphere bell used for search and observation; also called observation chamber. (See: bell, open bell.)

OBSS
Ocean Bottom Scanning Sonar; one of the first side-scan sonars, it sends narrow beams of sonic energy to either side of a towed body or a sub-

mersible, and receives a reflected pattern that shows a map of the terrain comparable to an aerial photograph.

occipital [ahk•sip•uh•ul]
Relating to the back part of the head.

ocean engineering [oh•shun en•juh•neer•ing]
The engineering concerned with the development of new equipment concepts and techniques which enable man to operate beneath the surface of the ocean.

oceanography [oh•shun•nag•ra•fee]
The study of the sea including physical boundaries, the chemistry and physics of sea water, and marine biology.

octopus [ahk•tuh•poos]
Although timid with its danger to man overrated, a marine animal having powerful parrot-like beak which can inflict a painful bite and some species are venomous; one species found off Australia, the blue-ringed octopus which is only four inches long, carries enough venom to kill ten humans. (See: hazardous marine animals.)

octopus rig [ahk•tuh•poos rig]
A single-hose regulator with an extra low-pressure port to which an additional second stage has been fitted; double regulator is for emergency shared-air breathing or in case of failure of the primary regulator.

O.D.
Outside diameter.

odograph [oh•duh•graf]
An instrument which records courses steered and distances (or time intervals) run on each course; a course recorder.

offset [awf•set]
A well bore which is set off from the vertical.
(See: directional drilling.)

offshore bar [awf•shor bahr]
Sandbar running parallel to coastline.

offshore currents [awf•shor kur•unts]
Prevailing nontidal current parallel to shore outside surf zone.

offshore structure [awf•shor struk•chur]
A steel or concrete structure installed on the sea bed for the purpose of supporting a drilling rig or oil or gas production equipment.

O.F.H.C.
Oxygen free high conductivity; copper which is free of oxygen, copper oxide, and residual copper deoxidants; commercially pure with high electrical conductance and a high resistance to hydrogen embrittlement.

ohm [om]
A measurement of the resistance to the flow of an electrical current through a conductor.

OHP
Oxygen high pressure; higher than normal partial pressure of oxygen within the body; also HPO.

oil field [oyl feeld]
An area where productive oil deposits have been located.

oil horizon [oyl hur•aye•zun]
The interface between oil and gas, or oil and water, in a reservoir. (See: interface.)

oil sand [oyl sand]
Porous sandstone formation containing oil.

oil show [oyl sho]
Indication of an oil reservoir by the presence of oil in the cuttings returning to surface, or of oil flowing into the well bore.

oil string [oyl streeng]
In drilling, the casing string which is run to keep the well open to bring fluid to the surface from an oil bearing formation. (See: casing string.)

olfactory [ol•fak•tur•ee]
Pertaining to the sense of smell.

OLP
Oxygen low pressure; lower than normal partial pressure of oxygen within the body.

omitted decompression [oh•mit•ud de•kum•presh•uh]
An ascent in which a diver comes to the surface at a rate greater than 60 feet salt water per minute, or without one or more decompression stops.

one-atmosphere diving suit
(See: one-atmosphere diving system.)

one-atmosphere diving system [wun-at•mus•feer dyv•ing sis•tum]
A pressure resistant, one-person system with articulated arms and legs, equipped with life-support capability and designed to operate at an internal pressure of one atmosphere, regardless of the external pressure.

one-circuit hot water suit
(See: suits — diving.)

one-man chamber
(See: chamber — monoplace.)

on the pump [ahn thuh pump]
Said of a well which will not flow because of low reservoir pressure; must be fitted with a down hole pump. (See: down hole pump.)

open bell [oh•pun bel]
A diving bell open at the bottom; containing a

gas pocket in the upper part; used as an elevator or haven. (See: bell.)

open center [oh•pun sen•tur]
Refers to hydraulic system in which oil is continuously cycled.

open circuit apparatus [oh•pun sur•kut ap•ur•at•us]
Diving life-support system in which the diver's exhalation is completely vented to the water.

open circuit voltage [oh•pum sur•kut vol•tuj]
The voltage between the terminals of a power source when no current is flowing in the circuit.

open hole [oh•pun hol]
The uncased portion of a well.

organism [org•uh•niz•um]
An individual animal or plant; any organized living thing.

oronasal mask [or•oh•nay•zul mask]
A breathing mask that covers and allows breathing through both nose and mouth. (See: mask, band mask, demand mask, full face mask, lightweight diving mask.)

osmosis [ahs•mo•sus]
The passage of a pure solvent, such as water, from a solution of lesser concentration to one of greater concentration, through a semipermeable membrane.

osseous [ahs•see•us]
Bony; resembling or having the quality of bone.

ostalgia [as•tal•ja]
Pain in a bone.

osteitis [as•tee•y•tis]
Inflammation the bone or bony tissue.

osteonecrosis
(See: dysbaric osteonecrosis, juxta-articular osteonecrosis, medullary osteonecrosis.)

osteoneuralgia [a•stee•oh•noo•ral•ja]
Pain of a bone.

otic [oh•tik]
Pertaining to the ear; aural.

otitis [oh•tyt•us]
Inflammation of the ear which may be marked by pain, fever, abnormalities of hearing, tinnitus and vertigo; a very common problem in diving. (See: externa otitis, media otitis.)

outcrop [owt•krahp]
Naturally protruding or erosionally exposed part of a rock, bed or formation, most of which is covered by overlying material.

outgassing [owt•gas•ing]
In vacuum terminology, the vaporization of contaminants within a vacuum system as pressure is decreased; commonly refers to the decom-

pression of a diver back to normal condition; the process of gas elimination.

out step well [owt step wel]
A well drilled to explore the extent of a field beyond the proven area.

overboard dump system
(See: dump system.)

overbreak [oh•vur•brayk]
In blasting, excessive breaking of rock beyond the line planned.

overexertion [oh•vur•eg•zur•shun]
Physical condition characterized by a feeling of suffocation, inability to breathe deeply enough for comfort; working beyond the limits of fitness; also called exhaustion.

overhand knot [oh•vur•hand naht]
One of three basic turns in knotting; the simplest of the end knots.

overhead position [oh•vur•hed puh•zish•un]
The position where welding is performed from the underside of the joint.

overlap [oh•vur•lap]
Protrusion of weld metal beyond the bond at the toe of the weld.

overpressure [oh•vur•presh•ur]
The pressure in excess of normal ambient levels, created by the detonation of an explosive; refers to either air or water.

overshot [oh•vur•shaht]
In drilling, a fishing tool fitted with slips with radial teeth which is designed to recover a string of pipe lost in a hole. (See: fishing tools, slips.)

oxidation [ahks•uh•day•shun]
Induction of chemical reaction or reactions in which oxygen is added to a substance; rust.

oxter plates [ahks•tur playts]
On a vessel, plates attached to the stern frame forming the counter in way of the rudderpost.

oxy acetylene cutting [ahk•see uh•set•uh•leen kur•ing]
An oxygen-cutting process where the severing of metals is effected by means of the chemical reaction of oxygen with the base metal at elevated temperatures, the necessary temperature maintained by means of gas flames obtained from the combustion of acetylene with oxygen.

oxy-fuel gas cutting [ahk•see-fyoo•ul gas kut•ing]
An oxygen cutting method where the severing of metals is effected by means of the chemical reaction of oxygen with the base metal at elevated temperatures, the necessary temperature being maintained by means of gas flames obtained from the combustion of a specified fuel and oxygen.

oxy-gas cutting
(See: oxygen cutting.)

oxygen [ahks•uh•jun]
A colorless, odorless, tasteless and, under normal conditions, non toxic gas; found free in the atmosphere; the most abundant element in the ocean; essential in cellular respiration of all animals and man, but may be toxic at elevated partial pressures.

oxygen-arc cutting [ahk•see•jun•ahrk kut•ing]
An oxygen-cutting process where the severing of metals is effected by means of the chemical reaction of oxygen with the base metal at elevated temperatures; also oxy-arc.

oxygen at high pressure
(See: hyperbaric oxygenation.)

oxygen breathing [ahks•uh•jun breeth•ing]
The breathing of 100 percent oxygen; in diving, used in some closed-circuit scuba and in the treatment of decompression sickness, also to enhance the elimination of inert gas during the final stages of decompression.

oxygen cleaning [ahks•uh•jun kleen•ing]
A method of cleaning a diving gas supply system in which high percentages of oxygen are to be used ensure elimination of all hydrocarbons and other potentially combustible contaminants.

oxygen cutting [ahks•uh•jun kut•ing]
A group of cutting processes where the severing or removing of metals is effected by means of the chemical reaction of oxygen with the base metal at elevated temperature; in the case of oxi oxidation-resistant metals, the reaction is facilitated by the use of a chemical flux or metal powder.

oxygen-cutting operator [ahks•uh•jun-kut•ing ah•pur•ay•tur]
One who operates a machine or automatic oxygen-cutting equipment.

oxygen dump system
(See: dump systems.)

oxygen high pressure (OHP) [ahks•uh•jun hy presh•ur]
In diving, higher than normal partial pressure of oxygen within the body.

oxygen-lance [ahks•uh•jun-lans]
A length of pipe used to convey oxygen to the point of cutting in oxygen-lance cutting.

oxygen-lance cutting [ahks•uh•jun-lans kut•ing]
An oxygen-cutting process where only oxygen is supplied by the lance and the preheat is obtained by other means.

oxygen lancing
(See: oxygen-lance cutting.)

oxygen poisoning
(See: oxygen toxicity)

oxygen toxicity [ahks•uh•jun tahk•sis•uh•tee]
Delterious effects caused by breathing high partial pressures of oxygen; rolonged exposure can result in effects which become progressively more severe as the inspired partial pressure and or the duration of exposure increases; depending on level and length of exposure, may cause lung damage, involvement of the central nervous system or convulsions.

oxy-hydrogen cutting [ahks•ee-hy•druh•jun kut•ing]
An oxygen cutting method where the severing of metal is effected by means of the chemical reaction of oxygen with the base metal at elevated temperatures, the necessary temperature being maintained by means of gas flames obtained from the combustion of hydrogen and oxygen.

oxy-natural gas cutting [ahks•ee-nach•ur•ul kut•ing]
An oxygen-cutting method where the severing of metals is effected by means of the chemical reaction of oxygen with the base metal at elevated temperatures, the necessary temperature being maintained by means of gas flames obtained from the combustion of natural gas with oxygen.

oxy propane cutting [ahk•see pro•payn kut•ing]
An oxygen-cutting method where the severing of metals is effected by means of the chemical reaction of oxygen with the base metal at elevated temperatures, the necessary temperature being maintained by means of gas flames obtained from combustion of propane with oxygen.

-P-

packer [pak•ur]
In drilling, an expanding rubber plug set in a hole to hold back the fluid.

packer's knot [pak•urz naht]
A figure-eight knot tied around the standing part.

padeye [pad•eye]
On a vessel, the combination of a circle of steel stock secured to a double plate which is attached to the deck, bulkhead, overhead or structural.

panting [**pant**•ing]
On a vessel, the tendency of the bow plating to move in and out as a result of the water pressure differential caused by pitching in a seaway.

paradoxical shivering [pair•uh•**dahk**•suh•kul **shiv**•ur•ing]
Uncontrollable shivering under conditions of high helium partial pressures, accompanied by a subjective feeling of warmth.

parallax [**pair**•uh•laks]
A visual phenomenon, the apparent displacement of an object as seen from two different points not on a straight line with the object.

parasite [**pair**•uh•syt]
Any organism that lives within or upon another at the expense of the other.

paresthesia [par•es•**thee**•zha]
Abnormal sensation without objective cause, such as numbness, pricking, etc.; heightened sensitivity.

partial pressure [**pahr**•shul **presh**•ur]
Pressure exerted by one component in a gaseous system, described by Dalton's law; the partial pressure of a gas is equal to the product of the ambient pressure and that fraction of the total pressure in a mixture which can be ascribed to that gas. (See: ambient pressure, atmospheric pressure, Dalton's law, design pressure, gauge pressure, hydrostatic pressure, pressure, working pressure.)

particle velocity [**pahr**•tuh•kul vuh•**lah**•suh•tee]
The oscillatory velocity of any given particle of earth caused by the detonation of an explosive; used as a measure of the magnitude of blast-induced ground motions.

Pascal's law [**pas**•culz law]
The component of the pressure in a fluid in equilibrium due to forces externally applied is uniform throughout the body of the fluid; externally applied pressure is transmitted equally throughout all fluid-filled spaces. (See: laws.)

pass [pas]
A single longitudinal progression of a welding operation along a joint or weld deposit; the result of a pass is a weld bead.

pathology [path•**ahl**•uh•jee]
The study or branch of medicine that deals with disease and the changes in body tissues and organs caused by disease or trauma.

Paul Bert effect [powl bair uh•**fekt**]
Convulsions caused by oxygen at raised pressures, first observed by the French physiologist for whom the condition is named.

pawl [pawl]
On a vessel, the metal cog used inside winches to prevent the winch from turning in order to lock the load in position.

payload [**pay**•lod]
On a research vessel, the amount of weight a vehicle can carry, excluding research crew, observers and their personal effects; usually, payload is made up of scientific instruments which are not a regular part of the boat's instruments.

pay sand [pay sand]
A sand reservoir which contains oil or gas of productive value.

peak [peek]
A seamount rising more than 500 fathoms from the sea floor and having a round or pointed top.

peak tanks [peek tangks]
Large compartments located at the bow and stern of a vessel for the storage of water or ballast.

peening [**peen**•ing]
The mechanical working of metal by means of blows with a hammer.

pelagic [puh•**laj**•ik]
Refers to free-swimming or floating organisms of the open sea.

pelican hook [**pel**•uh•kun hook]
A quick-release hinged hook used where speed in disconnecting is a prime requisite.

pendant [**pen**•dunt]
On a vessel, a length of rope having thimble or block spliced into the lower end for hooking on tackle.

penetration [pen•uh•**tray**•shun]
The distance into a target that the target material is broken and shattered by an explosive; for example, the depth of the hole produced by a conical shaped charge.

pennant [**pen**•unt]
Special flag usually having a greater length or "fly" than its breadth or "hoist."

perception of color underwater [pur•**sep**•shun uv **kul**•ur un•dur•**wah**•tur]
Conditions of lighting and water color may cause red and blue to appear black; in clear ocean water, however, yellow and dark blue retain their color and, in green water, red and blue-green retain theirs, to a considerable depth; proceding toward depth, red is filtered out first, then orange, then yellow, then green, then blue; factors other than depth affecting color underwater include salinity, turbidity and the degree of pollution of the water. (See: adaptation, night vision.)

percussion drilling
(See: drilling — percussion.)

perforating [**pur**•fur•ay•ting]
In drilling, piercing the casing by use of a gun opposite a producing formation, to allow the oil to flow into the casing. (See: gun-perforating.)

perfusion [pur•**fyoo**•zhun]
The flow of blood or lymph through an organ or tissue, by which gases and chemical substances are distributed and exchanged. (See: diffusion.)

pericardium [pair•uh•**kahr**•dee•um]
The serous membrane that lines the sac enclosing the heart.

perilymph fistula [**pair**•uh•limf **fis**•tyoo•luh]
A round or oval window rupture allowing the fluid (perilymph) surrounding the middle ear to escape into the inner ear; rupture of the round or oval windows is caused by stretching them beyond capacity or by a sudden reversal in position, usually occurring during a forceful attempt to clear the ears. (See: alternobaric.)

permeability [pur•me•uh•**bil**•uh•tee]
In drilling, the condition of a formation which allows or does not allow the flow of fluid to pass through the rock and into the well bore.

permissibles [pur•**mis**•ub•bulz]
In blasting, those explosives approved by the U.S. Bureau of Mines for nontoxic fumes and allowed in underground work.

personnel transfer capsule [pur•sun•**nel trans**•fur **kap**•sool]
A diving chamber for the transfer of personnel between the surface and the underwater work site that can be mated to the deck decompression chamber (DDC); can either be maintained at one atmosphere or pressurized, depending on the type of system used. (See: bell, deck decompression chamber.)

persuader [pur•**swayd**•ur]
A large tool used to exert excessive pull when unscrewing a very tight joint of pipe, etc.

petcock [**pet**•kahk]
A small valve placed at various points in a fluid circuit for draining purposes.

PETN
The high explosive core of primacord. (See: primacord.)

pH
Measure of relative acidity and alkalinity based on a 0 to 14 scale; seven is pH of pure water and represents neutrality; below 7 acidity increases as hydrogen ions increase, above 7 alkalinity increases as ions decrease.

pharyngeal [fur•in•jee•ul]
Referring to the pharynx.

pharynx [**fair**•ingks]
The saclike tube extending from the nose and mouth to the larynx and esophagus; also, the throat. (See: esophagus, larynx.)

phoria [**for**•ee•uh]
Any tendency of deviation of the eyes from normal.

photosensitive [fo•to•**sen**•suh•tiv]
Affected by light; also refers to photographic emulsions.

physical oceanography [**fiz**•uh•kul oh•shun•**ah**•gruh•fee]
The study of the physical aspects of the ocean: its density, temperature, ability to transmit light and sound, and sea ice; the movements of the sea, such as tides, currents and waves.

physics of diving [**fiz**•iks uv **dyv**•ing]
The application of physical laws and principles to underwater activities.

physio-diver [**fiz**•ee•oh-**dyv**•ur]
Colloquial for a scientific diver working in the field of underwater physiology or pyschology.

physiology [fiz•ee•**ahl**•uh•jee]
The science which deals with the activities or functions of the body and its parts.

physiology of diving [fiz•ee•**ahl**•uh•jee•uv **dyv**•ing]
The organic processes and phenomena dealing with life and the functions of organs of human beings while in a water environment.

pig [pig]
A device used for pumping through a pipeline to clean the walls of the pipe or to clean an obstruction; also a go devil. (See: rabbit.)

pilot [**py**•lut]
One who conducts a ship out of or into a harbor.

pilot bit [**py**•lut bit]
A bit used for starting a directional hole, i.e., a hole deviated from the true vertical. (See: directional drilling.)

pin [pin]
A tapered male thread connection.

ping [ping]
An acoustic pulse signal projected by an underwater transducer.

pinger
(See: beacon.)

pintles [**pin**•tulz]
On a vessel, vertical pins attached to rudders which fit into gudgeons on the rudderpost about which the rudder pivots.

pipe hitch [pyp hich]
A hitch used for lifting a bar or post straight up.

pipeline oil [pyp•lyn oyl]
Oil which is clean enough to be marketed.

pipeline, submarine [pyp•lyn, sub•mur•een]
A pipeline which is trenched into the sea bed; laid by special lay barge and fed off by means of a stinger (ramp) at the stern of the barge. (See: lay barge.)

pipe rack [pyp rak]
In drilling, a staging outside the derrick floor on which drill pipe or casing is stored and can be easily pulled into the derrick floor by way of the pipe ramp. (See: casing ramp, derrick.)

pirate sand [py•rut sand]
In drilling, a porous sandstone which allows fluid to escape from the bore hole.

pitch [pich]
On a vessel, the motion in the fore-and-aft plane, so the bow dips and rises.

pitch, propeller [pich, pruh•pel•ur]
The distance the blade of a propeller will advance during one complete revolution.

pitman [pit•mun]
In drilling, the rod which connects the walking beam to the drive crank on a percussion drilling rig. (See: drilling-percussion, walking beam.)

planking [plang•king]
On a vessel, the wood covering of the hull and decks.

plasma [plaz•muh]
The fluid portion of the blood.

plasmaarc cutting [plaz•muhahrk kut•ing]
An arc cutting process where severing of the metal is obtained by melting a localized area with a constricted arc and removing the molten material with a high velocity jet of hot, ionized gas.

plasma arc welding [plaz•muh ahrk weld•ing]
An arc welding process where coalescence is produced by heating with a constricted arc between an electrode and the workpiece (transferred arc) or the electrode and the constricting nozzle (non-transferred arc); shielding is obtained from the hot, ionized gas issuing from the orifice which may be supplemented by an auxiliary source of shielding gas.

plastic range [plas•tik raynj]
The stress range where material will take on permanent deformation due to some load above yield.

platelet [playt•lut]
A small, non-nucleated cell found in the blood of all animals, concerned with blood coagulation and contraction of a clot; platelet loss often occurs after decompression; also thrombocyte.

platform [plat•form]
Any man-made structure from which oceanographic instruments are suspended or on which they are installed, or from which diving operations are conducted.

pleura [ploo•ra]
A thin serous membrane, which covers the inside of the thorax and also envelopes the lungs separately, forming two closed sacs. The two layers covering the lungs and inner chest wall are held in opposition by surface tension and by positive barometric pressure inflating the lungs. These overcome the elastic recoil of the lungs.

pleurisy [ploor•uh•see]
Inflammation of the serous membrane covering the lungs and lining of the chest cavity; also, pleuritis.

plot [plaht]
To mark on a chart a ship's position, course or bearing.

plow steel [plow steel]
Intermediate grade of rope wire.

plug back [plug bak]
In drilling, to place a cement plug at the bottom of a hole to seal off an area.

plug, blow out [plug, blo owt]
A device installed in a cylinder valve assembly, designed to fail under pressure before the cylinder fails.

plumb line [plum lyn]
A weight line used to measure vertical dimensions and horizontal deflections.

pneumofathometer [noo•mo•fath•ahm•uh•tur]
A hollow tube, connected at the surface end to a gauge, and open at the diver's end under the surface; used to measure the water pressure at the diver's end of the tube.

pneumogauge hose [noo•mo•gayj hos]
A durable, lightweight, flexible hose attached to a low-pressure air supply source on the surface and open at the diver's end; used to monitor the diver's depth; usually attached to the umbilical with the open end terminating at the diver's chest. (See: pneumofathometer, umbilical.)

pneumonia [noo•mon•yuh]
Inflammation of the lungs.

pneumopericardium [noo•mo•pair•uh•kar•dee•um]
A condition in which gas is present in the membrane sac which contains the heart.

pneumothorax [noo•mo•thor•aks]
The presence of air between the lungs and the chest wall; possible collapse of lung tissues and

corresponding respiratory compromise; specifically, the result of rupture of cysts on the lung surface or dissection of gas along fascial planes to the mediastinum and thence around a lung to produce collapse.

point [poynt]
One of the 32 points of the compass equal to 11¼ degrees. Also, a sailboats ability to sail close to the wind.

point charge [poynt chahrj]
A charge with its length no more than two or three diameters; when detonated, it acts as if the explosion energy comes from a single point.

polarity [po•lair•uh•tee]
Refers to the positive or negative terminal of a battery or an electric circuit; also the north or south pole of a magnet.

polarization [pol•ur•uh•**zay**•shun]
Confinement of oscillation of light waves, or other radiating energy waves, to a certain plane.

polished rod [**pahl**•isht rahd]
In drilling, a highly polished rod operates a down hole pump or down hole tools in a well which may be under pressure condition.

pontoon [pahn•**toon**]
A portable steel tank or fabric balloon used to displace water and provide positive buoyancy. (See: positive buoyancy.)

poor boy [poor boy]
In drilling, said of a tool or operation which is done cheaply instead of making use of the most sophisticated equipment or service available.

porosity [por•**ahs**•uh•tee]
The percentage of void in a porous rock compared to the percentage of solid formation.

port [port]
Harbor; also, the left-hand side of a ship looking from aft toward the bow.

porthole [port•hol]
An aperture in a ship's side fitted with glass for admitting light.

Portuguese man-of-war [**Port**•chuh•geez man-uv-wor]
Often mistaken for a jellyfish, a marine animal, sometimes called a blue bottle, which floats on the surface of the water, drifting with the current in large concentrations; produces a toxin similar to that of a cobra, and has been responsible for many injuries, ranging from minor irritation to shock and respiratory arrest. (See: hazardous marine animals.)

position of welding [puh•**zish**•un uv **weld**•ing]
(See: flat welding, horizontal welding, overhead welding, vertical welding.)

positive buoyancy [**pahz**•uh•tiv booy•yun•see]
The state in which the weight of the displaced liquid is greater than the weight of the submerged body, so the body will float or be buoyed upward. (See: buoyancy, negative buoyancy, neutral buoyancy.)

positive pole [**pahz**•uh•tiv pol]
The point from where current flows to the circuit.

post heating [post **heet**•ing]
The application of heat to the work after welding or cutting.

potential energy [puh•**ten**•chul en•ur•jee]
The energy of a particle or system of particles derived from position, rather than motion, with respect to a specific fact in a field of force.

potential test [puh•**ten**•chul test]
In drilling, a test which provides information on the productive capacity of a well.

powder [**pow**•dur]
General term for all explosives and blasting agents.

powder factor [**pow**•dur **fak**•tur]
In blasting, the pounds of explosive used, divided by the cubic yards of material broken or moved by the powder.

power [**pow**•ur]
The ability or capacity to perform effectively; strength or force exerted.

preheating [pre•**heet**•ing]
The application of heat to the work prior to welding or cutting.

presplitting [pre•**split**•ing]
In blasting, a stress-relief technique involving a single row of holes drilled along a neat excavation line, where detonation of explosives in the holes causes breaking between the webs from hole to hole; holes are fired in advance of production shooting.

pressure [**presh**•ur]
The force distributed upon a surface, usually expressed in pounds per square inch (p.s.i.). (See: absolute pressure, ambient pressure, atmospheric pressure, design pressure, gauge pressure, hydrostatic pressure, partial pressure, standard atmospheric pressure, working pressure.)

pressure head [**presh**•ur hed]
The difference in pressure between two components of a system.

pressure-proof [**presh**•ur-proof]
Having the ability structurally to resist ambient pressure without leakage.

pressure tubing
(See: hydraulic tubing.)

primacord [**prym**•uh•kord]
A high explosive in cord form; originally a trademark, now often used generically.

primer [**pry**•mur]
A cartridge of explosive with a cap or detonating cord in place.

primer, cast [**pry**•mur, kast]
A priming charger consisting of a cylinder of military type explosive, used with a cap or detonating cord to prime ANFO or water gel slurry main charges. (See: ANFO.)

production platform [pro•**duk**•shun **plat**•form]
A platform over the field to handle the drilling of wells and the production of oil or gas from the reservoir.

profile [**pro**•fyl]
In diving, a graphic presentation of the depth-time relationships during a dive.

prognosis [prahg•**no**•sus]
A forecast of the probable results of a disorder; the outlook for recovery.

propane [pro•**payn**]
A petroleum hydrocarbon compound with a boiling point of about -44 degrees F; used as an engine fuel.

propogation [prahp•uh•**gay**•shun]
The transmission of a detonation reaction through an explosive column; in ditch or underwater blasting, the action of one explosive charge causing another unprimed charge to detonate.

propping agent [**prahp**•ing **ay**•junt]
In drilling, material such as walnut shells, glass balls or coarse sand which is injected into a formation to keep a fracture open. (See: formation, fracture.)

protein [**pro**•teen or **pro**•tee•un]
Any of a group of complex organic compounds consisting of carbon, hydrogen, oxygen and nitrogen (sometimes sulfur and phosphorus); the principal constituent of cell protoplasm.

protocol [**pro**•tuh•kahl]
A plan or set of procedures for conducting a dive or other formal activity.

proton [**pro**•tahn]
The positive particle of an atom; the smallest quantity of positive electricity which can exist in a free state. (See: electron.)

protoplasm [**pro**•tuh•plaz•um]
The living building material of all organisms, plants and animals.

psychomotor performance [sy•ko•mo•tur pur•for•muns]
The execution of actions involving the coordination of both mental and physical skills.

psychomotor tests [sy•ko•mo•tur tests]
Tests which measure psychomotor performance.

PTC
(See: personnel transfer capsule.)

puddle [**pud**•'ul]
That portion of a weld that is molten at the place the heat is supplied.

pufferfish [**puf**•ur•fish]
A marine animal which can inflict a damaging bite with its sharp teeth and powerful jaws, but hazardous only when handled. (See: hazardous marine animals.)

pulley [**pool**•ee]
A sheave wheel with grooved rim. (See: sheave.)

pull out [pool owt]
In drilling, to hoist the drill string out of the hole. (See: drill string.)

pulmonary [**pool**•mun•air•ee]
Pertaining to the lung (e.g. designating the artery conveying blood from the heart to the lungs, and the vein conveying blood from the lungs to the heart).

pulmonary barotrauma [**pul**•mun•air•ee bair•uh•trah•muh]
Damage to the lung alveoli due to changes in pressure; usually a result of increased internal pressure; may result in air embolism, pneumothorax or emphysema, and probably is second only to drowning as a cause of death in diving. (See: air embolism, alveoli, emphysema, pneumothorax.)

pulmonary function [[**pool**•mun•air•ee funk•shun]
The factors included in the act of breathing, including ventilatory mechanics (mechanics of breathing), alveolar ventilation, and gas exchange between the alveoli and the blood.

pulmonary ventilation [**pul**•mun•air•ee ven•tuh•lay•shun]
Movement of air or respirable gas in and out of the lungs and, by extension, the movement of the inspired gas into the blood through the alveolar wall.

pulmonic [pul•**mahn**•ik]
Referring or relating to the lungs or the pulmonary artery.

pulps [pulps]
Carbonaceous combustibles (wood, meal, rice hulls, nut shells, etc.) in dynamites to provide fuel source and control of density, fumes and other properties; also, dopes.

pumping jack [**pump**•ing jak]

The operating unit erected over a pumping well which operates the down hole pump. (See: down hole pump, put on pump.)

pump off [pump awf]

Said of the situation where a pumping well is pumped to a degree where the oil level falls below the level of the pump standing valve. (See: put on pump.)

put a well on [poot uh wel ahn]

To open up a well to production, either by pumping or flowing into the collecting system.

put on pump [poot ahn pump]

To install pumping equipment in a well which will not flow to the surface under the formation pressure.

PVHO

Pressure vessel for human occupancy; language adopted by the American Society for Mechanical Engineers (ASME) to describe hyperbaric chambers.

PWR

pressurized water reactor; a nuclear reactor that produces steam indirectly from nuclear fission be heating water under pressure.

-Q-

quadrant [Kwah•drunt]

In oceanography, a specific area marked off on the sea floor and used by biologists for long term animal counts.

Quarter deck [kwor•tur dek]

The term applied to the after portion of the weather deck of a vessel.

quebracho [kay•brah•choe]

Thinning agent added to the circulating mud to decrease its viscosity; otherwise known as tanic acid which is produced from the bark of a tree. (See: mud, viscocity.)

quicksand [kwik•sand]

Sand that is partly held in suspension by water; varying in depth, it easily yields to pressure of a person or an object; resembles ordinary sand or mud and occurs on flat shores and along rivers having shifting currents.

-R-

rabbet [rab•ut]

A step in the edge of a material to receive an adjoining material and make a fair surface.

rabbit [rab•ut]

In drilling, similar to a pig which is pumped through a pipeline to clean or test it for obstructions. (See: pig.)

rabbitfish [rab•ut•fish]

A marine animal which inflicts a venomous puncture wound with its fin spines when handled. (See: hazardous marine animals.)

racking seizing [rack•ing seez•ing]

Used to lash together two parallel ropes.

radar [ray•dahr]

From Radio Detection and Ranging; a system of determining the distance of an object by measuring the interval of time between transmission of a radio signal and reception of a signal returned as an echo.

radial movement [ray•dyul moov•munt]

The expansion or contraction of the diameter of tubing or pipe.

radiant energy [ray•dyunt enn•ur•jee]

Energy transferred by radiation, especially by an electromagnetic wave, i.e., visible light, heat or radio waves.

radiation [ray•dee•ay•shun]

The emission and propagation of waves or particles.

radiography [ray•dee•ah•gruf•ee]

The use of radiant energy in the form of X-rays or gamma rays for the non-destructive examination of metals.

rake [rayk]

On a vessel, an inclination from the vertical of a mast, stem, stack, etc., usually in a fore and aft direction.

ram plates [ram playtz]

On a vessel, vertical plates installed in the way of the inner bow spaces to prevent panting. (See: panting.)

Rankine temperature [rang•kun tem•pur•uh•choor]

An absolute temperature scale on which the unit of measurement equals a Fahrenheit degree. (See: temperature.)

rapture of the deep [rap•chur uv thu deep]
Euphamism for nitrogen narcosis. (See: nitrogen narcosis.)

rathole [rat•hole]
A shallow hole drilled near the corner of the derrick floor which is used to accommodate the kelly when it is removed from the drill string. (See: kelly.)

ream [reem]
To enlarge a hole.

reamer [ree•mur]
In drilling, a tool fitted with serrated rollers or expanding cutters which is used for enlarging the diameter of a bore hole.

rebreather [re•bree•thur]
A closed-circuit or semi-closed-circuit underwater breathing apparatus.

receiver tank [re•see•vur tank]
A volume tank mounted on a compressor unit.

recompression [re•cum•presh•un]
Returning a diver to the highest pressure experienced (or greater if necessary) for the purpose of minimizing and eliminating the effects of decompression sickness or air embolism; also, for treatment of these; accomplished in a chamber rather than return to depth underwater. (See: air embolism, decompression sickness.)

recompression chamber [re•cum•presh•un chaym•bur]
An enclosed space used to rapidly increase the pressure to which a diver has been exposed, to return the diver to the ambient underwater pressure; also, used when treating a diver for air embolism or decompression sickness. (See: air embolism, decompression sickness.)

recovery [re•cuv•ur•ee]
In diving, to retrieve an object from the deep.

red blood cell [red blud sell]
A blood corpuscle containing hemoglobin.

red clay [red klay]
A fine-grained deposit predominantly clay, of low carbonate and silica content, that covers most of the deeper portions of the ocean basins.

red mud [red mud]
A reddish-brown deep-sea mud which accumulates on the sea floor in the neighborhood of deserts and off the mouths of great rivers; contains calcium carbonate up to 25 percent.

red tide [red tyd]
A growth in the ocean of dinoflagellates (single-celled plant-like animals) in such quantities that the sea is colored red and marine animals are killed or made toxic.

reducer [re•doo•sur]
A device to regulate the flow or pressure in a gas system.

reef [reef]
A ridge or chain of rocks, sand or coral occurring in or causing a shallow area.

reef knot [reef naht]
A knot used to join two ropes or lines of the same size; it holds firmly and is easily untied; also a square knot.

reeved blocks [reevd blahks]
In rigging, a set of blocks with cable or rope passed through so there are no crossed or rubing lines; opposite of laced blocks. (See: laced blocks.)

RE factor [R E fak•tur]
The number describing the relative effectiveness of an explosive compared to an equal weight of TNT.

refraction [re•frak•shun]
The effect of the bending of light rays underwater, due to the fact that water is of a different density than air; causes objects to appear larger or smaller than they are, or to be in a position other than where they are actually located.

refractive index [re•frack•tiv in•dex]
The ratio of the speed of light in a vacuum to its speed in the substance.

regulator, demand [reg•yoo•lay•tur, duh•mand]
An apparatus in which the gas supply is activated by the negative pressure associated with inspiration.

relative humidity [rel•uh•tiv hyoo•mid•uh•tee]
The ratio of the amount of water vapor in the air at a specific temperature to the maximum capacity of the air at that temperature.

repetitive dive [ree•pet•uh•tiv dyv]
A dive whose decompression obligation is altered by the diver's previous exposure.

reserve buoyancy [ree•zurv boo•yun•see]
The amount of flooding water a ship can take before sinking, measured by the freeboard; also he amount of buoyancy a diver has available by detaching weights. (See: freeboard.)

reservoir [rez•ur•vwahr]
In drilling, a porous formation containing fluid or gas.

residual nitrogen [re•zij•oo•ul nite•roe•jun]
Denoting a concept which describes the amount of nitrogen remaining in a diver's tissues following a hyperbaric exposure. (See: residual nitrogen time.)

residual nitrogen time [re•zij•oo•ul nite•roe•jun time]

Time added to actual bottom time for calculating a decompression schedule for a repetitive dive; based on the concept of residual nitrogen. (See: residual nitrogen.)

residual volume [re•zij•oo•ul **vahl•**yoom]
The volume of air which remains in the lungs after the most forceful exhalation.

resistance [re•**zis•**tuns]
The difficulty in causing current to flow in an electrical circuit.

resolving power [re•**zahl•**veeng **pow'**r]
The ability of an optical system to form distinguishable images of objects separated by small angular distances.

respiration [res•pur•**ay•**shun]
The act or function of breathing; the oxidation reduction process by which energy in food is transformed to other kinds of energy for the continuance of life.

respiratory minute volume [res•pur•uh•tore•ee min•ut **vahl•**yoom]
The amount of air inhaled and exhaled per minute to maintain proper body function; variable, depending on the individual and the degree of exertion.

respiratory quotient [res•**pir•**a•toh•ree kwo•shent]
The rate between the volume of carbon dioxide expired and the volume of oxygen inspired in a given time.

respiratory rate [res•pur•uh•tore•ee rate]
The rate of breathing: normal range, 10 to 20 breath per minute (6 quarts of air); under exertion, approximately 20 times the individual's normal breath rate; an index of the degree of exertion.

reticulation [re•**tick•**yoo•**lay•**shun]
In photography, the mottling of film due to the use of solutions at different temperatures in the development process; caused by the unequal expansion and contraction of the sensitive emulsion and the backing material of the film.

retina [ret•'n•uh]
The innermost coating of the eyeball; the nerve coat of the eye, made of nerve cells and fibers.

reverse block [re•**vurs** blahk]
Referring to the inability of a diver to clear his ears or sinuses during ascent.

reverse circulation [re•vurs sur•kyoo•**lay•**shun]
In drilling, a procedure used when the circulating fluid is pumped down the annular space between the well wall and the drill pipe and is returned through the drill string. (See: circulating fluid, drill string.)

reversed ears
(See: squeeze.)

reversed polarity [re•**vurst** poe•**lair•**uh•tee]
The arrangement of arc welding leads where the work is the negative pole and the electrode is the positive pole in the arc circuit; also, direct current electrode positive (DCEP).

rhinitis [rye•**nye•**tus]
Inflammation of the nasal mucous membrane.

ribs [ribz]
Bone and cartilage that form the chest cavity and protect its contents; tissue between ribs allows for expansion of the chest cavity.

rider plate [**rye•**dur plate]
On a vessel, the horizontal center line plate fitted on top of the center vertical keelson; installed as a reinforcement in the total keel construction.

rig [rig]
On a vessel, the arrangement of sails and masts; to set up the rigging.

rig, drilling [rig, **drill•**ing]
The main drilling installation consisting of a derrick (or mast) substructure, drawworks, engines, pumps, boilers (if any), rotary table, crown block, travelling block, main hook, vibrating screen, storage tanks, cementing equipment, mud mixing plant, and all required tools; the term is frequently used by the layman when referring to a production platform. (See: crown block, derrick, drawworks, hook, production platform, rotary table, travelling block, vibrating screen.)

rigger [**rig•**ur]
One whose occupation is to prepare, fit and install the various pieces of rigging in a vessel.

rigging [**rig•**ing]
The guys, standing and running manila and wire ropes used to support and operate the movable parts of mast, booms and king posts of a vessel.

righting arm (R.A.) [**rite•**ing ahrm]
The perpendicular distance between lines of action when a vessel is inclined.

righting moment [**rite•**ing **mo•**munt]
The moment of buoyancy couple; the righting tendency of a ship at any given angle.

right lang lay [rite lahng lay]
Wire rope where strands and wire are both twisted to the right.

right regular lay [rite **reg•**yoo•lur lay]
Wire rope where strands are twisted to the right and wires in the strands are twisted to the left.

rig up [**rig** up]
To install a rig and equipment for drilling a well.

rip current [rip **kur**•unt]
A strong current of limited area, flowing outward from the shore, caused by the escape of water piled by wave action between shore and bar or reef; incorrectly called rip tide..

ripples [**rip**•ulz]
Very small, gentle waves with little undulation.

rise of floor [rize uv flor]
Commonly called the dead rise, the distance that the bottom of a vessel rises determined from a measurement between the keel and the turn of the bilge. (See: dead rise.)

riser [**rize**•ur]
A vertical section of pipeline extending from the sea bottom up to the drilling platform deck above the water.

riser clamp [**rize**•ur klamp]
A mechanical clamp which is bolted around a riser to prevent it from moving. (See: riser.)

R.M.S.
Root mean square; the measure of surface roughness obtained as the square root of the sum of the squares of micro-inch deviation from true flat.

rock [rock]
In engineering, a natural aggregate of mineral particles connected by strong and relatively permanent cohesive forces; in geology, the material that forms the essential part of the earth's solid crust and includes loose masses as well as very hard and solid masses.

rock bit [rok bit]
In drilling, a cone type bit which is run at the lower end of a drill string to dig into the formation being drilled.

rocker beam [**rok**•ur•beem]
A beam used for hoisting flimsy loads, or to equalize load weight.

rock hound [rok hound]
A geologist.

rocking [**rok**•ing]
Alternate pressurizing and releasing pressure to get a well to flow.

rock pressure [rok **presh**•ur]
In drilling, the pressure of the fluid in a reservoir.

rod [rod]
The rate of detonation of an explosive; also called detonation velocity.

roentgen [**ren(t)**•jun]
The international unit of radiation; a standard quantity of x or gamma radiation.

roentgenogram [**ren(t)**•jen•uh•gram]
A film produced by means of x-rays, also called roentgen rays; named after the discoverer of the x-ray.

roll [role]
On a vessel, motion about the longitudinal axis, from side to side.

roller bit
(See: rock bit.)

rolling chocks [**rol**•ing choks]
Longitudinal steel plates fitted externally along the bilge strake in order to decrease the transverse rolling of a vessel; sometimes called the bilge keel.

rolling hitch [**rol**•ing hich]
A knot used for lifting round loads such as pipe.

root of weld [root uv weld]
The points at which the bottom of a weld intersects the base metal surfaces.

root opening [root **oh**•pun•ing]
In welding, the separation between the members to be joined, at the root of the joint.

rope charge [rope charj]
A linear charge made up of a number of small charges, such as dynamite sticks, fastened lengthwise along a piece of rope.

rope spear [rope spear]
A fishing tool with projecting barbs, used to recover a broken wire line from a well hole. (See: fishing tools.)

rotary [**rot**•ur•ee]
Turning on an axis; pertaining to rotation.

rotary bushing [**rot**•ur•ee **bush**•ing]
In drilling, heavy steel liners which fit into the rotary table opening to accommodate the kelly bushing or the pipe slips. (See: kelly bushing, rotary table, slips.)

rotary drilling [**rot**•ur•ee **drill**•ing]
Drilling with a rock bit rotated by a string of drill pipe extending from the surface to the bottom of the hole. (See: drill string, rock bit.)

rotary inverter [**rote**•ur•ee in•**vurt**•ur]
An instrument that electronically changes DC power to AC, using a rotating device. (See alternating current.)

rotary table [**rot**•ur•ee **tay**•bul]
In drilling, equipment installed in the center of the derrick floor over the well bore, to support the weight of pipe or casing run into the hole, and to provide rotation by means of the kelly. (See: kelly.)

rotor [**rot**•ur]
Rotating valve or conductor for carrying fluid or

electrical current from a central source to individual outlets.

roughneck
(See: drilling crew.)

round seizing [rownd **see**•zing]
A small lashing that binds two ropes together or that holds a rope to a post.

round trip [rownd trip]
In drilling, refers to pulling the drill pipe out of the hole, changing the bit or tools, and running it back to the bottom.

round turn and two half hitches [rownd turn; too haff hichuz]
A knot used to secure a rope to a post.

round window rupture
(See: perilymph fistula.)

roustabout
(See: drilling crew.)

R.P.M.
Revolutions per minute.

rubber suit [rub•ur soot]
Partial or complete covering for a diver, primarily to insulate and preserve body heat; classified as wet and dry; wet suits, usually of foam neoprene, permit a thin layer of water to contact the diver's skin; dry, a rubber sheet prevents contact with the water, but requires the additional insulation afforded by cloth underclothing or a wet suit. (See: suits — diving.)

run in [run in]
In drilling, to run drill pipe, casing or tubing into the hole.

running bowline [run•ing boe•lyne]
A knot which can be tied more quickly than a bowline, and has its standing part free.

running sand [run•ing sand]
Grains of sand suspended in water or oil which can cause complications when drilling a hole.

running string [run•ing string]
In drilling, a short length of casing of the same size used to lower the regular casing string and its hanger into place. (See: casing string.)

running tool [run•ing tool]
In drilling, a tool used to lower and install a piece of equipment.

runout
(See: rip current.)

rupture [rup•chur]
The breaking apart or bursting under unequalized pressure of, for example, an ear drum.

-S-

saddling [sad•ling]
Refers to passing a choker around a pipeline and placing the eye back on the davit hook.

S.A.E.
Society of Automotive Engineers, Inc.

safe load [sayf lode]
In rigging, ratings, in tons, for proven safe capacity, depending on the hitch used.

safety factor [sayf•tee fak•tur]
Maximum load capacity, usually six time the expected use (a safety factor of six).

safety hitch or buckle [sayf•tee hich, buck•ul]
Any fastening device that may be operated to release easily with one hand.

safety joint [sayf•tee joint]
A safety tool with a fast left hand thread which, in drilling, is run in the drill pipe string above the bit or a fishing tool; permits the drill string above the safety joint to be backed off and recovered in case the bottom hole tools become stuck in the hole. (See: drill string, fishing tools.)

sagging [sag•ing]
The tendency of a vessel to sag in the middle.

salinity [suh•lin•uh•tee]
A measure of the quantity of dissolved salts in water.

saloon [suh•loon]
The officers' dining room on a merchantman vessel.

salvage [sal•vij]
The act of saving or rescuing a ship or its cargo.

salvor [sal•vur]
One who renders service in the salvage of property or lives of persons in distress or danger.

samples [sam•pulz]
Cuttings from the formation being drilled, returned to the surface in the circulating fluid and removed on the vibrating screen for examination by a geologist. (See: vibrating screen.)

Sampson post [Samp•sun post]
An upright post which supports a walking beam. (See: walking beam.)

sand bar [sand bahr]
A body of sand built up by the action of waves or currents.

sand hog [sand hawg]
Colloquial term meaning caisson or compressed air tunnel worker.

sand line [sand lyne]
In drilling, a wire line used to run a sand pump, a bailer or a swab into the hole. (See: bailer, swab.)

sand reel [sand reel]
The drum reel for handling the sand line. (See: sand line.)

sand up [sand up]
In drilling, refers to the condition where sand enters the well with the oil being produced, and chokes the tail pipe or down hole pump. (See: down hole pump, tail pipe.)

saturation [sach•ur•ay•shun]
The condition in which the partial pressure of a gas dissolved in a fluid is equal to its maximum possible partial pressure, under the existing ambient conditions of temperature and pressure. (See: steady state.)

saturation depth [sach•ur•ay•shun depth]
The depth or pressure at which a diver's tissues are saturated; also called storage depth.

saturation dive [sach•ur•ay•shun dyv]
An exposure of sufficient duration so that the diver's tissue gases reach equilibrium with the pressure environment; once this occurs, the decompression time required at the end of a dive does not increase with additional time spent at any depth; the diver works out of a habitat or other pressurized chamber.

saturation diving system [sach•ur•ay•shun dyv•ing sis•tum]
A pressurized diving system that incorporates a life support system for long term saturation dives. (See: diving system, one-atmosphere diving system.)

saversub [save•ur•sub]
In drilling, a short substitute which is run on the lower end of the kelly to connect with the drill string, and which can be easily replaced when worn. (See: drill string, kelly.)

sawfish [saw•fish]
A marine animal of the ray family, somewhat resembling a shark in appearance; commonly reaching a length of 16 feet; the snout is equipped with teeth on both sides and can be a hazard for divers. (See: hazardous marine animals.)

scaffold hitch [skaff•old hich]
A hitch used for fastening single planks or beams so they will hang level.

SCAL
Skin-diver contact air lens.

scaled distance [skayld dis•tuns]
In blasting, the actual distance from the charge divided by the charge weight to the one- half or two-thirds power.

SCFH
Standard cubic feet per hour.

SCFM
Standard cubic feet per minute at maximum working pressure.

schedule, decompression
(See: decompression schedule.)

Schlemberger [shlum•bur•gur]
A system of electrically logging a bore hole; named for the French scientist who invented the system.

sciatica [sigh•at•i•kuh]
A form of neuritis characterized by severe pain along the sciatic nerve and its branches.

scoliosis [skoe•lee•oh•sus]
An abnormal sideways (lateral) curvature from the normal vertical line of the spine.

scope [skop]
The length of the anchor rope or chain. 6 to 1 scope means that the length of the anchor rope from the boat to the anchor is 6 times the depth of the water.

scorpionfish [skore•pee•un•fish]
A family of marine animals (stone- fish, lionfish, etc.) that inflict venomous puncture wounds with spines on their fins and other parts of their bodies. (See: hazardous marine animals.)

scratcher [skrach•ur]
A device fitted to a casing joint which cleans the well wall as the casing is being run.

screen pipe [skreen pype]
In drilling, a short piece of perforated or slotted casing to protect the face of a producing formation.

scrubber [skrub•ur]
The part of a diver's life support system that removes carbon dioxide.

scuba [skoo•buh]
Derived from the acronym for self-contained underwater breathing apparatus, now the word used to describe apparatus in which the inspired gas is delivered by demand regulator and exhaled into the surrounding water (open-circuit), and the gas supply is carried on the diver's back. (See: closed circuit scuba, semi closed circuit scuba.)

SDC
(See: submersible decompression chamber.)

sea [see]
Denoting that all seas (except inland seas) are physically interconnected parts of the earth's total salt water system.

sea anchor [see **ang**•kur]
A drag thrown overside to keep a craft headed into the wind.

sea anemone [see uh•**nem**•uh•nee]
A marine animal attached to rocks, venomous when touched. (See: hazardous marine animals.)

sea bass [see bass]
In the tropics, a fish that can grow to more than 7 feet in length; their mouths are large enough to engulf a diver; size makes them a potential hazard. (See: hazardous marine animals.)

sea bottom slide [see **baht**•um slyde]
A landslide underwater, usually causing a tsunami, or dislocation wave.

sea breeze [see breez]
A breeze blowing over land from the sea.

sea chest [see chest]
On a vessel, a structure fitted to the internal shell plating below the waterline to which valves and pipes are attached for supplying water to condensers and engines, sanitary water, etc.

sea floor [see flore]
The bottom of the ocean where there is a generally smooth, gentle gradient; also, seabed and seabottom.

sea floor habitat [see flore **hab**•uh•tat]
Undersea living quarters for aquanauts in saturation.

seal [seel]
Acronym for a military assault force trained to operate in all three environments: sea, air and land.

seal [seel]
Any device used to prevent the passage of a gas or liquid.

sea level pressure [see **lev**•ul **presh**•ur]
Atmosphere pressure at mean sea level, either directly measured or determined from observed station pressure.

seal force [seel fors]
The force that presses structural sealing members together.

sea lion [see **lye**•un]
Sea lions and harbor seals normally are playful and not aggressive; however, during breeding season the bulls become irritable and may object to intruders, and females may nip if they feel their young are in danger. (See: hazardous marine animals.)

sea news [see nooz]
A rip current. (See: rip current.)

search pattern, underwater [surch **pat**•urn, un•dur•**wah**•tur]
A systematic procedure used to locate something underwater. (See: arc search, circular search, jackstay search, "Z" search.)

sea slick [see slick]
An area of sea surface, variable in size, markedly different in appearance; usually caused by plankton blooms.

sea snake [see snake]
A water snake; related to the cobra; generally does not bite humans unless roughly handled. (See: hazardous marine animals.)

sea urchin [see **ur**•chun]
A sometimes venomous marine animal found in large numbers and variety in the shallow coastal waters of the world; some spines are long, sharp and brittle, and secrete a painful or even a deadly venom; spines break off and are extremely difficult to remove; the black sea urchin, probably is responsible for the greatest number of diver injuries. (See: hazardous marine animals.)

seaward [**see**•wurd (or) **soo**•urd]
Away from land toward the open sea.

seaway [see way]
One of the sea traffic lanes or routes; a vessel's headway; an area where a moderate or rough sea is running.

seaworthy [**see**•wur•thee]
Fit for sailing hazards; able to withstand usual sea conditions.

secondary recovery [**seck**•un•dair•ee re•**kuv**•ur•ee]
In drilling, artificial recovery of oil by some means such as water injection or gas injection when a field's reservoir pressure is falling off. (See: gas drive, water flooding.)

sector [**seck**•tur]
An arc of the horizon through which a light is designed either to show in a particular color, or not be visible.

sediment [**sed**•uh•munt]
Organic and inorganic matter which accumulates in a loose, unconsolidated form.

seepage [**see**•puj]
A natural oil spring which occurs at the surface where there is a fissure at the oil reservoir.

seiche [saysh]
A geological term for a wave that oscillates in lakes, bays or gulfs as a result of seismic or atmospheric disturbances.

seismograph [**size**•mo•graff]
A device for detecting vibrations in the earth's crust; in drilling, an artificial earthquake may be created in order to investigate underground formations as detected by the seismograph; these may be created by high pressure air injection, firing small charges from a vessel, or by thumping (dropping a weight).

seize [seez]
To wrap, bind or secure with a small line.

seizure [**see**•zhur]
A physical condition involving a sudden convulsion or mental aberration or collapse.

self-contained diving
(See: scuba.)

self-propelled submersible [self-pro•**peld** sub•**mur**•suh•bul]
A submersible operating under its own power. (See: dry submersible, lock-out submersible, submersible, wet submersible.)

semicircular canals [**sem**•ee•**sur**•kyoo•lur kuh•**nalz**]
The parts (lateral, superior and posterior) of the inner ear's vestibular system which contain the receptors sensitive to acceleration and body position.

semi-closed circuit scuba [**sem**•ee-klozed sur•kut skoo•ba]
A self-contained underwater breathing apparatus in which the breathing gas is recirculated through purifying and oxygen replenishing systems; oxygen levels are maintained by regulating the flow of the gas; a portion of the exhaled gas is lost into the surrounding water. (See: closed-circuit scuba, scuba.)

semi-submersible rig [**sem**•ee-sub•**mur**•shu•bul rig]
A large offshore drilling rig built on huge caissons; some self-propelled, ballasted to drill depth, held by anchors; allows drilling to greater depths in areas of severe wave conditions.

sensitive [**sen**•suh•tiv]
Referring to an explosive very easily detonated.

sensitivity [sen•suh•**tiv**•uh•tee]
The measure of ease with which an explosive can be initiated.

sensor [**sen**•sore]
A device that responds to a physical stimulus and transmits the resulting impulse; in diving, most commonly used in connection with oxygen, pressure or temperature monitoring.

separated gas [sep•ur•ay•tud gas]
Describing the presence of gas in the body in joints and between muscles where the word

bubble would not be appropriate; also used by extension to describe all unspecified collections of gas, including bubbles. (See: breathing gas, diluent gas, gas, inert gas, mixed gas.)

separator [sep•ur•ay•tur]
A vessel or device for separating mixtures of oil/water/gas.

sepsis [**sep**•sis]
Poisoned state due to absorption of pathogenic bacteria and their products into the blood stream, blood poisoning.

sepsis gas [**sepsis**•gas]
Poisoning due to gas bacillicus.

sepsis intestinal [**sep**•sis intestinal]
Poisoning due to ingestion of decaying food.

set [set]
The direction in motion of a current, wind or sea, or a combination of these.

set casing [set **kay**•sing]
In drilling, landing a casing string and cementing it into place.

shackle [**shack**•ul]
In rigging, any one of various devices to make something fast.

shallow water blackout
(See: hyperventilation.)

shank [shank]
The main body of an anchor.

shaped charge [shaypt chahrj]
An explosive charge formed with a cavity at one end designed to increase penetration; cavities are usually conical in shape; may be lined with metal or high density glass.

shark [shark]
Probably are the most feared of all marine animals, the shark is completely unpredictable; approximately 250 species of sharks inhabit all the oceans of the world, but only a few are considered potentially dangerous to divers; statistically, the greater danger of shark attack is in tropical and subtropical waters; sharks known to have attacked humans are gray, white-tip, blue, tiger, sand, mako, white, hammerhead. (See: hazardous marine animals.)

shear lashing [sheer **lash**•ing]
In rigging, used for forming shear legs of timbers with their but ends spread apart, or to lash two spars together to keep them parallel.

shear legs [sheer legz]
Usually two or more timbers or spars erected on a vessel in the shape of an A-frame with tower ends spread out and upper ends fastened together from which lifting tackle is suspended.

sheave [sheev]
A pulley.

sheepshank [**sheep**•shangk]
A knot used to shorten a rope that is fastened at both ends.

sheer strake [sheer strayk]
On a vessel, the uppermost side shell row of plates secured longitudinally to the gunwale bar.

sheet bend [sheet bend]
A knot used for joining two rope ends, especially if the ropes are of different sizes.

shellfish, poisonous [**shell**•fish, **poy**•zun•us]
A "red tide" due to unusually great quantities of plankton; mussels and clams ingest this poison without damage to themselves, and if they are eaten by humans, the toxin acts directly on the central nervous system affecting respiratory and vasomotor centers, and on the peripheral nervous system resulting in profound depression; death can occur from respiratory paralysis; normal cooking methods do not remove the toxin. (See: hazardous marine animals.)

shielded metal-arc cutting [**sheel**•dud **met**•ul-ahrk **kut**•ing]
A method of metal-arc cutting where the severing of metals is effected by melting with the heat of an arc between a covered metal electrode and the base metal.

shielded metal-arc welding [**sheel**•dud **met**•ul-ahrk **well**•ding]
An arc-welding process where coalescence is produced by heating with an electric arc between a covered metal electrode and the work; shielding is obtained from decomposition of the electrode covering; pressure is not used.

ship [ship]
Among seamen, a ship is a sailing vessel with bowsprit and 3 masts, i.e., foremast, main mast and mizzenmast.

shoal [shole]
A place where a sea, river, etc., is shallow because of a bank or bar.

shock [shahk]
A condition characterized by decreased effective circulating fluid volume in the body.

shoe, casing
(See: casing shoe.)

shoe, drive [shoo, dryv]
In drilling, a short length of heavy pipe run on the lower end of a casing string as it is forced into a hole. (See: casing string.)

shoe, float [shoo, flote]
In drilling, casing shoe fitted with a non-return valve to facilitate floating a string of casing into a well to relieve the hoisting gear. (See: casing string, shoe-casing.)

shoestring knot [**shoo**•string naht]
A square knot with the ends slippery (not pulled all the way through).

shorting strip [**short**•ing strip]
In blasting, a piece of metal connecting two ends of leg wires to prevent stray currents from accidentally detonating the cap.

short splice [short splys]
A maximum strength splice used where it is not necessary to run a spliced rope through the pulley block.

shot [shaht]
The detonation of one or more charges, with or without delays between charges; initiated by a single action.

shotline [**shaht**•lyne]
A graduated line, with a weight at one end, used originally for measuring depth; often put down at a diving site, suspended either from a buoy or the side of a boat, to act as an underwater reference point; diver's descending line.

shunt [shunt]
To by-pass around or turn aside; in electrical apparatus, an alternate path for the current; in blasting, a shorting device on cap wires.

shunt winding [shunt **wynd**•ing]
An electric coil of wire which forms a bypass or alternate path for electric current.

shuttle valve [**shut**•ul valv]
A valve for diverting pressure from one channel to another.

sidetrack [**syde**•track]
Drilling past a fish which, for some reason, is permanently left in the hole. (See: fish.)

side wall coring
(See: coring — side wall.)

signal [**sig**•nul]
Coded communication other than voice; in diving, flags, line pulls, hammer taps and hand signals commonly are used.

signature [**sig**•nuh•chur]
Any characteristic pattern by which an object can be detected or identified; in diving, usually used to define the acoustic or magnetic characteristics of an object.

silent bubbles [**sigh**•lunt **bubb**•ulz]
Gas bubbles which may be detected in the blood vessels or tissues, but which cause no signs or symptoms of decompression sickness; may be demonstrated by ultrasonic flow techniques such as Doppler; also called covert bubbles. (See: Doppler effect.)

silica gel [sill•uh•kuh jell]
A desiccant or substance that absorbs water; can be purchased as crystals; normally blue but turns pink when saturated with water.

silver chloride [sil•vur klore•ide]
Material used in a type of battery used in a blaster's galvanometer. (See: galvanometer.)

single [sing•gul]
One joint of drill pipe (20-30 feet, 6.1-9.1 millemeters) fitted with a tool joint box connection on the top and a tool joint pin connection on the bottom. (See: drill pipe, tool joint.)

single blackwall [sing•gul black•wahl]
A simple half hitch over a hook; it will hold only when subjected to a constant strain.

single carrick bend [sing•gul kahr•uk bend]
One of the strongest of knots, requiring that both ends be seized onto their standing parts.

single hose unit [sing•gul hoze yoo•nut]
Open-circuit scuba having a single intermediate pressure hose with first-stage pressure reduction at the yoke (tank attachment), and second or ambient reduction at the mouthpiece; the exhaust is at the mouthpiece. (See: scuba.)

single lock chamber [sing•gul lahk chaym•bur]
A pressure chamber with only one pressurized compartment; usually having a small lock for the passage of supplies, poses a compromising restriction where interchange of personnel is required, as in treatment of decompression sickness. (See: altitude chamber, chamber, compression chamber, deck compression chamber, double-lock chamber, hyperbaric chamber, monoplace chamber, multiplace chamber, submersible decompression chamber.)

single Matthew Walker knot [sing•gul math•hyoo wahk•ur not]
A modified wall knot.

sinker [sink•ur]
A heavy steel bar used in cable tool drilling and run above the bit and jars to provide weight for operating the jars. (See: drilling — cable tool, jar.)

sinus [sigh•nus]
A cavity or hollow space in the skull connecting with ear, nose or throat.

sinusitis [sigh•nus•eye•tus]
Inflammation of the membranes lining the sinuses. (See: sinus.)

sinus squeeze [sigh•nus skweez]
A squeeze caused by blockage of the opening between one of the sinuses and the nose; may be due to a common cold or sinusitis; or, due to a failure to equalize sinus pressure with ambient pressure, usually due to the presence of sinusitis accompanying the common cold. (See: squeeze.)

skag [skag]
A heavy chain used when necessary in close waters as a drag for steadying a towed barge with a tendency to sheer about.

skeg [skehg]
The lower extension of the stern frame of a vessel that extends aft of the sternpost and is used to support the rudderpost; it confines the lower limit of the aperture.

skeletal system [skell•uh•tul sis•tum]
The bones of the body.

skids [skidz]
Parallel timbers or other members upon which boats, casks and other objects are lashed.

skiff [skiff]
A light, open boat, usually for rowing but sometimes equipped for sailing.

skin diving
(See: dive — breath-hold.)

slack water [slack wah•tur]
The state of a tidal current when its velocity is near zero, especially the moment when a reversing current changes direction; occurs at high and low tides.

slag inclusion [slag in•kloo•zhun]
Non-metallic solid material entrapped in weld metal or between weld metal and base metal.

slate, diver's [slayt, dye•vur'z]
A piece of equipment used for writing messages or recording data underwater.

slick [slick]
A smooth area of water, often caused by the sweep of a vessel's stern during a turn, or by a film of oil.

sling [sling]
A strap, chain or rope used to hold something to be hoisted or lowered.

slipknot [slip•naht]
An overhand knot around the standing part, not as satisfactory as two half hitches.

slippery clove hitch [slip•ur•ee klove hich]
A quick, easy knot used for lifting light loads.

slippery half hitch [slip•ur•ee haff hich]
A temporary hitch which can be quickly untied by pulling on the free end.

slippery sheet bend [slip•ur•ee sheet bend]
A sheet bend knot with a bight left in the right-hand rope; can be untied quickly by a tug on the free end of the rope.

slips [slips]
In drilling, steel wedges for the rotary table

master bushings, with replaceable tooth-like inserts to hold the drill pipe or casing in the rotary table when connecting or disconnecting pipe. (See: rotary table.)

slotted liner completion [slah•tud lye•nur kum•plee•shun]
A method of well completion; a length of casing having narrow vertical slots, placed through producing sand which consists of coarse material. (See: completion.)

sludging, blood
(See: blood sludging.)

slurp gun [slurp gun]
A plastic syringe type of gun used to pull in small fish as research specimens; a modification for submersibles uses an electrically driven propeller to suck water into a funnel.

slurry [slur•ee]
A mixture of water and cement pumped into a well to cement a casing string. (See: casing string.)

slush pit [slush pit]
A pit used for storing drilling mud. (See: mud.)

slush pump [slush pump]
A piston type pump with changeable liners used for handling the circulating fluid in a well. (See: mud.)

snake hole [snayk hole]
A hole drilled or bored under a rock or tree stump for the placement of explosives.

snatch block [snach blahk]
A block which can be opened at one end to receive the bight of a rope. (See: bight.)

SNG
Synthetic natural gas; the process of gassification of light liquid hydrocarbons.

snorkel [snor•kul]
A tube in the mouth with the open end above the surface of the water, allowing the swimmer or diver to breathe comfortably without turning the head.

snubber [snub•ur]
A device used for forcing drill pipe into, or recovering it from, a hole which is under pressure.

soft patch [sahft pach]
On a vessel, a temporary repair to a crack or hole in a plate; the small steel patch is secured with bolts and made tight with a gasket and sealing compound; an opening on deck through which machinery is accessible.

soldering [sahd•ur•ing]
A metal joining process performed by melting a tin-lead alloy.

solid [sahl•ud]
Distinct from liquid or gaseous; of definite shape and volume.

sonar [so•nahr]
Previously an acronym, now the word for sound navigation and ranging; the method or equipment for determining by underwater sound techniques the presence, location or nature of objects in the sea.

sound [sownd]
The perception of vibrations transported to the ear through some form of matter; travels more rapidly through denser substances such as water; underwater hearing is affected by reverberations off the bottom, heat and salinity of the water, microorganisms, noises from the surface, and the diver's head covering; to measure depth with a line and weight.

sound pressure, underwater [sownd presh•ur, un•dur•wah•tur]
Expressed in decibels or in dynes per square centimeter.

sound velocity [sownd vu•loss•uh•tee]
The rate of travel at which sound energy moves through a medium, usually expressed in feet per second.

sour gas [sowr gas]
Gas which has an unpleasant odor and often contains hydrogen sulphide.

spacing [spay•sing]
The distance between two or more production wells drilled into the same reservoir.

spaghetti [spu•get•ee]
Tubing or drill pipe of very small diameter.

spanner [span•ur]
A form of open-head wrench.

spar [spahr]
On a vessel, a length of wood or steel of circular cross section serving as a mast, boom or yard.

spark [spahrk]
An electrical current possessing sufficient pressure to jump through the air from one conductor to another.

spatter [spat•ur]
In arc and gas welding, the metal particles expelled during welding which do not form part of the weld.

spear [speer]
A fishing tool used to enter the bore of a lost drill string. (See: fishing tools.)

spear gun [speer gun]
Any device which propels a spear from a gunlike frame; usually rubber, spring or gas powered.

specific gravity [spuh•**siff**•ik **gra**•vuh•tee]
The relative weight of a substance as compared to water.

specific heat [spuh•**siff**•ik heet]
The amount of heat required to raise the temperature of a unit mass of a substance by one unit of temperature compared to the amount of heat required to raise a similar mass of water by the same amount.

sphygmomanometer [**sfig**•moe•man•**ahm**•uh•tur]
An instrument for measuring arterial blood pressure.

spider [**spy**•dur]
In drilling, a heavy duty steel housing fitted with wedged slips, used to support casing being run into a hole. (See: slips.)

spindrift [**spin**•drift]
Sea spray, sometimes called spoondrift; the spray and water driven from the tops of waves by the wind.

spinning chain [**spin**•ing chane]
A chain wrapped around the drill pipe and operated from the drawworks to assist in breaking out and making up lengths of pipe when round tripping. (See: breaking out, drawworks, round trip.)

spiny dogfish [**spine**•ee **dahg**•fish]
A small shark, approximately three and one-half feet long, found in tropical and temperate seas; two short spines, in front of the dorsal fins, can cause painful and venomous wounds. (See: hazardous marine animals.)

spit [spit]
In blasting, the flame produced by the safety fuse inside the fuse cap.

spitcock [**spit**•kahk]
An auxiliary exhaust valve in a diving helmet.

splash zone [splash zone]
The area high upshore, above the tideline, which may be splashed with sea water from breaking waves.

splice [splys]
A method of joining two ropes together by interlacing strands.

splicing [**splys**•ing]
Uniting two ropes by interlacing strands.

spontaneous pneumothorax [spahn•**tayn**•ee•us noo•moe•**thor**•aks]
Pnemothorax without known cause. (See: pneumothorax.)

sport diver [sport **dyv**•ur]
One who dives (with or without scuba) for recreation. (See: scuba.)

spot weld [spot weld]
To attach in spots by localized fusion of metal parts, with the aid of an electric current.

spreaders [**spred**•urz]
In rigging, a set of chokers or slings of equal length used to lift a load.

spring tides [spring tydz]
The highest and the lowest course of tides, occurring every new moon and every full moon.

spudding in [**spud**•ing in]
Drilling the first foot of a new hole.

spume [spyoom]
Frothy matter, foam or scum which collects at the edgewater line of a body of water.

squall [skwahl]
A gust of wind, generally accompanied by rain or snow with nimbus clouds of intense and short duration.

square lashing [skwair **lash**•ing]
A lashing used whenever spars cross at an angle, touching each other where they cross.

squeeze [skweez]
An injury caused by a difference in pressure in an enclosed space within the body. (See: body squeeze, dry suit squeeze, external ear squeeze, eye squeeze, face squeeze, middle ear squeeze, sinus squeeze.)

squeeze job [skweez jahb]
Pumping cement slurry into a porous drilling formation under pressure. (See: slurry.)

stab [stab]
The operation of guiding one end of a pipe into the connection of another pipe to make up a connection.

stabbing board [**stab**•ing bord]
In drilling, a temporary platform set in the derrick above the derrick floor, to allow the derrick man to handle joints of casing when running a string of casing into a hole. (See: casing string, derrick, derrick man.)

stabilizer [**stay**•bul•eye•zur]
In drilling, a tool run above the bit in a drilling string to help drill a directional hole, or to maintain the direction of a vertical hole. (See: directional drilling, drill string, rock bit.)

staggers [**stag**•urz]
A descriptive term referring to the dysequilibrium of decompression sickness when the inner ear is involved. (See: decompression sickness.)

stainless steel [**stane**•luss steel]
Acid and heat resistant metal.

stand [stand]
A length of drill pipe usually made up of three singles. (See: single.)

standard atmospheric pressure [stan•durd at•mus•fear•ik presh•ur]
The unit of pressure, called one atmosphere, used in underwater practice.

standard dress [stan•durd dress]
A diving system consisting of a copper diving helmet, breastplate, heavy dry suit, weighted shoes, weighted belt, hose, compressor and communications.

standard suit [stan•durd soot]
British term for deep deep sea diving suit. (See: closed circuit hot water suit, constant volume dry suit, deep sea diving suit, dry suit, hot water open circuit suit, suit — diving, variable volume dry suit, wet suit.)

standby diver [stand•by dyv•ur]
A suited or partially suited diver, ready to assist the working diver should an emergency arise.

stand pipe [stand pype]
In drilling, a steel pipe located in the derrick next to a leg to which the kelly hose is attached to connect the slush pump disharge line to the kelly hose and onto the swivel. (See: derrickes, hose-rotary, kelly, slush pump, swivel.)

starboard [star•burd]
The right side of a vessel, marked by green lights at night.

static electricity [stat•ik ee•lek•tris•uh•tee]
Atmospheric electricity as distinguished from electricity produced by a mechanical device; usually has extremely high tension.

static inverter [stat•ik in•vur•tur]
An instrument that electronically changes DC power to AC using solid state electronic components.

static seal [stat•ik seel]
A seal designed to work between parts having no relative motion.

statute mile [stach•oot myle]
4,280 ft. or 1.6093 km., or 0.869 nautical miles.

STD
An instrument developed to measure continuously the variables (salinity, temperature and depth) which are important to physical oceanography.

steady state [sted•dee stayt]
In diving, the term used to describe the condition in which there is no net gain or loss of gas molecules, into or from the tissues, exchanged with the environment. (See: saturation.)

stem [stem]
On a vessel, the foremost upper timber in the hull with all planks or plates being fastened to it.

stem [stem]
The bow frame casting at the extreme forward end of a ship to which the number one plates of all strakes are attached; the nose plating is fitted around the forward end of the stem. (See: strake.)

stemming [stem•ing]
Material placed in the top of a borehole to seal off escaping gases and to reduce noise from the detonation of explosives in the hole.

step out well [step owt well]
A well drilled away from a discovery well to allow for the assessment of the reservoir area.

stern [sturn]
The hind part of ship where the rudder is placed.

stethoscope [steth•us•skope]
An instrument used for conveying sounds from one person's body to another person's ears.

stevedore's knot [steve•uh•dorz naht]
A knot the same as a figure eight, except that it has an extra loop.

stiffener [stiff•un•ur]
On a vessel, any shape used to provide rigidity and strength to the plating of a bulkhead; the shapes most commonly used for stiffeners are the angle bar, tee bar, flat bar, zee bar and bulb angle bar.

stinging coral [sting•ing kore•ul]
Also called fire coral, actually is not a true coral but is found among the true corals in warm waters; contacts are relatively common, with symptoms generally limited to a stinging sensation and redness of the skin. (See: hazardous marine animals.)

stingray [sting ray]
A marine animal inhabiting shallow depths of tropical and subtropical seas; it lies partially buried in sand or mud and, if disturbed, will strike upward with its tail and drive a sharp spine into a diver's foot or leg; wounds in the chest or abdomen can be fatal. (See: hazardous marine animals.)

Stokes law [Stokes law]
The expression of the relation between the size of spherical particles and their settling velocity in a fluid; used in determining proportion and size distribution of silt and clay in sediment samplers.

stonefish [stone•fish]
A variety of scorpion fish found in tidepool areas; lies motionless while concealed or partly

buried, and is equipped with as many as 18 venomous spines; has the most potent sting of all scorpionfish, and has caused death. (See: hazardous marine animals.)

stopper hitch [stop•ur hich]
A hitch formed the same way as a taut-line hitch, except reversed; useful because the hitches will slip downward.

storage depth
(See: saturation depth.)

storm [storm]
Winds of 56 to 65 knots (64 to 75 miles per hour); in relative force, between a gale and a hurricane.

stove pipe [stove pyp]
Riveted casing once used in old cable tool holes. (See: drilling cable tool.)

STPD
Indicates that a volume has been corrected to standard conditions of temperature (0°C), (760 mm Hg) and dry gas. This correction is universally used for Vco_2 and Vco_2.

straddle test [strad•ul test]
In drilling, the technique of setting down hole packers above and below a reservoir formation to conduct a flow test. (See: flow test.)

straight polarity [strayt pole•air•uh•tee]
The arrangement of arc welding leads where the work is the positive pole and the electrode is the negative pole of the arc circuit; also, direct current electrode negative (DCEN).

strain [strayn]
The movement of material within a fixed length of dimension.

strake [strayk]
On a vessel, a continuous row of plating from the bow to the stern, identified by letters beginning with "A" strake which is the garboard strake, and continuing outward and upward to the sheer strake; the letter "I" is not used to identify a strake and is always omitted.

stranded [stran•dud]
The condition of a grounded vessel incapable of freeing itself unassisted.

strangle knot [strang•gul naht]
Similar to a miller's knot, used as an emergency whipping, a tie for a finger bandage, or in place of the miller's knot.

strangulation [strang•gyoo•lay•shun]
Obstruction of breathing.

strap knot [strap naut]
A knot designed especially for tying flat leather straps.

strength [strength]
Refers to the energy content of an explosive in relation to an equal amount of nitroglycerine dynamite; may also refer to the pushing effect of an explosive due to gas pressure.

stress [stress]
The amount of load placed on material, usually expressed in pounds per square inch.

stress relief, heat treatment [stress re•leef, heet treet•munt]
The uniform heating of structures to a sufficient temperature below the critical range to relieve the major portion of the residual stresses followed by uniform cooling.

string bead [string beed]
A type of weld bead made without appreciable transverse oscillation.

stringer [string•ur]
On a vessel, a longitudinal side shell internal stiffener; diagonal side frames to which the treads and handrails of ladders are attached; the outboard plating of any deck.

string shot [string shaht]
In drilling, a charge run inside the drill pipe on an electric cable, which blows off the pipe above an obstruction when the drill string is stuck in the hole; allows recovery of the free section of the string and simplifies fishing the remaining pipe. (See: fish.)

strip a well [strip uh well]
To pull out rods and tubing simultaneously from a well.

stripper [strip•ur]
A well which will produce only a very small amount of oil.

stroke [stroke]
In an engine, the distance moved by the piston.

strong breeze [strong breez]
A wind of 22 to 27 knots (25 to 31 miles per hour).

strong gale [strong gale]
A wind of 41 to 47 knots (47 to 54 miles per hour).

stuck pipe [stuck pyp]
In drilling, drill pipe, casing or tubing which sticks in a hole and cannot be raised or lowered.

sub-bottom profiler [sub-baht•um pro•fyl•ur]
An acoustic instrument carried on submersibles; emits a sonar pulse of high frequency which penetrates the upper layers of sediment; the hydrophone receives the returned signal and a recorder shows geologic strata.

subcutaneous [sub•kyoo•tane•ee•us]
Occurring or located beneath the skin.

submarine [sub•muh•reen]
Any manned vessel that is able to operate inde-

pendently of the surface and also can operate under its own power on the surface.

submersible [sub•**mur**•suh•b'l]
A one-atmosphere vehicle for underwater operation. (See: dry submersible, lock out submersible, self propelled submersible, wet submersible.)

submersible decompression chamber [sub•**mur**•suh•b'l de•kum•**presh**•un **chaym**•bur]
A chamber that can be lowered into the water to transport divers between the surface and the work site; can be mated to the deck decompression chamber. (See: altitude chamber, chamber, compression chamber, deck compression chamber, double-lock chamber, hyperbaric chamber, monoplace chamber, multiplace chamber, single lock chamber.)

submersible work chamber (SWC) [sub•**murs**•uh•b'l wurk **cham**•bur]
A single-wall, pressure-proof, helium-tight tank of steel mounted on a support frame, designed to accommodate two divers.

sub-sea completion [sub-see kum•**plee**•shun]
A method of completing production wells when the well heads are located on the sea floor; piping oil or gas from the well heads to a loading buoy, a fixing platform, or to shore. (See: completion.)

sub-sea drilling [sub-see **drill**•ing]
A type of drilling operation where all well heads and blow out preventer equipment are on the ocean floor.

substitute [sub•stuh•**toot**]
A screwed connection joint for matching pipes having different threads; also called a sub.

substructure [sub•**struck**•choor]
In drilling, the structure on which the derrick engines and drawworks are installed. (See: derrick, drawworks.)

subsurface geology [sub•**sur**•fuss gee•**all**•uh•gee]
The method by which a geologist studies information gained from wells that have already been drilled in an area; an electric log is lowered and shows the depth of the formations and, to some degree, if any of the sands are oil bearing. (See: electric log, logging a well.)

sucker rods [**suck**•ur rahdz]
In drilling, rods about 20 feet (6.1 millemeter) long, which make up a string to operate a down hole pump. (See: down hole pump.)

suction bailer [**suck**•shun **bay**•lur]
A tubular device with a foot valve, used for bailing mud or fluid from a well. (See: mud.)

sudoriferous [**sood**•ur•if•ur•us]
Producing or secreting sweat.

suffocation [suff•uh•**kay**•shun]
Stoppage of breathing from any cause, or the resulting asphyxia; may be due to a lack of oxygen, or a foreign body, water or vomitus in the wind pipe.

sugar sand [**shoog**•ur sand]
Very fine sand common to delta areas.

suits, diving [soots, **dyv**•ing]
Specialized protective clothing used by divers underwater. (See: closed circuit hot water suit, constant volume dry suit, deep sea diving suit, dry suit, hot water open circuit suit, rubber suit, standard suit, variable volume dry suit, wet suit.)

suit squeeze [soot skweez]
Injury resulting from unequal ambient pressure in a diving suit. (See: squeeze.)

superstructure [**soop**•ur•struck•chur]
On a vessel, a bridge, pilothouse, cabin, mast or other structure built above the main deck.

sur-D tables
(See: surface decompression.)

surf [surf]
Waves breaking upon a shore.

surface decompression [**sur**•fuss de•kum•**presh**•un]
The procedure in which a portion of the in-water decompression is omitted, and the diver is brought to the surface and recompressed in a chamber to complete the decompression; sometimes confused with decanting.

surface geology [**sur**•fuss jee•**ahl**•uh•jee]
The method by which the surface of the earth is studied and predictions are made as to what type of structures lie beneath the surface.

surface interval [**sur**•fuss in•tur•vul]
The elapsed time between surfacing from a dive and the moment when the diver leaves the surface for the next dive.

surface string [**sur**•fuss string]
The first string of casing set in a well to act as an anchor for the drilling well head and blow out preventer stack. (See: blow out preventer stack.)

surface supplied [**sur**•fuss suh•**plyd**]
A form of diving in which the breathing gas is supplied from a compressor or cylinder(s) on the surface.

surge [surj]
A great rolling swell of water; a violent rising and falling.

surgeonfish [**sur**•jun fish]
A marine animal which can inflict venomous puncture wounds with fin spines; many also can

cause deep lacerations with knife-like spines carried on either side of their bodies, by a fast lashing motion. (See: hazardous marine animals.)

surgeon's knot [**sur**•jun'z not]
A square knot with an extra twist to give added friction to the hold.

swab [swahb]
A tool fitted with rubber cups and run on a wire line; used for removing fluid from a well bore.

swage [swayj]
A term meaning to overwork (or permanently deform) a piece of metal.

SWC
(See: submersible work chamber.)

swell [swell]
A large and fairly smooth wave.

swim fins [swim finz]
Devices worn on the feet of a diver or swimmer to increase the propulsive force of the legs.

swimmer delivery vehicle (SDV) [swim•ur de•**liv**•ur•ee ve•hik•ul]
A type of wet submersible used for the underwater transport of divers.

swimmer vehicle [swim•ur ve•hik•ul]
Any one of a number of devices used to aid a swimmer in attaining speeds greater than he could accomplish using fins.

swimming ascent [swim•ing uh•**sent**]
Controlled ascent with a breathing device, but without the aid of a buoyancy device or line. (See: ascent, buoyant ascent, emergency ascent, emergency buoyant ascent, emergency controlled ascent, exhaling ascent, hooded ascent.)

swivel [swiv•ul]
An assembly suspended from the rig hook and fastened to the top end of the kelly; the swivel supports the drilling string and allows rotation of the pipe. (See: hook, kelly.)

symbiosis [sim•bee•**oh**•sus]
The living together of two or more organisms in an association which is mutually advantageous.

sympathetic detonation [sim•puh•**thet**•ik det•uh•nay•shun]
A detonation set off by shock waves from another detonation in which the explosive charges are not in direct contact.

symptoms [**simp**•tums]
Perceptible changes in body state or function that may be indicative of disease or injury; the word applies to changes perceptible to the individual himself, but is often used to include signs which are abnormalities that can be detected by an observer or examiner.

syncline [sin•klyne]
In drilling, a saucer shaped formation.

syndrome [sin•drome]
A group of symptoms that indicate a specific disorder; a complex of symptoms and signs that occur together.

system, demand
(See: regulator, demand)

systemic [sis•**tem**•ik]
Affecting the whole body; generalized.

systole [sis•**tole**•ee]
The period of heart muscle contraction, especially that of the ventricles; adjective: systolic.

-T-

tachometer [tack•**ahm**•uh•tur]
A device for measuring and indicating the rotative speed of an engine.

tachycardia [tack•uh•**kahrd**•ee•uh]
A rapid heart beat; the term usually applies to a resting pulse rate above 100 per minute.

tackle [**tack**•ul]
In rigging, a term applied to the combination of falls and blocks used to gain advantage in power, or for fairlead. (See: fairlead.)

tack weld [tack weld]
A weld, generally short made to hold parts of a weldment in proper alignment until the final welds are made; used only for assembly purposes.

tail board [tale bord]
In drilling, the rear extension of a walking beam. (See: walking beam.)

tail out rods [tale owt rodz]
To pull the lower end of a sucker rod away from a well when laying down rods. (See: sucker rods.)

tail pipe [tale pype]
In drilling, a length of pipe which is run below a packer (anchor) and rests on the bottom of the hole. (See: anchor.)

tamping [**tam**•ping]
The act of pressing an explosive charge into a hole or covering it with a dense material; also stemming.

tank
(See: bottle.)

tank farm [tank fahrm]
A storage area for large oil storage tanks and their pipe manifolds and pumping units.

tank strapper [tank **strap**•ur]
The operator who measures the level of liquid in a tank to establish the contents.

tank top [tank tahp]
The plating, sometimes called the inner bottom, which confines the upper limits of a double-bottom tank.

tap, fishing [tap, **fish**•ing]
A tapered thread cutting tool which is run into the hole and connects to a pipe lost in the hole. (See: fishing tools.)

T.D.C.
Top dead center.

tearing down [**tair**•ing down]
Dismantling a rig when a well has been completed.

telemetry [tu•**lem**•uh•tree]
The technique of measuring a variety of quantities in place, transmitting the value to a station, and there interpreting, indicating or recording the quantities; transmission may be electrical, electromagnetic or sonic.

telephoto lens [**tel**•uh•**foe**•toe lenz]
In photography, a lens with a long focal length and a small acceptance angle; can be used to make small or distant objects occupy more of the frame than possible with a standard lens.

telescoping derrick [**tel**•uh•**scope**•ing **dair**•ik]
A portable mast whose sections nest inside each other and can be extended and installed by means of tackle or hydraulics.

temperature [**tem**•pur•uh•choor]
The degree of hotness or coldness measured on a definite scale; may be measured in Celsius, centigrade, Fahrenheit, Kelvin or Rankine temperature scale. (See: Celsius temperature, centigrade temperature, Fahrenheit temperature, Kelvin temperature, Rankine temperature.)

temperature, absolute [**tem**•p'ruh•choor, **ab**•so•loot]
Temperature measured or calculated on a scale having absolute zero as the minimum and scale units equal in magnitude to centigrade degrees.

temperature, Celsius [**tem**•p'ruh•choor, **sell**•see•us]
Thermometer scale in which water boils at 100° C and freezes at 0° C (absolute zero is 273° below Celsius zero).

temperature, Fahrenheit [**tem**•p'ruh•choor, **Fair**•un•hite]
Thermometer scale where water boils at 212° F, and freezes at 32^0 F above Fahrenheit zero, and where absolute zero is 159.6^0 below Fahrenheit zero.

temperature, Rankine [**tem**•p'ruh•choor, **Rang**•kun]
Temperature in which the difference between boiling and freezing points of water is 212^0 and zero is absolute zero of temperature; freezing point of water is 491.7^0 F, and one degree Rankine equals one degree Fahrenheit.

temperature survey [**tem**•p'ruh•choor **sur**•vay]
Operation of an instrument which records the change of temperature in a hole; used to locate the correct cementation or the amount of water flowing in.

template [**tem**•plut]
A pattern shaped to the dimensions and form of a piece of work to be fabricated; includes information such as sizes of lap, thickness of plate, location of rivet holes, type of weld, etc.

tender [**ten**•dur]
The individual responsible for seeing that the diver receives care both topside and underwater; also called the attendant; a support vessel.

tensile force [**ten**•sul fors]
A force exerted to stretch or pull apart a material.

tensile strength [**ten**•sul strength]
The highest stress that a material can withstand before failure or rupture occurs; also, ultimate strength.

tensor [**ten**•sore]
Any muscle that stretches or pulls on a part to make it tense.

terminal [**tur**•min•ul]
In electrical work, a junction point where connections are made.

tethered diving [**teth**•urd **dyv**•ing]
Diving with a lifeline and a tender.

tetrytol [**tet**•ri•tall]
A high explosive.

TFE
A tetrafluoroethylene polymer with excellent chemical resistance and a self-lubricating quality.

therapy [**thair**•uh•pee]
The treatment of disease or disorder.

thermal balance [**thur**•mul **bal**•uns]
A state characterized by stable body temperature in which heat gain equals heat loss.

thermal stress [**thur**•mul stress]
A condition in which the body attempts to maintain normal temperature when the surrounding temperature is either higher or lower than that of the body.

thermocline [thur•mo•klyne]
An abrupt change in temperature encountered at varying depths.

thermogenesis [thur•mo•jen•uh•sus]
The production of heat, especially in the animal body.

thermostat [thur•muh•stat]
A heat controlled valve used in the cooling system of an engine to regulate the flow of water, or in an electrical circuit to control the current.

thief formation
(See: lose returns.)

thoracic squeeze [thor•ass•ik skweez]
Injury to the lung due to chest air spaces not being equalized to ambient pressure.

thorax [thor•aks]
That portion of the body between the head and the abdomen; enclosed by the ribs in vertebrates.

thoriated tungsten [thor•ee•ay•tud tung•stun]
Tungsten containing a small percentage of thorium; improves the electronic emission quality of an electrode.

threshold [thresh•old]
As a visual term, the minimum amount of background luminance, size of an object, contrast, or duration of the visual stimulus required to effect a visual response.

thrible [thrib•ul]
A drill pipe stand made up of three singles. (See: single.)

throat of a fillet weld [throte uv uh fill•ut weld]
Shortest distance from the root of a fillet weld to the face.

thrombocyte
(See: platelet.)

thrombosis [throm•boh•sis]
Coagulation of the blood in some part of the circulary system, forming a clot that obstructs circulation in that part.

throwing the chain [throe•ing thu chayn]
In drilling, the technique of throwing (flipping) the spinning chain from the joint of pipe in the rotary table to the joint of pipe being made up; the chain is wrapped around the pipe and the power for spinning the pipe is applied by the drawworks cathead. (See: cathead, spinning chain.)

thrust [thrust]
The force trying to push a tube out of its fitting; results from system pressure against the exposed tube area.

thruster [thrus•tur]
A propeller or water jet, usually located at the bow and stern, used to give lateral thrust to aid in slow speed steering or maneuvering.

tidal volume [tide•ul vahl•yoom]
The amount of gas exchanged in respiration cycle, measured by averaging over several breaths.

tide [tyde]
The periodic rise and fall of the water level, due to the gravitational attraction of the moon and sun acting on the earth's rotating surface.

tide rip [tyde rip]
Waves and eddies in shoal water caused by tide.

tide wave [tyde wayv]
A long-lasting wave that has its origin in the tide-producing force, and which displays itself in the rising and falling of the tide.

T.I.G.
Tungsten insert gas; a form of welding used to weld hard-to-weld metals.

tight formation [tite fore•may•shun]
In drilling, a reservoir formation which has poor porosity or permeability, and does not allow the free flow of fluid into the hole. (See: permeability.)

TIG welding [tig weld•ing]
An arc welding process where coalescence is produced by heating with an electric arc between a single tungsten (nonconsumable) electrode and the work; shielding is obtained from a gas or gas mixture; pressure may or may not be used; also, gas tungsten arc welding.

timber hitch [tim•bur hich]
A hitch for dragging a heavy object.

tissue half time
(See: half time.)

toe of weld [toe uv weld]
The junction between the face of the weld and the base metal.

toggle [togg•ul]
A small piece of wood or metal often used to lock a knot that may have to be loosened quickly, or to help it hold better.

tong line [tong lyne]
In drilling, wire or rope used for pulling on the pipe tongs, which are used for making up and breaking out sections of the drill string above the rotary table. (See: drill string, rotary table.)

tongman [tong•man]
In drilling, the floorman who handles the tongs which are used for making up or breaking out joints of pipe from the drilling string.

tongs [tongz]
Large pipe wrenches hanging in the derrick, used for making up or breaking out lengths of drill pipe, casing or tubing.

tongs, power [tongz, pow•ur]
Pneumatically or hydraulically operated tools which spin the drill pipe and take the place of the normal hand operated tongs. (See: tongs.)

tooker patch [took•ur pach]
A small folding patch used to make an airtight seal on the portholes of a vessel.

tool joint [tool joint]
In drilling, a heavy steel coupling, screwed or welded to the end of drill pipe singles, for making up a drill string.

tool pusher
(See: drilling crew.)

tooth squeeze [tooth skweez]
Pain or injury caused by an air pocket between a tooth and a filling; also called barodontalgia.

torch
(See: cutting torch.)

torch tip
(See: cutting tip.)

torque [tork]
A force that produces or tends to produce rotary motion.

torr [tore]
A unit of pressure equal to 1/760 of an atmosphere and approximately equal to the pressure of a column of mercury one millimeter high at 0°C and standard gravity.

torus [tore•us]
A surface generated by the revolution of a circle about an axis lying in its plane; an O-Ring is one example.

total bottom time
(See: bottom time.)

total time [toe•tul tym]
In diving, refers to the time of descent in addition to the time at maximum pressure. (See: bottom time.)

tour [toor]
The shift worked by a drilling crew, either eight or twelve hours long, known as: morning tour (0800—1600); evening tour (1600 to midnight); graveyard tour (midnight to 0800).

toxemia [tahk•see•me•uh]
A general toxic condition in which poisonous products are present into the blood stream.

toxic [tahk•sik]
Poisonous.

Toynbee maneuver [Toyn•bee mun•oo•vur]
A maneuver to equalize the pressure in the middle ear with the ambient pressure against the outer surface of the eardrum; the nose is compressed shut, the mouth is closed, the glottis is closed; one swallows, reducing the pressure and opening the eustachian tube, allowing equalization.

trachea [tray•kee•uh]
The wind pipe, formed of cartilage rings to maintain an open airway; carries air to the bronchial tubes.

tracheobronchial [tray•kee•oh•brahng•kyul]
Relating to the trachea and the bronchi. (See: bronchi, trachea.)

tracheostomy [tray•kee•ahs•tuh•mee]
A surgical opening into the trachea, for the introduction of a tube through which the patient may breathe.

traction steel [track•shun steel]
A specific grade of rope wire used in some hoist ropes.

trainee driller
(See: drilling crew.)

transducer [trans•doo•sur]
Any device for converting energy from one form to another (electrical, mechanical or acoustical).

TRANSEC
Transverse section; line of survey used in underwater biological and geological surveys.

transformer [trans•fore•mur]
An electrical device, such as a high tension coil, which transforms or changes the characteristics of an electrical current.

transmural pressure [trans•myoo•rul pre•shur]
The differential between the pressure acting on the inside and outside of a surface; e.g. the tubes in the lungs, or the chambers of the heart.

transom [tran•sum]
On a vessel, one of several beams and timbers fixed across the sternpost to strengthen the after part.

transponder [trans•pahn•dur]
A sonar device triggered by a signal; a transmitter that replies with a sonic output, usually on a separate frequency. (See: sonar.)

transpulmonary pressure [trans•pool•mun•air•ee pre•shur]
The difference between the oral pressure and the pressure exerted on the visceral pleural cavity of the lung.

trauma [traw•muh]
An injury or wound which may be produced by external force or by shock.

travelling block [trav•ul•ing blahk]
The block containing sheaves, attached to the hook to hoist or lower drill pipe and casing loads.

trawl [trawl]
A bag or funnel-shaped net to catch bottom fish by dragging along the bottom.

treatment depth [treet•munt depth]
The depth (pressure) to which a patient is compressed during decompression treatment.

treatment mix, gas [treet•munt miks, gas]
The breathing gas mixture used in the treatment of decompression sickness.

treatment table [treet•munt tay•bul]
A collection of decompression schedules used to treat decompression sickness or air embolism; sometimes loosely used as a synonym for an individual schedule.

tricone bit [try•kone bit]
A rock bit having three cutting cones mounted on high duty roller bearings. (See: rock bit.)

triggerfish [trig•ur•fish]
A fish with teeth and jaws adapted to feeding on heavily armored prey; can inflict a damaging bite; generally hazardous to divers only when handled. (See: hazardous marine animals.)

trimix [try•miks]
A gas misture involving three gases, usually oxygen, helium and nitrogen.

trim system [trim sis•tum]
On a vessel, any of several variable ballast or weight systems used to change trim fore and aft.

trip gas [trip gas]
In drilling, gas which enters the hole when a round trip is underway; often pulled in from the formation by pulling the pipe and bit at high speed. (See: round trip.)

tripod lashing [try•pahd lash•ing]
A method for forming a tripod, similar to shear lashing.

trochoidal waves [tro•koy•dul wavz]
Deep-water trains of waves that have great distance between crests with gentle slopes; the result of wind pressure, local or distant.

troposphere [tro•pus•fear]
The lower layer of the earth's atmosphere, extending from the surface of the earth to an altitude of ten miles.

trough [trahf]
The hollow or low area between crests of waves.

true crater dimensions [troo kray•tur duh•men•shunz]
In blasting, the crater dimensions that would exist if none of the ejected material fell back into the crater.

true north [troo north]
The direction from any point on the earth's surface toward the geographic North Pole.

tube fitting [toob fit•ing]
A device used with tubing for connection in a fluid system.

tubing [toob•ing]
Small pipe that is run into a production well to handle fluid flow from the formation to the surface.

tubing job [toob•ing jahb]
The operation of pulling or running tubing. (See: tubing.)

tumblehome [tum•bul•home]
The gradual narrowing of a vessel's beam from the water line to the top of the sheer strake. (See: sheer strake.)

tungsten electrode [tung•stun ee•lek•trode]
A non-filler-metal electrode used in arc welding, consisting of a tungsten wire.

tunnel vision [tun•ul vizh•un]
The narrowing of the field of vision; in diving, most commonly encountered in connection with oxygen toxicity. (See: oxygen toxicity.)

turbidity [tur•bid•uh•tee]
Reduced water clarity resulting from the presence of suspended matter.

turbo drill [tur•bo drill]
In drilling, the turbine situated at the bottom of the drill string; operated by the circulation of the mud; turns the rotary bit. (See: drill string, mud, rotary bit.)

turbulence [tur•byoo•luns]
A disturbed or disordered, irregular motion of fluids or gases.

turbulent work [tur•byoo•lent wurk]
That work performed in the act of breathing to overcome the effect of turbulent flow in the lung caused by high gaseous densities and/or rapid breathing.

turnbuckle [turn•buck•ul]
In rigging, a sleeve with screw thread at one end and a swivel at the other. (See: sleeve.)

twist off [twist off]
In drilling, failure of the drill string due to faulty pipe or too much tortion stress.

two-blocked [too•blahkt]
Situation when blocks are against each other and can go no farther; so that the load cannot be lifted any higher by extension, any situation where one can go no farther; also known as block-and-block.

two-part explosive [too•pahrt eks•plo•siv]
An explosive made up of two components, both

of which may be nonexplosive by themselves, that can be mixed on site prior to use.

tympanic membrane [tim•**pan**•ik **mem**•brayn]
The membrane separating the external auditory canal from the middle ear; also called the ear drum.

typhoon [tie•**foon**]
A storm originating over water; consists of winds rotating in counterclockwise motion at tremendous velocity (75 to 150 miles per hour; develops in a low-pressure center and is accompanied by high tides; seldom travels faster than 12 miles per hour; diameter may range from 150 to 300 miles.

-U-

U boom [yoo boom]
An inverted-U-shaped davit used to swing the bell out over the vessel. (See: bell, davit.)

UHF
Ultra High Frequencies (300—3000 megacycles).

ulcer [**ul**•sir]
An open lesion upon the skin or mucous membrane of the body, will loss of substance, accompanied by formation of pus.

ulcer duodenal [**ul**•sir duodenal]
An ulcer in the first section of the small intestine, between the stomach and the jejunum, due to the action of the gastric juice.

ultimate strength [**ul**•tuh•mut strayngth]
(See: tensile strength.)

ultrasonics [ul•truh•**sahn**•iks]
The technology of sound at frequencies above the audio range; i.e., above 20,000 cycles per second.

ultrasound detector [ul•truh•sound de•**tek**•tur]
A device using high frequency sound waves, used in diving to detect bubbles in the diver's body.

umbilical [um•**bill**•uh•cull]
The composite of hoses and lines supplying life support to the diver.

underbead crack [**un**•dur•beed krack]
In welding, a crack in the heat-affected zone not extending to the surface of the base metal.

undercut [**un**•dur•kut]
A groove melted into the base metal adjacent to the toe of a weld and left unfilled by weld metal.

under ream [**un**•dur reem]
In drilling, enlarging a hole below a casing shoe by means of using an under reamer tool having expanding blades. (See: casing shoe, ream.)

undertow [**un**•dur•toe]
An often misused term meaning a seaward current near the bottom of a sloping beach; caused by the return, under the action of gravity, of the water carried up to the shore by wave action. (See: backwash.)

unit pulmonary toxicity dose [**you**•nut **pull**•mun•air•ee tok•**sis**•uh•tee dose]
A unit of measure devised by the Institute for Environmental Medicine at the University of Pennsylvania; used for calculating the total oxygen exposure incurred during all phases of a dive, including decompression.

unloaded [un•**low**•dud]
When air is drawn into a cylinder, then pumped back out the suction side of a compressor.

uphill welding [up•**hill** wel•ding]
A pipe welding term indicating that the welds are made from the bottom of the pipe to the top of the pipe, without rotating the pipe.

UPTD
(See: unit pulmonary toxicity dose.)

UQC
U.S Navy designation for a wireless, underwater telephone which uses sonic energy in the water to communicate between the surface support ship and a submerged submersible.

URV
Underseas research vehicle.

USN
United States Navy.

-V-

vaccine [vack•**seen**]
A substance inoculated into the body, used to cause antibody formation in order to prevent a specific disease.

vacuum [**vack**•yoo'm]
The absence or partial absence of the standard pressure exerted by the atmosphere.

vacuum bakeout [**vack**•yoom **bayk** owt]
The addition of heat to a vacuum system to promote vaporization of contaminants and reduce pump-down time.

Valsalva maneuver [Val•**sal**•vuh muh•**noo**•vur]
A maneuver to equalize the pressure in the middle ear with the ambient pressure against the outer surface of the eardrum; the nose is compressed shut, the mouth is shut, the glottis is open, and an attempt is made to exhale through the nose; results in forcing air through the eustachian tube into the middle ear, but also causes increased pulmonary pressure which has been known to cause rupture of lung tissues and the round window of the ear.

valve [valv]
A device that starts, stops or regulates the flow of gas or air in diving equipment.

valve, non-return [valv, nahn-re•**turn**]
A valve which prevents reverse flow through the gas supply umbilical.

vapor pressure [vay•pur **presh**•ur]
The pressure exerted by a vapor in equilbrium with its solid or liquid phase.

variable ballast system [vair•ee•uh•bul **bal**•ust sis•tum]
Any of several types of pumping systems that can change ballast by admitting or expelling seawater.

variable volume dry suit [vair•ee•uh•bul **vahl**•yoom dry soot]
A dry suit with both an inlet gas valve and an exhaust valve; together with a weighted belt, the diver can maintain buoyancy control. (See: closed circuit hot water suit, dry suit, hot water open circuit suit, standard suit, suit-diving, wet suit.)

vascular [vas•kyoo•lur]
Pertaining to or composed of blood vessels.

vascular system [vas•kyoo•lur system]
The heart, blood vessels, lymphatics and their parts considered collectively. It inludes the pulmonary and portal system.

vasoconstriction [vas•oh•kun•**strik**•chun]
A decrease in the diameter of blood vessels, especially constriction of arterioles; leads to decreased blood flow to a part of the body.

vasodilation [vas•oh•dye•**lay**•shun]
An increase in the diameter of blood vessels, especially the dilation of the smallest arteries (arterioles) resulting in an increase of the blood to a part of the body.

vasomotor [vas•oh•moh•tur]
Regulating the size (i.e. caliber) of blood vessels by causing contraction or dilation, said of a nerve, nerve center or drug.

V door [Vee dore]
In drilling, an opening in the derrick structure at floor level to permit the pulling in of lengths of drill pipe or casing from the racks outside the derrick. (See: casing, derrick, drill pipe.)

velocimeter [vuh•loss•uh•mee•tur]
An instrument that measures the speed of sound in seawater.

velocity [vuh•**loss**•uh•tee]
In blasting, the rate of the detonation wave traveling through a column of explosive material.

vena cava [vee•nuh **kah**•vuh]
Either of the two large veins that enter into and return blood to the right atrium of the heart.

ventilate [ven•tuh•late]
Procedure in which a diver increases gas flow to ventilate or flush the life-support system.

ventilatory capacity [ven•til•a•tor•ee ka•**pas**•i•tee]
A function of maximum breathing capacity, timed vital capacity, and maximum expiratory flow rate, all of which are maximum — effort dynamic ventilatory measures and all reflect the work limits of the anatomical respiratory apparatus.

ventricle [ven•trik•ul]
A small cavity or pouch in the heart.

vertebra [vur•tuh•brah]
Any one of the bones of the spinal column.

vertical position [vur•tik•ul puh•**zish**•un]
The position of welding where the axis of the weld is vertical.

vertigo [vur•ti•go]
A disoriented state in which the individual or the surrounding seems to rotate dizzily; objective vertigo: the sensation that the external world is revolving around one, subjective vertigo: the sensation that one is revolving in space.

vessel [vess•ul]
A hollow structure designed for carrying or transporting something underwater or on water.

vest [vest]
Diving equipment designed to provide positive buoyancy at the surface when desired, and to afford buoyancy control by means of diver-initiated volume variation; buoyancy control below the surface is maintained either by oral inflation or by valve-controlled gas supply.

vestibular bends [ves•tib•yoo•lur bendz]
Decompression sickness involving the inner ear; often associated with vertigo. (See: decompression sickness.)

vestibular system [ves•tib•yoo•lur sis•tum]
That part of the inner ear concerned with balance.

vestibule [ves•ti•byool]
Any cavity or space serving as an entrance to another cavity or space, as the vestibule of the inner leading into the cochlea.

vibrating screen [vye•bray•ting skreen]
In drilling, the shale shaker used for removing cuttings from the circulating fluid; wire mesh screens vibrate at high speed, causing the fluid to flow through and the cuttings to remain for examination.

vibration [vye•**bray**•shun]
The ground motion caused by an explosion.

viewport [**vyoo**•port]
The observation window of a bell, submersible chamber or habitat.

viscera [vis•sur•uh]
The organs in the three large body cavities, such as the stomach and the liver in the abdominal cavity.

visceral [vis•sur•ul]
Pertaining to the internal organs.

viscosity [vis•**kahs**•uh•tee]
The property of a fluid or gas that resists change in the shape or arrangement of its elements during flow; thickness.

viscous work [vis•kus•wurk]
That work performed in the act of breathing to overcome the effect of increased viscosity of the inspired gaseous medium.

visible light [viz•uh•bul lite]
Wavelengths between 400 nm (violet) and 700 nm (red).

visor [vye•zur]
On a vessel, a small inclined canvas or metal awning extending around the pilothouse over the portholes or windows to reduce sun glare.

visual acuity [viz•yoo•ul uh•**kyoo**•uh•tee]
The ability of the eye to see or resolve fine details; expressed in distance for normal eyesight as 20/20.

visual angle [viz•shoo•ul ang•gul]
A measure of the size of a visual object at the eye; represented by the tangent of the size of the object divided by the viewing distance.

visual field [viz•shoo•ul feeld]
That portion of the external environment, measured in degrees, which is represented on the retina of the eye.

vital capacity [vye•tul kuh•**pass**•uh•tee]
The maximum volume of air that can be expired after a maximum inspiration.

volatility [vahl•uh•**till**•uh•tee]
The tendency of fluid to evaporate rapidly or pass off in the form of vapor.

voltmeter [volt•mee•tur]
An instrument for measuring the voltage in an electrical circuit.

volume [vahl•yoom]
Space measured by cubic units.

volume of breathing [vol•yoom uv bree•thing]
The amount of air moved in and out of the lungs during normal respiratory cycle.

vortex [vor•teks]
A whirling movement or mass of liquid or air.

-W-

waiting on cement [wayt•ing ahn see•**ment**]
In drilling, the expression used for the period during which a rig is shut down to allow cement to set after a casing string has been cemented into the hole or a cement plug has been placed; also, w.o.c. (See: casing string, cement plug.)

walking beam [wahk•ing beem]
A moveable beam from which drilling tools are suspended in cable tool drilling. (See: cable tool drilling.)

walking the line [wahk•ing thuh lyne]
Underwater inspection of a length of pipeline.

wall hook [wahl hook]
A fishing tool used to pull the top of a fish into the center of the hole, so an overshot or similar device can be connected to recover the fish. (See: fish, fishing tools, overshot.)

wall knot [wahl naht]
A firm, round, semipermanent stopper knot tied with the end strands of a rope.

wall scraper [wahl **skray**•pur]
In drilling, a tool used for scraping the wall of a hole to remove mud cake opposite a deposit. (See: lose returns, mud-cake.)

warp [wahrp]
To move a vessel by hauling on a line fastened to or around a piling, anchor or pier.

washout [wahsh•owt]
Enlargement in a well bore because of erosion or caving due to the solubility of a salt formation.

washover [wahsh•oh•vur]
In drilling, working a pipe fitted with a cutter head over a stuck pipe, by rotating to remove whatever is causing the fish to be stuck. (See: fish.)

water, bottom [wah•tur, baht•um]
In drilling, water entering the hole from below

the oil in a producing sand, or from a sand below the producing sand.

water breathing
(See: liquid breathing.)

water, connate [**wah**•tur, **kahn**•ayt]
Water which was trapped in a drilling formation millions of years ago.

water drive [**wah**•tur dryv]
When a well flows oil because of pressure caused by water in the formation.

water flooding [**wah**•tur **flud**•ing]
The process of injecting water into a reservoir formation in order to flood out the oil towards a production well; special injection wells are drilled for this purpose.

water head [**wah**•tur hed]
Pressure caused by a column of water.

water overburden [**wah**•tur **oh**•vur•bur•dun]
Water which lies over the rock to be blasted.

water penetration [**wah**•tur **pen**•uh•**tray**•shun]
In blasting, the seepage into or absorption of water by an explosive.

water shock [**wah**•tur shahk]
The shock wave, or overpressure, in water caused by an explosion.

water string [**wah**•tur streeng]
In drilling, a string of casing for shutting out formation water. (See: casing string.)

water table [**wah**•tur **tay**•bul]
In drilling, the platform at the top of a derrick on which the crown block is located. (See: crown block.)

watt [waht]
A measuring unit of electrical power, obtained by multiplying amperes by volts.

wave [wayv]
An oscillatory movement in a body of water which results in an alternate rise and fall of the surface; the result of wind, water displacement (earthquake, landslide), and the gravitational pull of sun and moon (tides).

wave age [wayv ayj]
The ratio of wave velocity to wind velocity.

wave height [wayv hite]
The vertical distance from preceding trough to crest.

wavelength of sound [**wayv**•layngth uv sownd]
The ratio of speed to frequency of sound waves.

wave period [wayv **peer**•ee•ud]
The time required for one full wavelength to pass a given point.

weaving [**wee**•ving]
A technique of depositing weld metal in which the electrode is oscillated.

weeverfish [**wee**•vur•fish]
Small but extremely venomous fish possessing a well-developed venom apparatus; they bury themselves with only part of the head exposed, and dart out suddenly to strike with venomous spines, causing stab wounds. (See: hazardous marine animals.)

weight [wayt]
A measure of the heaviness or mass of an object.

weight belt
(See: belt.)

weight indicator [wayt in•duh•**kay**•tur]
In drilling, an instrument which records the weight of the drilling string or casing string hanging from the travelling block and hook assembly; provides the driller with information as to the weight he is applying to the bit during the drilling operation. (See: casing string, drill string, hook, travelling block.)

weighting material [**wayt**•ing muh•**teer**•ee•ul]
In drilling, a heavy material such as barium sulphate which is added to the circulating fluid to increase its specific gravity; to control high pressures encountered when drilling into reservoir formations or to support caving formations.

weld [weld]
A localized coalescence of metal where coalescence is produced by heating to suitable temperatures, with or without the application of pressure and with or without the use of filler metal.

welding rod [**weld**•ing rahd]
Filler metal, in wire or rod form, used in gas welding and brazing processes, and in arc welding processes where the electrode does not furnish the filler metal.

weldment [**weld**•munt]
An assembly of which the component parts are joined by welding. (See: weld.)

weld metal [weld **met**•ul]
That portion of a weld which has been melted during welding. (See: weld.)

well [well]
The means of getting oil, gas or water from an underground reservoir formation to the surface; varying from a few hundred feet to more than 30,000 feet in depth.

well log
(See: log — well.)

wet boat [wet bote]
A free flooding, ambient pressure submersible designed to be operated by swimmers using

breathing apparatus, either air or mixed gas; wet means that the inside is flooded.

wet gas [wet gass]
Natural gas containing condensate; a wet gas tends to indicate the presence of an oil reservoir.

wet oil
(See: cut oil.)

wet pot [wet paht]
One chamber of a hyperbaric facility capable of being filled with water and pressurized to simulate a given underwater depth.

wet submersible [wet sub•**mur**•suh•bul]
A free-flooding submersible in which the occupants are exposed to the ambient environment. (See: dry submersible, lock out submersible, self propelled submersible, submersible.)

wet suit [wet soot]
A closed cell, synthetic rubber diving suit which provides a thermal barrier by trapping a thin layer of body-warmed water next to the diver's skin; may include boots, gloves, hood or vest. (See: closed circuit hot water suit, constant volume dry suit, deep sea diving suit, dry suit, hot water open circuit suit, standard suit, suits — diving, variable-volume dry suit.)

wet welding [wet **weld**•ing]
Underwater welding without the use of a protective habitat.

whaler [**whayl**•ur]
On a vessel, a length of heavy timber or steel structural shape to which planks are fastened to form a bulkhead or cofferdam; sometimes used to temporarily shore or stiffen bulkheads or decks.

whipping [**whip**•ing]
In rigging, winding the end of a rope to prevent fraying; in welding, a term applied to an inward and upward movement of the electrode which is employed in vertical welding to avoid undercut.

whipstock [**whip**•stahk]
A steel wedge which is set in a hole and kicks off the hole to start a directional drilling operation.

WHOI
Woods Hole Oceanographic Institution; located at Woods Hole, Massachusetts.

whole gale [hole gale]
Wind of 48 to 55 knots (55 to 63 miles per hour).

wide angle lens [wyd **ang**•gul lenz]
A photographic lens of short focal length, with a wide acceptance angle.

widow maker [**wid**•oh **mak**•ur]
Anything which could cause the death or serious injury of a workman.

wild cat [wyld kat]
A well drilled in an area which is unproven, where conditions are not fully known.

wildcatter [**wyld**•kat•ur]
An operator who drills in the hope of discovering oil or gas in an area which is not a proven oil field.

wild well [wyld well]
A well which is out of control and flowing fluid or gas from the down hole reservoir.

windlass [**wind**•las]
A hauling or lifting machine consisting of a drum or cylinder wound with rope and turned by a crank.

window [**win**•doe]
In drilling, an opening milled in a casing joint to allow a new hole to be drilled away from the original hole.

windward [**wind**•wurd]
The point or side from which the wind blows; toward the wind; in the direction from which the wind blows. (See: leeward.)

W.O.C.
(See: waiting on cement.)

WOO
World Oceanographic Organization.

working pressure [**wurk**•ing **presh**•ur]
The approximate pressure required to operate a system over its intended mission range. (See: ambient pressure, absolute pressure, atmospheric pressure, design pressure, gauge pressure, hydrostatic pressure, partial pressure, pressure.)

work of breathing [wurk uv **bree**•thing]
The amount of effort a diver must exert to breathe through the equipment; the work of breathing depends on depth, type of equipment, gas mixture and the condition of the lungs. (See: breathing resistance.)

work over job [wurk **oh**•vur jahb]
A remedial operation on a production well, such as plugging back, pulling a liner, cementing a squeeze, fracturing; etc. (See: cement squeeze, fracturing-formation, plugging back.)

WOW [wow]
Waiting on weather.

wrenching [**rench**•ing]
To pull alternately in opposite directions on the outside end of a stranded vessel in an attempt to wrench the vessel free of the ground.

-X-

xenon flasher [zee•nahn flash•ur]
A light that emits a bright flash for the purpose of surface identification; visible for two miles at night.

X-ray [eks-ray]
Artificial radiations, the same as gamma rays except that they originate outside the nucleus, produced by electronic means; used in photographing opaque bodies, etc.

-Y-

yaw [yah]
On a vessel, motion about the vertical axis.

yield point [yeeld point]
The stress at which elongation takes place with little or no increase in applied force.

yoke [yoke]
A device for attaching regulators to cylinders in order to make a leak-proof seal.

-Z-

zebrafish [zee•bruh•fish]
Beautiful, ornate fish with fan-like fins which swim around coral reefs; the fins contain 18 venom-equipped, potentially lethal spines. (See: hazardous marine animals.)

zoom lens [zoom lenz]
A compound photographic lens with a variable focal length, with which different focal lengths are achieved by varying the separation of the elements of the lens.

"Z" search [zee surch]
Underwater search of an area using a single jackstay, and moving one end at a time, forming the letter "Z"; using two divers in contact with each other, the most thorough but also the slowest of the search methods. (See: search patterns underwater.)

CONVERSION
FACTORS

ACRE: =

0.0015625	square miles or sections
0.004046875	square kilometers
0.1	square furlongs
0.4046875	square hektometers
10	square chains
40.46875	square dekameters
160	square rods
4,046.875	square meters
4,840	square yards
5,645.41213	square varas (Texas)
43,560	square feet
77,440	square spans
100,000	square links
400,000	square hands
404,687.5	square decimeters
40,468.750	square centimeters
6,272,640	square inches
4,046,875,000	square millimeters
0.4046875	hectares
40.46875	ares
4,046.875	centares (centiares)

ATMOSPHERE: =

0.103327	hektometers of water @ 60° F.
1.03327	dekameters of water @ 60° F.
10.3327	meters of water @ 60° F.
33.9007	feet of water @ 60° F.
406.8084	inches of water @ 60° F.
103.327	decimeters of water @ 60° F.
1,033.27	centimeters of water @ 60° F.
10,332.7	millimeters of water @ 60° F.
0.00760	hektometers of mercury @ 32° F.
0.0760	dekameters of mercury @ 32° F.
0.760	meters of mercury @ 32° F.
2.49343	feet of mercury @ 32° F.
29.9212	inches of mercury @ 32° F.
7.6	decimeters of mercury @ 32° F.
76	centimeters of mercury @ 32° F.
760	millimeters of mercury @ 32° F.
113,893.88	tons per square hektometer
1,138.9388	tons per square dekameter
11.389388	tons per square meter
1.0581	tons per square foot
0.00734792	tons per square inch
0.11389388	tons per square decimeter
0.0011389388	tons per square centimeter
0.000011389388	tons per square millimeter
103,327,000	kilograms per square hektometer
1,033,270	kilograms per square dekameter
10,332.7	kilograms per square meter

ATMOSPHERE: (cont'd)

959.931252	kilograms per square foot
6.666189	kilograms per square inch
103.327	kilograms per square decimeter
1.03327	kilograms per square centimeter
0.0103327	kilograms per square millimeter
227,774,851.2	pounds per square hektometer
2,277,748.512	pounds per square dekameter
22,777.48512	pounds per square meter
2,116.080	pounds per square foot
14.696	pounds per square inch
227.7748512	pounds per square decimeter
2.277748512	pounds per square centimeter
0.02277748512	pounds per square millimeter
1,033,270,000	hektograms per square hektometer
10,332,700	hektograms per square dekameter
103,327	hektograms per square meter
9,599,31252	hektograms per square foot
66.66189	hektograms per square inch
1,033.27	hektograms per square decimeter
10.3327	hektograms per square centimeter
0.103327	hektograms per square millimeter
10,332,700,000	dekagrams per square hektometer
103,327,000	dekagrams per square dekameter
1,033,270	dekagrams per square meter
95,993.1252	dekagrams per square foot
666.6189	dekagrams per square inch
10,332.7	dekagrams per square decimeter
103.327	dekagrams per square centimeter
1.03327	dekagrams per square millimeter
3,644,397,619.2	ounces per square hektometer
36,443,976.192	ounces per square dekameter
364,439.76192	ounces per square meter
33,857.28	ounces per square foot
235.136	ounces per square inch
3,644.39762	ounces per square decimeter
36.44398	ounces per square centimeter
0.36444	ounces per square millimeter
103,327,000,000	grams per square hektometer
1,033,270,000	grams per square dekameter
10,332,700	grams per square meter
959,931.252	grams per square foot
6,666,189	grams per square inch
103,327	grams per square decimeter
1,033.27	grams per square centimeter
10.3327	grams per square millimeter
1,033,270,000,000	decigrams per square hektometer
10,332,700,000	decigrams per square dekameter
103,327,000	decigrams per square meter
9,599,312.52	decigrams per square foot
66,661.89	decigrams per square inch
1,033,270	decigrams per square decimeter
10,332.7	decigrams per square centimeter

ATMOSPHERE: (cont'd)

103.327	decigrams per square millimeter
10,332,700,000,000	centigrams per square hektometer
103,327,000,000	centigrams per square dekameter
1,033,270,000	centigrams per square meter
95,933,125.2	centigrams per square foot
666,618.9	centigrams per square inch
10,332,700	centigrams per square decimeter
103,327	centigrams per square centimeter
1,033.270	centigrams per square millimeter
103,327,000,000,000	milligrams per square hektometer
1,033,270,000,000	milligrams per square dekameter
10,332,700,000	milligrams per square meter
959,931,252	milligrams per square foot
6,666,189	milligrams per square inch
103,327,000	milligrams per square decimeter
1,033,270	milligrams per square centimeter
10,332.7	milligrams per square millimeter
101,325,000,000,000	dynes per square hektometer
1,013,250,000,000	dynes per square dekameter
10,132,500,000	dynes per square meter
941,343,587	dynes per square foot
6,537,096	dynes per square inch
101,325,000	dynes per square decimeter
1,013,250	dynes per square centimeter
10,132.5	dynes per square millimeter
1.01325	bars

BARREL: =

0.158987	kiloliters
0.158987	cubic meters
0.20794	cubic yards
1.58987	hectoliters
4.5112274	bushels—U.S. (dry)
4.373766	bushels—Imperial (dry)
5.6146	cubic feet
15.89871	dekaliters
18.045097	pecks
42	gallons—U.S. (liquid)
36.09798	gallons—U.S. (dry)
34.99089	gallons—Imperial
168	quarts (liquid)
144.408516	quarts (dry)
158.987146	liters
158.987146	cubic decimeters
336	pints
1,344	gills
1,589.87146	deciliters
9,702.0288	cubic inches
15,898.71459456	centiliters
158,987.1459456	milliliters
158,987.1459456	cubic centimeters

BARREL: (cont'd)

158,987,145.9456	cubic millimeters
0.174993	tons (short) of water @ 62° F.
0.1562438	tons (long) of water @ 62° F.
0.1587512	tons (metric) of water @ 62° F.
158.7512	kilograms of water @ 62° F.
349.986	pounds of water @ 62° F.
15.87512	hektograms of water @ 62° F.
1.587512	dekagrams of water @ 62° F.
5,599.776	ounces of water @ 62° F.
0.1587512	grams of water @ 62° F.
0.01587512	decigrams of water @ 62° F.
0.001587512	centigrams of water @ 62° F.
0.0001587512	milligrams of water @ 62° F.
5.1042	sacks of cement
2,449,902	grains
404.25	pounds of salt water @ 60° F. of 1.155 specific gravity

BTU(60° F.) =

25,030	foot poundals
300,360	inch poundals
777.97265	foot pounds
9,335.67120	inch pounds
0.00027776	ton (short) calories
0.25198	kilogram calories
0.55552	pound calories
2.5198	hektogram calories
25.198	dekagram calories
8.88832	ounce calories
251.98	gram calories
2,519.8	decigram calories
25,198	centigram calories
251.980	milligram calories
0.000012201	kilowatt days
0.00029283	kilowatt hours
0.01757	kilowatt minutes
1.0546	kilowatt seconds
0.012201	watt days
0.29283	watt hours
17.57	watt minutes
1,054.6	watt seconds
0.11856	ton meters
107.56	kilogram meters
237.12678	pound meters
1,075.6	hektogram meters
10,756	dekagram meters
3,794.02848	ounce meters
107,560	gram meters
1,075,600	decigram meters
10,756,000	centigram meters
107,560,000	milligram meters

BTU(60°F.) (cont'd)

0.0011856	ton hektometers
1.0756	kilogram hektometers
2.37127	pound hektometers
10.756	hektogram hektometers
107.56	dekagram hektometers
37.94028	ounce hektometers
1,075.6	gram hektometers
10,756	decigram hektometers
107,560	centigram hektometers
1,075,600	milligram hektometers
0.011856	ton dekameters
10.756	kilogram dekameters
23.7127	pound dekameters
107.56	hektogram dekameters
1,075.6	dekagram dekameters
379.40285	ounce dekameters
10,756	gram dekameters
107,560	decigram dekameters
1,075,600	centigram dekameters
10,756,000	milligram dekameters
0.388977	ton feet
352.887473	kilogram feet
777.97265	pound feet
3,528.874731	hektogram feet
35,288.747308	dekagram feet
12,447.611780	ounce feet
352,887.473080	gram feet
3,528.875	decigram feet
35,288.747	centigram feet
352,887,473	milligram feet
4.667724	ton inches
4,234.649677	kilogram inches
9,335.671800	pound inches
42,346.496772	hektogram inches
423,464.96772	dekagram inches
149,371.34136	ounce inches
4,234,650	gram inches
42,346,497	decigram inches
423,464,968	centigram inches
4,234,649,677	milligram inches
1.1856	ton decimeters
1.0756	kilogram decimeters
2,371.2678	pound decimeters
10,756	hektogram decimeters
107,560	dekagram decimeters
37,940.2848	ounce decimeters
1,075,600	gram decimeters
10,756,000	decigram decimeters
107,560,000	centigram decimeters
1,075,600,000	milligram decimeters
11.856	ton centimeters
10,756	kilogram centimeters

BTU(60°F.) (cont'd)

23,712.678	pound centimeters
107,560	hektogram centimeters
1,075,600	dekagram centimeters
379,402.848	ounce centimeters
10,756,000	gram centimeters
107,560,000	decigram centimeters
1,075,600,000	centigram centimeters
10,756,000,000	milligram centimeters
118.56	ton millimeters
107,560	kilogram millimeters
237,126.780	pounds millimeters
1,075,600	hektogram millimeters
10,756,000	dekagram millimeters
3,794,028.48	ounce millimeters
107,560,000	gram millimeters
1,075,600,000	decigram millimeters
10,756,000,000	centigram millimeters
107,560,000,000	milligram millimeters
0.0104028	kiloliter-atmospheres
0.104028	hektoliter-atmospheres
1.040277	dekaliter-atmospheres
10.40277	liter-atmospheres
104.0277	deciliter-atmospheres
1,040.277	centiliter-atmospheres
10,402.77	milliliter-atmospheres
0.0000000000104104	cubic kilometer-atmospheres
0.0000000104104	cubic hektometer-atmospheres
0.000010410	cubic dekameter-atmospheres
0.0104104	cubic meter-atmospheres
0.3676637	cubic feet-atmospheres
635.277597	cubic inch-atmospheres
10.410432	cubic decimeter-atmospheres

BUSHEL—U.S. (DRY): =

0.035238	kiloliters
0.035238	cubic meters
0.04609	cubic yards
0.304785	barrels—U.S
0.35238	hectoliters
0.96945	bushels—Imp.(dry)
1.24446	cubic feet
3.5238	dekaliters
4	pecks
9.3088	gallons—U.S. (liquid)
8	gallons—U.S. (dry)
7.81457	gallons—Imp.
37.2353	quarts (liquid)
32	quarts (dry)
35.238	liters
35.238	cubic decimeters
64	pints (dry)

BUSHEL—U.S. (DRY): (cont'd)

74.8706	pints (liquid)
299.4824	gills (liquid)
352.38	deciliters
2,150.42	cubic inches
3,523.8	centiliters
35,238	milliliters
35,238	cubic centimeters
35,238,000	cubic millimeters
0.053335	tons (short)
0.047621	tons (long)
0.048385	tons (metric)
48.38492	kilograms
106.67048	pounds
483.84924	hektograms
4,838.4924	dekagrams
7,741.58787	ounces
48,384.924	grams
483,849.24	decigrams
4,838,492.4	centigrams
48,384,924	milligrams

BUSHEL—IMPERIAL: =

0.036348	kiloliters
0.036348	cubic meters
0.047542	cubic yards
0.31439	barrels
0.36348	hectoliters
1.03151	bushels—U.S.
1.2843	cubic feet
3.63484	dekaliters
4.12604	pecks
9.60212	gallons—U.S. (liquid)
8.25208	gallons—U.S. (dry)
8	gallons—Imp.
38.40858	quarts (liquid)
33.00832	quarts (dry)
36.34835	liters
36.34835	cubic decimeters
66.01664	pints (dry)
76.81716	pints (liquid)
307.26856	gills (liquid)
363.4835	deciliters
2,219.3	cubic inches
3,634.835	centiliters
36,348.35	milliliters
36,348.35	cubic centimeters
36,348,350	cubic millimeters
0.055016	tons (short)
0.049122	tons (long)
0.049910	tons (metric)
49.90953	kilograms

BUSHEL—IMPERIAL: (cont'd)

110.031667	pounds
499.095330	hektograms
4,990.95330	dekagrams
7,985.52530	ounces
49,909.53296	grams
499,095.32955	decigrams
4,990,953.29552	centigrams
49,909,532.95524	milligrams

CUBIC FOOT: =

0.000000000017596	cubic miles
0.000000000028317	cubic kilometers
0.0000000034783	cubic furlongs
0.000000028317	cubic hektometers
0.0000034783	cubic chains
0.000028317	cubic dekameters
0.00022261	cubic rods
0.028317	cubic meters
0.028317	kiloliters
0.037036	cubic yards
0.046656	cubic varas (Texas)
0.17811	barrels
0.28317	hectoliters
0.80358	bushels—U.S. (dry)
0.77860	bushels—Imperial (dry)
2.37033	cubic spans
2.8317	dekaliters
3.2143	pecks
3.48327	cubic links
7.48050	gallons—U.S. (liquid)
6.42937	gallons—U.S. (dry)
6.22889	gallons—Imperial
27.08096	cubic hands
29.92257	quarts (liquid)
25.71410	quarts (dry)
28.317	liters
28.317	cubic decimeters
59.84515	pints (liquid)
51.4934	pints (dry)
239.38060	gills (liquid)
283.17	deciliters
1,727.98829	cubic inches
2,831.7	centiliters
28,317	milliliters
28,317	cubic centimeters
28,317,000	cubic millimeters
957.51104	ounces (fluid)
7,660.03167	drams (fluid)
0.9091	sacks of cement (set)
62.35	pounds of water @ 60° F.

CUBIC FOOT: (cont'd)

64.3 . . . . pounds of salt water
72.0 . . . . pounds of salt water @ 60° F. at 1.155 specific gravity
489.542 . . . . pounds of steel of 7.851 specific gravity

CUBIC INCH: =

0.000000000000010183 . . . . cubic miles
0.000000000000016387 . . . . cubic kilometers
0.0000000000020129 . . . . cubic furlongs
0.000000000016387 . . . . cubic hektometers
0.0000000020129 . . . . cubic chains
0.000000016387 . . . . cubic dekameters
0.00000012883 . . . . cubic rods
0.000016387 . . . . .cubic meters
0.000016387 . . . . kiloliters
0.000021434 . . . . .cubic yards
0.000027000 . . . . cubic varas (Texas)
0.00010307 . . . . barrels
0.00016387 . . . . hectoliters
0.00046503 . . . . bushels—U.S. (dry)
0.00045058 . . . . bushels—Imperial (dry)
0.0005787 . . . . cubic feet
0.0013717 . . . . cubic spans
0.0016387 . . . . dekaliters
0.0018601 . . . . pecks
0.0020129 . . . . cubic links
0.0043290 . . . . gallons—U.S. (liquid)
0.003721 . . . . gallons—U.S. (dry)
0.003607 . . . . gallons (Imperial)
0.015672 . . . . cubic hands
0.017316 . . . . .quarts (liquid)
0.014881 . . . . quarts (dry)
0.016387 . . . . liters
0.016387 . . . . cubic decimeters
0.034632 . . . . pints (liquid)
0.029762 . . . . .pints (dry)
0.13853 . . . . gills (liquid)
0.16387 . . . . .deciliters
1.63871 . . . . centiliters
16.38716 . . . . .milliliters
16.38716 . . . . cubic centimeters
16,387.16 . . . . cubic millimeters
4.4329 . . . . .drams (fluid)
0.2833 . . . . pounds of steel (specific gravity—7.851)
0.03607 . . . . pounds of water @ 60° F.
0.5541 . . . . ounces of fluid
0.041667 . . . . pounds of salt water @ 60° F. and 1.155 specific gravity
0.0005216 . . . . sacks of cement (set)
0.000016387 . . . . kiloliters per day
0.00000068278 . . . . kiloliters per hour
0.000000011380 . . . . kiloliters per minute
0.00000000018966 . . . . kiloliters per second

CUBIC INCH: (cont'd)

0.000016387	cubic meters per day
0.00000068278	cubic meters per hour
0.000000011380	cubic meters per minute
0.00000000018966	cubic meters per second
0.000021434	cubic yards per day
0.00000089309	cubic yards per hour
0.000000014885	cubic yards per minute
0.00000000024808	cubic yards per second
0.00010307	barrels per day
0.0000042944	barrels per hour
0.000000071574	barrels per minute
0.0000000011929	barrels per second
0.00016387	hectoliters per day
0.0000068278	hectoliters per hour
0.00000011380	hectoliters per minute
0.0000000018966	hectoliters per second
0.0005787	cubic feet per day
0.000024112	cubic feet per hour
0.00000040187	cubic feet per minute
0.0000000066979	cubic feet per second
0.0016387	dekaliters per day
0.000068278	dekaliters per hour
0.0000011380	dekaliters per minute
0.000000018966	dekaliters per second
0.0043290	gallons per day
0.00018037	gallons per hour
0.0000030062	gallons per minute
0.000000050104	gallons per second
0.003607	gallons (Imperial) per day
0.00015029	gallons (Imperial) per hour
0.0000025049	gallons (Imperial) per minute
0.000000041748	gallons (Imperial) per second
0.016387	liters per day
0.00068278	liters per hour
0.000011380	liters per minute
0.00000018966	liters per second
0.016387	cubic decimeters per day
0.00068278	cubic decimeters per hour
0.000011380	cubic decimeters per minute
0.00000018966	cubic decimeters per second
0.017316	quarts per day
0.00072151	quarts per hour
0.000012025	quarts per minute
0.00000020042	quarts per second
0.034632	pints per day
0.0014430	pints per hour
0.000024050	pints per minute
0.00000040083	pints per second
0.13853	gills per day
0.0057722	gills per hour
0.000096024	gills per minute

CUBIC INCH: (cont'd)

0.0000016034	gills per second
0.16387	deciliters per day
0.0068278	deciliters per hour
0.00011380	deciliters per minute
0.0000018966	deciliters per second
1.0	cubic inches per day
0.041666	cubic inches per hour
0.00069444	cubic inches per minute
0.000011574	cubic inches per second
1.63871	centiliters per day
0.068278	centiliters per hour
0.0011380	centilters per minute
0.000018966	centiliters per second
16.38716	milliliters per day
0.68278	milliliters per hour
0.011380	milliliters per minute
0.00018966	milliliters per second
16.38716	cubic centimeters per day
0.68278	cubic centimeters per hour
0.011380	cubic centimeters per minute
0.00018966	cubic centimeters per second
16,387.16	cubic millimeters per day
682.7760	cubic millimeters per hour
11.3796	cubic millimeters per minute
0.18966	cubic millimeters per second

CUBIC METER: =

0.00000000062139	cubic miles
0.000000001	cubic kilometers
0.00000012283	cubic furlongs
0.000001	cubic hektometers
0.00012283	cubic chains
0.001	cubic dekameters
0.0078613	cubic rods
1	kiloliters
1.307943	cubic yards
1.64763	cubic varas (Texas)
6.28994	barrels
10	hectoliters
28.37798	bushels (U.S.) dry
27.49582	bushels (Imperial) dry
35.314445	cubic feet
83.70688	cubic spans
100	dekaliters
113.51120	pecks
122.83316	cubic links
264.17762	gallons (U.S.) liquid
227.026407	gallons (U.S.) dry
219.97542	gallons (Imperial)
956.34894	cubic hands
1,000	liters

CUBIC METER: (cont'd)

1,000	cubic decimeters
1,056.71088	quarts (liquid)
908.10299	quarts (dry)
2,113.42176	pints (liquid)
1,816.19834	pints (dry)
8,453.68704	gills (liquid)
10,000	deciliters
61,022.93879	cubic inches
100,000	centiliters
1,000,000	milliliters
1,000,000	cubic centimeters
1,000,000,000	cubic millimeters
2,204.62	pounds of water @ 39° F.
2,201.82790	pounds of water @ 60° F.
2,542.608	pounds of salt water @ 60ºF. and 1.155 specific gravity
32.10396	sacks of cement (set)
33,813.54487	ounces (fluid)
270,506.35839	drams (fluid)

DEGREE PER MINUTE: =

4.0	revolutions per day
0.16667	revolutions per hour
0.0027778	revolutions per minute
0.000046297	revolutions per second
15.99869	quadrants per day
0.66661	quadrants per hour
0.01111	quadrants per minute
0.00018517	quadrants per second
25.13203	radians per day
1.04717	radians per hour
0.017453	radians per minute
0.00029088	radians per second
1,440	degrees per day
60	degrees per hour
1.0	degrees per minute
0.016667	degrees per second
1,440	hours per day
60	hours per hour
1.0	hours per minute
0.016667	hours per second
86,400	minutes per day
3,600	minutes per hour
60	minutes per minute
1	minutes per second
5,184,000	seconds per day
216,000	seconds per hour
3,600	seconds per minute
60	seconds per second
240	revolutions per day
10	revolutions per hour

DEGREE PER MINUTE: (cont'd)

0.16667	revolutions per minute
0.0027778	revolutions per second
959.904	quadrants per day
39.9960	quadrants per hour
0.6666	quadrants per minute
0.01111	quadrants per second
1,507.9392	radians per day
62.83080	radians per hour
1.047180	radians per minute
0.017453	radians per second
86,400	degrees per day
3,600	degrees per hour
60	degrees per minute
1.0	degrees per second
86,400	hours per day
3,600	hours per hour
60	hours per minute
1.0	hours per second
5,184,000	minutes per day
216,000	minutes per hour
3,600	minutes per minute
60	minutes per second
311,040,000	seconds per day
12,960,000	seconds per hour
216,000	seconds per minute
3,600	seconds per second

DRAM (AVOIRDUPOIS): =

0.0000017439	tons (long)
0.0000017718	tons (metric)
0.0000019531	tons (short)
0.001771845	kilograms
0.00390625	pounds (Avoir.)
0.0047471788	pounds (Troy)
0.01771845	hektograms
0.1771845	dekagrams
0.056966146	ounces (Troy)
0.0625	ounces (Avoir.)
0.4557292	drams (Troy)
1.139323	pennyweights
1.3671875	scruples
1.771845	grams
17.71845	decigrams
27.34375	grains
177.1845	centigrams
1,771.845	milligrams
8.85923	carats (metric)

DRAM (FLUID): =

0.0000036966	kiloliters
0.0000036966	cubic meters
0.0000048352	cubic yards
0.000023252	barrels
0.000036966	hektoliters
0.00013055	cubic feet
0.00036966	dekaliters
0.00097658	gallons (U.S.) liquid
0.00081318	gallons (Imperial) liquid
0.00390625	quarts (liquid)
0.0036966	liters
0.0036966	cubic decimeters
0.0078125	pints (liquid)
0.03125	gills (liquid)
0.036966	deciliters
0.225586	cubic inches
0.36966	centiliters
3.69661	milliliters
3.69661	cubic centimeters
3,696.61	cubic millimeters
0.125	ounces (fluid)
60	minims

DRAM (TROY OR APOTHECARY): =

0.0000038265308	tons (long)
0.0000038879351	tons (metric)
0.0000042857145	tons (short)
0.0038879351	kilograms
0.008571429	pounds (Avoir.)
0.010416667	pounds (Troy)
0.038879351	hektograms
0.38879351	dekagrams
0.12500	ounces (Troy)
0.1371429	ounces (Avoir.)
2.194286	drams (Avoir.)
2.50	pennyweight
3.0	scruples
3.8879351	grams
38.879351	decigrams
60.0	grains
388.79351	centigrams
3,887.9351	milligrams
19.43968	carats (metric)

FOOT (OR ENGINEER'S LINK): =

0.0001893939	miles
0.0003048006	kilometers
0.00151515	furlongs
0.003048006	hektometers
0.0151515	chains
0.03048006	dekameters

FOOT (OR ENGINEER'S LINK): (cont'd)

0.0606061	rods
0.3048006	meters
0.33333	yards
0.3600	varas (Texas)
1.33333	spans
1.515152	links
3.00	hands
3.048006	decimeters
30.48006	centimeters
12	inches
304.8006	millimeters
12,000	mils
304,801	microns
304,801,200	millimicrons
304,801,200	micromillimeters
473,404	wave lengths of red line of cadmium
3,048,012,000	Angstrom Units

GALLON (DRY): =

0.00044040	kiloliters
0.00044040	cubic meters
0.0057601	cubic yards
0.027701	barrels
0.0044040	hektoliters
0.12497	bushels—U.S. (dry)
0.12116	bushels—Imperial (dry)
0.15553	cubic feet
0.44040	dekaliters
1.16342	gallons—U.S. (liquid)
1	gallons—U.S. (dry)
0.96874	gallons—Imperial
4.65368	quarts (liquids)
4	quarts (dry)
4.4040	liters
4.4040	cubic decimeters
9.30736	pints (fluid)
37.22943	gills (fluid)
44.04010	deciliters
268.75	cubic inches
440.40097	centiliters
4,404.00974	milliliters
4,404.00974	cubic centimeters
4,404,009.74	cubic millimeters
0.14139	sacks of cement
71,481	minims
148.91775	ounces (fluid)
1,191.34199	drams (fluid)
0.0043301	tons (long) of water @ 62° F.
0.0043996	tons (metric) of water @ 62° F.
0.0048498	tons (short) of water @ 62° F.
4.40005	kilograms of water @ 62° F.

GALLON (DRY): (cont'd)

9.69943	pounds (Avoir) of water @ 62° F.
11.78750	pounds (Troy) of water @ 62° F.
44.00054111	hektograms
440.0054111	dekagrams
141.45004	ounces (Troy) of water @ 62° F.
155.19091	ounces (Avoir.) of water @ 62° F.
1,131.60029	drams (Troy) of water @ 62° F.
2,483.05454	drams (Avoir.) of water @ 62° F.
2,829.00071	pennyweights of water @ 62° F.
3,394.80086	scruples (Avoir.) of water @ 62° F.
4,400.054111	grams of water @ 62° F.
44,000.54111	decigrams of water @ 62° F.
67,896.022703	grains of water @ 62° F.
440,005.41110	centigrams of water @ 62° F.
4,400,054.1197	milligrams of water @ 62° F.

GALLON (IMPERIAL): =

0.00045460	kiloliters
0.00045460	cubic meters
0.0059459	cubic yards
0.028594	barrels
0.045460	hektoliters
0.12900	bushels—U.S. (dry)
0.125066	bushels—Imperial (dry)
0.16054	cubic feet
0.45460	dekaliters
1.20094	gallons—U.S. (liquid)
1.032184	gallons—U.S. (dry)
1	gallon—Imperial
4.80376	quarts (liquid)
4.12820	quarts (dry)
4.54596	liters
4.54596	cubic decimeters
9.60752	pints (liquid)
38.43008	gills (liquid)
45.4596	deciliters
277.41714	cubic inches
454.596	centiliters
4,545.96	milliliters
4,545.96	cubic centimeters
4,545.960	cubic millimeters
0.14595	sacks of cement
73,785.7536	minims
153.72032	ounces (fluid)
1,299.76256	drams (fluid)
0.0044698	tons (long) of water @ 62° F.
0.0045415	tons (metric) of water @ 62° F.
0.0050061	tons (short) of water @ 62° F.
4.54196	kilograms of water @ 62° F.
10.012237	pounds (Avoir.) of water @ 62° F.
12.16765	pounds (Troy) of water @ 62° F.

GALLON (IMPERIAL): (cont'd)

45.41955	hektograms of water @ 62° F.
454.19551	dekagrams of water @ 62° F.
146.011774	ounces (Troy) of water @ 62° F.
160.19579	ounces (Avoir.) of water @ 62° F.
1,168.094195	drams (Troy) of water @ 62° F.
2,563.13262	drams (Avoir.) of water @ 62° F.
2,902.23549	pennyweights of water @ 62° F.
3,504.28258	scruples of water @ 62° F.
4,541.95508	grams of water @ 62° F.
45,419.5508	decigrams of water @ 62° F.
70,085.65746	grains of water @ 62° F.
454,195.508	centigrams of water @ 62° F.
4,541,955.08	milligrams of water @ 62° F.

GALLON (LIQUID): =

0.0037854	kiloliters
0.0037854	cubic meters
0.004951	cubic yards
0.0238095	barrels
0.037854	hektoliters
0.10742	bushels—U.S. (dry)
0.10414	bushels—Imperial (dry)
0.133681	cubic feet
0.37854	dekaliters
1	gallons—U.S. (liquid)
0.85948	gallons—U.S. (dry)
0.83268	gallons—Imperial
4	quarts (liquid)
3.43747	quarts (dry)
3.78544	liters
3.78544	cubic decimeters
8	pints (liquid)
32	gills (liquid)
37.8544	deciliters
231	cubic inches
378.544	centiliters
3,785.44	milliliters
3,785.44	cubic centimeters
3,785,440	cubic millimeters
0.12153	sacks of cement
61,440	minims
128	ounces (fluid)
1,024	drams (fluid)
0.0037219	tons (long) of water @ 62° F.
0.0037816	tons (metric) of water @ 62° F.
0.0041685	tons (short) of water @ 62° F.
3.7820	kilograms of water @ 62° F.
8.337	pounds (Avoir.) of water @ 62° F.
10.13177	pounds (Troy) of water @ 62° F.
37.820	hektograms of water @ 62° F.
378.20	dekagrams of water @ 62° F.

GALLON (LIQUID): (cont'd)

121.58124 . . . . ounces (Troy) of water @ 62° F.
133.392 . . . . ounces (Avoir.) of water @ 62° F.
972.64992 . . . . drams (Troy) of water @ 62° F.
2,134.272 . . . . drams (Avoir.) of water @ 62° F.
2,431.6284 . . . . pennyweights of water @ 62° F.
2,917.94976 . . . . scruples (Avoir.) of water @ 62° F.
3,782 . . . . grams of water @ 62° F.
37,820 . . . . decigrams of water @ 62° F.
58,359 . . . . grains of water @ 62° F.
378,200 . . . . centigrams of water @ 62° F.
3,782,000 . . . . milligrams of water @ 62° F.

GRAIN (AVOIRDUPOIS): =

0.000000637755089 . . . . tons (long)
0.000000647989857 . . . . tons (metric)
0.0000007142857 . . . . tons (short)
0.000064798918 . . . . kilograms
0.00014285714 . . . . .pounds (Avoir.)
0.00017361111 . . . . pounds (Troy)
0.00064798918 . . . . hektograms
0.0064798918 . . . . dekagrams
0.00208333 . . . . .ounces (Troy)
0.0022857 . . . . .ounces (Avoir.)
0.03657143 . . . . .drams (Avoir.)
0.0166667 . . . . drams (Troy)
0.0416667 . . . . pennyweights (Troy)
0.05000 . . . . .scruples (Troy)
0.064798918 . . . . .grams
0.64798918 . . . . decigrams
6.4798918 . . . . centigrams
64.798918 . . . . .milligrams
0.3240 . . . . carats (metric)

GRAM: =

0.00000098426 . . . . tons (long)
0.000001 . . . . .tons (metric)
0.00000110231 . . . . .tons (short)
0.001 . . . . kilograms
0.00220462 . . . . .pounds (Avoir.)
0.00267923 . . . . pounds (Troy)
0.01 . . . . hektograms
0.1 . . . . dekagrams
0.0321507 . . . . .ounces (Troy)
0.03527392 . . . . .ounces (Avoir.)
0.257206 . . . . drams (Troy)
0.564383 . . . . .drams (Avoir.)
0.6430149 . . . . pennyweights
0.771618 . . . . scruples
5.0 . . . . carats (metric)
10.0 . . . . decigrams

GRAM: (cont'd)

15.4324 . . . . grains
100 . . . . centigrams
1,000 . . . . .milligrams

HORSEPOWER: =

47,520,000 . . . . foot pounds per day
1,980,000 . . . . foot pounds per hour
33,000 . . . . foot pounds per minute
550 . . . . foot pounds per second
570,240,000 . . . . .inch pounds per day
23,760,000 . . . . .inch pounds per hour
396,000 . . . . inch pounds per minute
6,600 . . . . inch pounds per second
15,390.720 . . . . kilogram calories (mean) per day
641.280 . . . . kilogram calories (mean) per hour
10.688 . . . . .kilogram calories (mean) per minute
0.178133 . . . . kilogram calories (mean) per second
33,930.724525 . . . . pounds calories (mean) per day
1,413.780189 . . . . pounds calories (mean) per hour
23.563003 . . . . pounds calories (mean) per minute
0.392716 . . . . pounds calories (mean) per second
542,891.59248 . . . . ounce calories (mean) per day
22,620.483024 . . . . ounce calories (mean) per hour
377.008048 . . . . ounce calories (mean) per minute
6.283456 . . . . ounce calories (mean) per second
15,390,720 . . . . .gram calories (mean) per day
641,280 . . . . .gram calories (mean) per hour
10,688 . . . . gram calories (mean) per minute
178.133 . . . . gram calories (mean) per second
61,081.344 . . . . BTU (mean) per day
2,545.5600 . . . . BTU (mean) per hour
42.41760 . . . . BTU (mean) per minute
0.70696 . . . . BTU (mean) per second
0.7452 . . . . kilowatts (g=980)
0.74570 . . . . kilowatts (g=980.665)
745.2 . . . . watts (g=980)
745.70 . . . . watts (g=980.665)
1.0139 . . . . horsepower (metric)
1.0139 . . . . Cheval-vapeur hours
0.174 . . . . pounds carbon oxidized with 100% efficiency
2.62 . . . . pounds water evaporated from and @ 212° F.
635.769600 . . . . kiloliter-atmospheres per day
24.490400 . . . . kiloliter-atmospheres per hour
0.441507 . . . . kiloliter-atmospheres per minute
0.00735844 . . . . kiloliter-atmospheres per second
635,769.599962 . . . . liter-atmospheres per day
26,490.399998 . . . . liter-atmospheres per hour
441.506667 . . . . liter-atmospheres per minute
7.358844 . . . . liter-atmospheres per second
635,769,599.962 . . . . .milliliter-atmospheres per day

HORSEPOWER: (cont'd)

26,490,399.998	milliter-atmospheres per hour
441,506.666667	milliliter-atmospheres per minute
7,358.444444	milliliter-atmospheres per second

INCH: =

0.00001578	miles
0.00002540	kilometers
0.000126263	furlongs
0.0002560	hektometers
0.00126263	chains
0.002540	dekameters
0.00505051	rods
0.02540	meters
0.027777	yards
0.030000	varas (Texas)
0.083333	feet
0.111111	spans
0.126263	links
0.25000	hands
0.2540	decimeters
2.5400	centimeters
1	inches
25.40	millimeters
1000	mils
25,400	microns
39,450.33	wave lengths of red line of cadmium
25,400,000	millimicrons
25,400,000	micromillimeters
254,000,000	Angstrom Units

JOULE (ABSOLUTE): =

23.730	foot poundals
284.760	inch pounds
0.73756	foot pounds
8.85072	inch pounds
0.000000263331	ton (net) calories
0.00023889	kilogram calories (mean)
0.00526661	pound calories
0.00842658	ounce calories
0.23889	gram calories (mean)
238.89	milligram calories
0.0000000115740	kilowatt days
0.0000002778	kilowatt hours
0.0000166667	kilowatt minutes
0.001	kilowatt seconds
0.0000115740	watt days
0.0002778	watt hours
0.0166667	watt minutes
1	watt seconds
0.000112366	ton (net) meters
0.101937	kilogram meters

JOULE (ABSOLUTE): (cont'd)

0.224733	pounds meters
3.595721	ounce meters
101.937	gram meters
101,937	milligram meters
0.000368654	tons (net) feet
0.334438	kilogram feet
0.737311	pound feet
11.796960	ounce feet
334.438274	gram feet
334,438.273531	milligram feet
0.00442385	ton (net) inches
4.013259	kilogram inches
8.847732	pound inches
141.563520	ounce inches
4,013.259288	gram inches
4,013,259	milligram inches
0.0112366	ton (net) centimeters
10.1937	kilogram centimeters
22.4733	pound centimeters
359.5721	ounce centimeters
10,193.7	gram centimeters
10,193,700	milligrams centimeters
0.112366	ton (net) millimeters
101.937	kilogram millimeters
224.733	pound millimeters
3,595.721	ounce millimeters
101,937	gram millimeters
101,937,000	milligram millimeters
0.0000098705	kiloliter-atmosphere
0.000098705	hektoliter-atmosphere
0.0003485	cubic foot-atmosphere
0.00098705	dekaliter-atmosphere
0.0098705	liter-atmosphere
0.098705	deciliter-atmosphere
0.98705	centiliter-atmosphere
9.8705	millimeter-atmosphere
1	joules
0.0000003775	Cheval-vapeur hours
0.0000000155208	horsepower days
0.0000003725	horsepower hours
0.0000223500	horsepower minutes
0.00134100	horsepower seconds
0.00000000642	pounds of carbon oxidized with perfect efficiency
0.0000009662	pounds of water evaporated from and at 212° F.
0.0009480	BTU (mean)
100,000,000	ergs

KILOWATT: =

63,725,184	foot pounds per day
2,655,216	foot pounds per hour
44,253.60	foot pounds per minute

KILOWATT: (cont'd)

737.56 . . . . foot pounds per second
764,702,208 . . . . inch pounds per day
31,862,592 . . . . inch pounds per hour
531,043.20 . . . . inch pounds per minute
8,850.72 . . . . inch pounds per second
20,640.09600 . . . . kilogram calories (mean) per day
860.004 . . . . kilogram calories (mean) per hour
14.33340 . . . . .kilogram calories (mean) per minute
0.23889 . . . . kilogram calories (mean) per second
45,503.615916 . . . . pound calories (mean) per day
1,895.983996 . . . . pound calories (mean) per hour
31.599733 . . . . pound calories (mean) per minute
0.526662 . . . . pound calories (mean) per second
728,057.85472 . . . . ounce calories (mean) per day
30,335.743936 . . . . ounce calories (mean) per hour
505.595728 . . . . ounce calories (mean) per minute
8.426592 . . . . ounce calories (mean) per second
20,640,096 . . . . gram calories (mean) per day
860.004 . . . . gram calories (mean) per hour
14,333.40 . . . . gram calories (mean) per minute
238.89 . . . . gram calories (mean) per second
81,930.52800 . . . . BTU (mean) per day
3,413.77200 . . . . BTU (mean) per hour
56.89620 . . . . BTU (mean) per minute
0.94827 . . . . BTU (mean) per second
1 . . . . kilowatts
1,000 . . . . watts
3,600,000 . . . . joules
1.341 . . . . horsepower
1.3597 . . . . horsepower (metric)
1.3597 . . . . Cheval-vapeur hours
0.234 . . . . pounds carbon oxidized with 100% efficiency
3.52 .pounds water evaporated from and at 212°F.
852.647040 . . . . kiloliter-atmospheres per day
35.52695 . . . . kiloliter-atmospheres per hour
0.592116 . . . . kiloliter-atmospheres per minute
0.0098686 . . . . kiloliter-atmospheres per second
852,647 . . . . liter-atmospheres per day
35,526.95 . . . . liter-atmospheres per hour
592.116 . . . . liter-atmospheres per minute
9,8686 . . . . liter-atmospheres per second

LITER: =

0.001 . . . . kiloliters
0.001 . . . . .cubic meters
0.0013080 . . . . .cubic yards
0.00628995 . . . . barrels
0.01 . . . . hektoliters
0.028378 . . . . .bushels (U.S.) dry
0.027497 . . . . .bushels (Imperial) dry
0.0353144 . . . . cubic feet

LITER: (cont'd)

0.1	dekaliters
0.113512	pecks (U.S.) dry
0.264178	gallons (U.S.) liquid
0.22702	gallons (U.S.) dry
0.21998	gallons (Imperial)
1.056710	quarts (liquid)
0.908102	quarts (dry)
1	cubic decimeters
1.8162	pints (U.S.) dry
2.1134	pints (U.S.) liquid
7.0392	gills (Imperial)
8.4538	gills (U.S.)
10	decilliters
61.025	cubic inches
100	centilliters
1,000	milliliters
1,000	cubic centimeters
1,000,000	cubic millimeters
33.8147	ounces (U.S.) fluid
35.196	ounces (Imperial) fluid
270.5179	drams (fluid)
16,231.0740	minims
2.20462	pounds of water at maximum density

METER: =

0.00053961	miles (nautical)
0.00062137	miles (statute)
0.001	kilometers
0.00497097	furlongs
0.01	hektometers
0.0497097	chains
0.1	dekameters
0.198839	rods
1	meters
1.093611	yards
1.811	varas (Texas)
3.280833	feet
4.374440	spans
4.970974	links
9.84250	hands
10	decimeters
100	centimeters
39.370	inches
1,000	millimeters
39,370	mils
1,000,000	microns
1,000,000,000	millimicrons
1,000,000,000	micromillimeters
1,553,164	wave lengths of red line cadmium
1,000,000	Angstrom Units
0.54681	fathoms

MILE (STATUTE): =

0.86836	miles (nautical)
1	miles (statute)
1.60935	kilometers
8	furlongs
16.0935	hektometers
80	chains
160,935	dekameters
320	rods
1,609.35	meters
1,760	yards
1,900.8	varas (Texas)
5,280	feet
7,040	spans
8,000	links
15,840	hands
16,093.5	decimeters
160,935	centimeters
63,360	inches
1,609,350	millimeters
63,360,000	mils
1,609,344,000	microns
$1,609,344 \times 10^6$	millimicrons
$1,609,344 \times 10^6$	micromillimeters
2,499,572,909	wave lengths of red line of cadmium
$16,093,440 \times 10^6$	Angstrom Units

MINUTE (ANGLE): =

0.00018519	quadrants
0.000290888	radians
0.0166667	degrees
60	seconds
0.0000462963	circumference or revolutions

OHM (ABSOLUTE): =

0.00000000000111263	electrostatic cgs unit or statohm
0.000001	megohm (absolute)
0.99948	International ohm
1,000,000	microhms (absolute)
1,000,000,000	electromagnetic cgs or abohms

ohm per kilometer = 0.3048 ohms per 1,000 feet
ohm per 1,000 feet = 3.280833 ohms per kilometer
ohm per 1,000 yards = 1.0936 ohms per kilometer

OUNCE (AVOIRDUPOIS): =

0.0000279018	tons (long)
0.0000283495	tons (metric)
0.00003125	tons (short)
0.0282495	kilograms
0.0759549	pounds (Troy)
0.0625	pounds (Avoir.)

OUNCE (AVOIRDUPOIS): (cont'd)

0.283495	hektograms
2.834953	dekagrams
0.9114583	ounces (Troy)
1	ounces (Avoir.)
28.349527	grams
283.49527	decigrams
2,834.9527	centigrams
28,349.527	milligrams
437.5	grains
7.29166	drams (Troy)
16	drams (Avoir.)
18.22917	pennyweights
21.875	scruples
141.75	carats (metric)

OUNCES (FLUID): =

0.0000295729	kiloliters
0.0000295729	cubic meters
0.0000386814	cubic yards
0.000186012	barrels
0.000295729	hektoliters
0.000839221	bushels (U.S.—dry)
0.000813167	bushels (Imperial—dry)
0.00104435	cubic feet
0.00295729	dekaliters
0.00335688	pecks (U.S.—dry)
0.00781252	gallons (U.S.—liquid)
0.00671365	gallons (U.S.—dry)
0.00650545	gallons (Imperial)
0.03125	quarts (liquid)
0.0268552	quarts (dry)
0.0295729	liters
0.0295729	cubic decimeters
0.0537104	pints (U.S.—dry)
0.0625	pints (U.S.—liquid)
0.208170	gills (Imperial)
0.25	gills (U.S.)
0.295729	deciliters
1.80469	cubic inches
2.957294	centiliters
29.572937	milliliters
29.572937	cubic centimeters
29,572.9372	cubic millimeters
1	ounces (U.S.—fluid)
1.0408491	ounces (Imperial—fluid)
8	drams (fluid)
480	minims
0.0651972	pounds of water @ maximum density

OUNCE (TROY): =

0.0000306122	tons (long)
0.0000311034	tons (metric)
0.000034285	tons (short)
0.0311035	kilograms
0.0833333	pounds (Troy)
0.0685714	pounds (Avoir.)
0.311035	hektograms
3.110348	dekagrams
1	ounces (Troy)
1.09714	ounces (Avoir.)
31.103481	grams
311.03481	decigrams
3,110,3481	centigrams
31,103.481	milligrams
480	grains
8	drams (Troy)
17.55428	drams (Avoir.)
20	pennyweights
24	scruples
155.52	carats (metric)

OUNCE (WEIGHT) PER SQUARE INCH: =

0.000439419	hektometers of water @ 60° F.
0.00439419	dekameters of water @ 60° F.
0.0439419	meters of water @ 60° F.
0.144174	feet of water @ 60° F.
1.730092	inches of water @ 60° F.
0.439419	decimeters of water @ 60° F.
4.394188	centimeters of water @ 60° F.
43.941875	millimeters of water @ 60° F.
0.0000323219	hektometers of mercury @ 32° F.
0.000323219	dekameters of mercury @ 32° F.
0.00323219	meters of mercury @ 32° F.
0.0106042	feet of mercury @ 32° F.
0.127250	inches of mercury @ 32° F.
0.0323219	decimeters of mercury @ 32° F.
0.323219	centimeters of mercury @ 32° F.
3.232188	millimeters of mercury @ 32° F.
484.379356	tons per square hektometer
4.843794	tons per square dekameter
0.0484379	tons per square meter
0.00450014	tons per square foot
0.0000312500	tons per square inch
0.000484379	tons per square decimeter
0.00000484379	tons per square centimeter
0.0000000484379	tons per square millimeter
439,419	kilograms per square hektometer
4,394.1875	kilograms per square dekameter
43.941875	kilograms per square meter
4.0823252	kilgrams per square foot
0.0283494	kilograms per square inch

OUNCE (WEIGHT) PER SQUARE INCH: (cont'd)

0.439419 . . . . kilograms per square decimeter
0.00439419 . . . . .kilograms per square centimeter
0.0000439419 . . . . kilograms per square millimeter
968,758 . . . . pounds per square hektometer
9,687.58 . . . . pounds per square dekameter
96.8758 . . . . pounds per square meter
90 . . . . .pounds per square foot
0.0625 . . . . pounds per square inch
0.968758 . . . . pounds per square decimeter
0.00968758 . . . . pounds per square centimeter
0.0000968758 . . . . pounds per square millimeter
4,394,190 . . . . hektograms per square hektometer
43,941.875 . . . . hektograms per square dekameter
439.41875 . . . . hektograms per square meter
40.823252 . . . . hektograms per square foot
0.283494 . . . . hektograms per square inch
4.394188 . . . . .hektograms per square decimeter
0.043919 . . . . hektograms per square centimeter
0.000439419 . . . . .hektograms per square millimeter
43,941,900 . . . . dekagrams per square hektometer
439,419 . . . . dekagrams per square dekameter
4,394.1875 . . . . dekagrams per square meter
408.232519 . . . . dekagrams per square foot
2.834944 . . . . .dekagrams per square inch
43.941875 . . . . dekagrams per square decimeter
0.439419 . . . . dekagrams per square centimeter
0.00439419 . . . . dekagrams per square millimeter
15,500,139 . . . . ounces per square hektometer
155,001 . . . . .ounces per square dekameter
1,550.0139 . . . . ounces per square meter
144 . . . . ounces per square foot
1 . . . . ounces per square inch
15.500139 . . . . ounces per square decimeter
0.155001 . . . . .ounces per square centimeter
0.00155001 . . . . ounces per square millimeter
439,419,000 . . . . grams per square hektometer
4,394,190 . . . . grams per square dekameter
43,941.875 . . . . grams per square meter
4,082.325187 . . . . .grams per square foot
28.349438 . . . . grams per square inch
439.4187 . . . . grams per square decimeter
4.394187 . . . . grams per square centimeter
0.0439419 . . . . grams per square millimeter
4,394,190,000 . . . . .decigrams per square hektometer
43,941,900 . . . . decigrams per square dekameter
439,419 . . . . decigrams per square meter
40,823.25187 . . . . decigrams per square foot
283.494375 . . . . decigrams per square inch
4,394.1875 . . . . decigrams per square decimeter
43.94187 . . . . decigrams per square centimeter
0.439419 . . . . .decigrams per square millimeter

OUNCE (WEIGHT) PER SQUARE INCH: (cont'd)

43,941,900,000 . . . . centrigrams per square hektometer
439,419,000 . . . . centigrams per square dekameter
4,394,190 . . . . centigrams per square meter
408,233 . . . . centigrams per square foot
2,834.943750 . . . . centigrams per square inch
43,941.875 . . . . centigrams per square decimeter
439.41875 . . . . .centigrams per square centimeter
4.394188 . . . . centigrams per square millimeter
439,419,000,000 . . . . milligrams per square hektometer
4,394,190,000 . . . . milligrams per square dekameter
43,941,900 . . . . milligrams per square meter
4,082,325 . . . . milligrams per square foot
28,349.43750 . . . . milligrams per square inch
439,419 . . . . .milligrams per square decimeter
4,394.1875 . . . . milligrams per square centimeter
43.941875 . . . . milligrams per square millimeter
430,920,000,000 . . . . dynes per square hektometer
4,309,200,000 . . . . .dynes per square dekameter
43,092,000 . . . . dynes per square meter
4,003,324 . . . . .dynes per square foot
28,050.875 . . . . dynes per square inch
430,920 . . . . dynes per square decimeter
4,309.2 . . . . .dynes per square centimeter
43.092 . . . . dynes per square millimeter
0.00430919 . . . . bars
0.00425288 . . . . atmosphere

PARTS PER MILLION: =

0.00000110231 . . . . tons (net) per cubic meter
0.001 . . . . kilograms per cubic meter
0.00220462 . . . . pounds (Avoir.) per cubic meter
0.0352739 . . . . ounces (Avoir.) per cubic meter
1.0 . . . . grams per cubic meter
15.4324 . . . . grains per cubic meter
0.000000175250 . . . . tons (net) per barrel
0.000158984 . . . . kilograms per barrel
0.000350499 . . . . .pounds (Avoir.) per barrel
0.00560799 . . . . ounces (Avoir.) per barrel
0.158984 . . . . grams per barrel
2.453505 . . . . grains per barrel
0.0000000312133 . . . . tons (net) per cubic foot
0.0000283162 . . . . kilograms per cubic foot
0.0000624264 . . . . pounds (Avoir.) per cubic foot
0.000998823 . . . . .ounces (Avoir.) per cubic foot
0.0283162 . . . . .grams per cubic foot
0.436987 . . . . .grains per cubic foot
0.00000000417262 . . . . tons (net) per gallon (U.S.—liquid)
0.00000378524 . . . . kilograms per gallon (U.S.—liquid)
0.00000834522 . . . . pounds (Avoir.) per gallon (U.S.—liquid)
0.000133524 . . . . ounces (Avoir.) per gallon (U.S.—liquid)
0.00378534 . . . . .grams per gallon (U.S.—liquid)

PARTS PER MILLION: (cont'd)

0.0584168	grains per gallons (U.S.—liquid)
0.00000000501107	grains per gallon (Imperial—liquid)
0.00000454585	kilograms per gallon (Imperial—liquid)
0.0000100221	pounds (Avoir.) per gallon (Imp.—liquid)
0.000160355	ounces (Avoir.) per gallon (Imp.—liquid)
0.00454597	grams per gallon (Imperial—liquid)
0.0701552	grains per gallon (Imperial—liquid)
0.00000000110231	tons (net) per liter
0.000001	kilograms per liter
0.00000220462	pounds (Avoir.) per liter
0.0000352739	ounces (Avoir.) per liter
0.001	grams per liter
0.0154324	grains per liter
0.0000000000180663	tons (net) cubic inch
0.0000000163867	kilograms per cubic inch
0.0000000361264	pounds (Avoir.) per cubic inch
0.000000578023	ounces (Avoir.) per cubic inch
0.0000163867	grams per cubic inch
0.000252886	grains per cubic inch
8.345	pounds per million gallons

POUND (TROY): =

0.000367347	tons (long)
0.000373242	tons (metric)
0.000411429	tons (net)
0.373242	kilograms
1	pounds (Troy)
0.822857	pounds (Avoir.)
3.732418	hektograms
37.324176	dekagrams
12	ounces (Troy)
13.165714	ounces (Avoir.)
373.241762	grams
3,732.417621	decigrams
37,324.176213	centigrams
373,242	milligrams
5,760	grains
96	drams (Troy)
210.651425	drams (Avoir.)
240	pennyweights
288	scruples
1,866.239964	carats (metric)

POUND (AVOIRDUPOIS):=

0.000446429	tons (long)
0.000453593	tons (metric)
0.0005	tons (net)
0.453592	kilograms
1.215278	pounds (Troy)
1	pounds (Avoir.)

POUND (AVOIRDUPOIS): (cont'd)

4.535924 . . . . hektograms
45.359243 . . . . dekagrams
14.5833 . . . . ounces (Troy)
16 . . . . ounces (Avoir.)
453.592428 . . . . grams
4,535.92428 . . . . decigrams
45,359.2428 . . . . centigrams
453,592 . . . . milligrams
7,000 . . . . grains
116.666675 . . . . drams (Troy)
256 . . . . drams (Avoir.)
291.6667 . . . . pennyweights
350.1 . . . . scruples
2,268 . . . . carats (metric)

POUND (PRESSURE) PER SQUARE INCH: =

0.0070307 . . . . hektometers of water @ 60° F.
0.070307 . . . . dekameters of water @ 60° F.
0.70307 . . . . meters of water @ 60° F.
2.306787 . . . . feet of water @ 60° F.
27.681473 . . . . inches of water @ 60° F.
7.0307 . . . . decimeters of water @ 60° F.
70,307 . . . . centimeters of water @ 60° F.
703.07 . . . . millimeters of water @ 60° F.
0.00051715 . . . . hektometers of mercury @ 32° F.
0.0051715 . . . . dekameters of mercury @ 32° F.
0.051715 . . . . meters of mercury @ 32° F.
0.169667 . . . . feet of mercury @ 32° F.
2.0360 . . . . inches of mercury @ 32° F.
0.51715 . . . . decimeters of mercury @ 32° F.
5.1715 . . . . centimeters of mercury @ 32° F.
51.715 . . . . millimeters of mercury @ 32° F.
7,750.0696898 . . . . tons per square hektometer
77.500697 . . . . tons per square dekameter
0.775007 . . . . tons per square meter
0.0720023 . . . . tons per square foot
0.0005 . . . . tons per square inch
0.00775007 . . . . tons per square decimeter
0.0000775007 . . . . tons per square centimeter
0.000000775007 . . . . tons per square millimeter
7,030,700 . . . . kilograms per square hektometer
70,307 . . . . kilograms per square dekameter
703.07 . . . . kilograms per square meter
65.317203 . . . . kilograms per square foot
0.453592 . . . . kilograms per square inch
7.0307 . . . . kilograms per square decimeter
0.070307 . . . . kilograms per square centimeter
0.00070307 . . . . kilograms per square millimeter
15,500,130 . . . . pounds per square hektometer
155,001 . . . . pounds per square dekameter
1,550.0130 . . . . pounds per square meter

POUND (PRESSURE) PER SQUARE INCH: (cont'd)

144 . . . . .pounds per square foot
1 . . . . pounds per square inch
15.500130 . . . . pounds per square decimeter
0.155001 . . . . pounds per square centimeter
0.00155001 . . . . pounds per square millimeter
70,307,000 . . . . hektograms per square hektometer
703,070 . . . . hektograms per square dekameter
7,030.70 . . . . hektograms per square meter
653.172168 . . . . hektograms per square foot
4.535933 . . . . hektograms per square inch
70.3070 . . . . .hektograms per square decimeter
0.70307 . . . . hektograms per square centimeter
0.0070307 . . . . .hektograms per square millimeter
703,070,000 . . . . dekagrams per square hektometer
7,030,700 . . . . dekagrams per square dekameter
70,307 . . . . dekagrams per square meter
6,531.721544 . . . . dekagrams per square foot
45.359332 . . . . .dekagrams per square inch
7,030.7 . . . . dekagrams per square decimeter
70.307 . . . . .dekagrams per square centimeter
0.70307 . . . . dekagrams per square millimeter
248,002,217 . . . . ounces per square hektometer
2,480,022 . . . . .ounces per square dekameter
24,800.22 . . . . ounces per square meter
2,303.985941 . . . . .ounces per square foot
16 . . . . ounces per square inch
248.0022 . . . . ounces per square decimeter
2.480022 . . . . .ounces per square centimeter
0.0248002 . . . . ounces per square millimeter
7,030,700,000 .grams per square hektometer
70,307,000 . . . . grams per square dekameter
703,070 . . . . grams per square meter
65,317.215135 . . . . .grams per square foot
453.593927 . . . . grams per square inch
7,030.7 . . . . grams per square decimeter
70.307 . . . . grams per square centimeter
0.70307 . . . . grams per square millimeter
70,307,000,000 . . . . .decigrams per square hektometer
703,070,000 . . . . decigrams per square dekameter
7,030,700 . . . . decigrams per square meter
653,172 . . . . decigrams per square foot
4,535.939265 . . . . decigrams per square inch
70,307 . . . . .decigrams per square decimeter
703.07 . . . . decigrams per square centimeter
7.0307 . . . . .decigrams per square millimeter
703,070,000,000 . . . . centigrams per square hektometer
7,030,700,000 . . . . .centigrams per square dekameter
70,307,000 . . . . centigrams per square meter
6,531,720 . . . . .centigrams per square foot
45,359.392595 . . . . centigrams per square inch
703,070 . . . . centigrams per square decimeter
7,030.70 . . . . .centigrams per square centimeter

POUND (PRESSURE) PER SQUARE INCH: (cont'd)

70.3070 . . . . centigrams per square millimeter
$70,307 \times 10^8$ . . . . milligrams per square hektometer
$70,307 \times 10^6$ . . . . milligrams per square dekameter
$70,307 \times 10^4$ . . . . milligrams per square meter
65,317,200 . . . . milligrams per square foot
453,594 . . . . milligrams per square inch
70,307,000 . . . . milligrams per square decimeter
703,070 . . . . milligrams per square centimeter
7,030.70 . . . . milligrams per square millimeter
$68,947 \times 10^8$ . . . . dynes per square hektometer
68,947,000,000 . . . . dynes per square dekameters
689,470,000 . . . . dynes per square meter
64,053,184 . . . . dynes per square foot
448,814 . . . . dynes per square inch
6,894,700 . . . . dynes per square decimeter
68,947 . . . . .dynes per square centimeter
689.47 . . . . dynes per square millimeter
0.068947 . . . . bars
0.068046 . . . . .atmospheres

POUND (WEIGHT) PER SQUARE FOOT: =

48,824,306 . . . . grams per square hektometer
488,243 . . . . grams per square dekameter
4,882.430555 . . . . grams per square meter
453.591783 . . . . .grams per square foot
3.149953 . . . . grams per square inch
48.824306 . . . . grams per square decimeter
0.488243 . . . . grams per square centimeter
0.00488243 . . . . grams per square millimeter
488,243,056 . . . . .decigrams per square hektometer
4,882,431 . . . . decigrams per square dekameter
48,824.305552 . . . . decigrams per square meter
4,535.917833 . . . . decigrams per square foot
3.149953 . . . . decigrams per square inch
488.243056 . . . . .decigrams per square decimeter
4.882431 . . . . decigrams per square centimeter
0.0488243 . . . . .decigrams per square millimeter
4,882,430,555 . . . . .centigrams per square hektometer
48,824,306 . . . . .centigrams per square dekameter
488,243 . . . . centigrams per square meter
45,359.178330 . . . . centigrams per square foot
31.499535 . . . . centigrams per square inch
4,882.430555 . . . . centigrams per square decimeter
48.824306 . . . . .centigrams per square centimeter
0.488243 . . . . centigrams per square millimeter
48,824,305,552 . . . . .milligrams per square hektometer
488,243,056 . . . . milligrams per square dekameter
4,882.431 . . . . milligrams per square meter
453,592 . . . . milligrams per square foot
314.995347 . . . . milligrams per square inch
48,824.305552 . . . . milligrams per square decimeter

POUND (WEIGHT) PER SQUARE FOOT: (cont'd)

488.243056 . . . . milligrams per square centimeter
4.882431 . . . . milligrams per square millimeter
47,879,860,000 . . . . dynes per square hektometer
478,798,600 . . . . dynes per square dekameter
4,787,986 . . . . dynes per square meter
444,814 . . . . dynes per square foot
3,116.763889 . . . . dynes per square inch
47,879.861108 . . . . dynes per square decimeter
478.798611 . . . . dynes per square centimeter
4.787986 . . . . dynes per square millimeter
0.00047880 . . . . bars
0.00047254 . . . . atmospheres

QUADRANT (ANGLE): =

324,000 . . . . seconds
5,400 . . . . minutes
90 . . . . degrees
1.57080 . . . . radians
0.25 . . . . circumference of revolution
0.7854 . . . . pi (π)

QUART (U.S.—DRY): =

0.000110089 . . . . kiloliters
0.000110089 . . . . cubic meters
0.00143968 . . . . cubic yards
0.00692448 . . . . barrels
0.0110089 . . . . hektoliters
0.0312402 . . . . bushels (U.S.—dry)
0.0302863 . . . . bushels (Imperial—dry)
0.0388775 . . . . cubic feet
0.110089 . . . . dekaliters
0.290823 . . . . gallons (U.S.—liquid)
0.249956 . . . . gallons (U.S.—dry)
0.242162 . . . . gallons (Imperial)
1.163290 . . . . quarts (liquid)
1 . . . . quarts (dry)
1.100889 . . . . liters
1.100889 . . . . cubic decimeters
2 . . . . pints (U.S.—dry)
2.326580 . . . . pints (U.S.—liquid)
7.749187 . . . . gills (Imperial)
9.306320 . . . . gills (U.S.)
11.00888839 . . . . deciliters
67.18 . . . . cubic inches
110.0888839 . . . . centiliters
1,100.888839 . . . . millimeters
1,100.888839 . . . . cubic centimeters
1,100,889 . . . . cubic millimeters (fluid)
17,868.135060 . . . . minims (fluid)
37.225281 . . . . ounces (fluid)
297.802251 . . . . drams (fluid)

QUART (U.S.—DRY) (cont'd)

0.00108241	tons (long)
0.00109977	tons (metric)
0.00121230	tons (short)
1.0997744	kilograms
2.424587	pounds (Avoir.)
2.946547	pounds (Troy)
10.997744	hektograms
109.977441	dekagrams
35.358561	ounces (Troy)
38.793396	ounces (Avoir.)
282.868492	drams (Troy)
620.694342	drams (Avoir.)
707.171230	pennyweights
848.605475	scruples
1,099.774407	grams
10,997.744067	decigrams
16,972.110905	grains
109,977	centigrams
1,099,774	milligrams

QUART (U.S.—LIQUID) =

0.0000946358	kiloliters
0.0000946358	cubic meters
0.00123775	cubic yards
0.0059525	barrels
0.00946358	hektoliters
0.026855	bushels (U.S.—dry)
0.026035	bushels (Imperial—dry)
0.0334203	cubic feet
0.0946358	dekaliter
0.25	gallons(U.S.—liquid)
0.21487	gallons (U.S.—dry)
0.20817	gallons (Imperial)
1	quarts (liquid)
0.859368	quarts (dry)
0.946358	liters
0.946358	cubic decimeters
1.718733	pints (U.S.—dry)
2	pints (U.S.—liquid)
6.66144	gills (Imperial)
8	gills (U.S.)
9,46358	deciliters
57.75	cubic inches
94.6358	centiliters
946.358	milliliters
946.358	cubic centimeters
946,358	cubic millimeters
15,360	minims
32	ounces (fluid)
256	drams (fluid)
0.000930475	tons (long) water @ 62° F.

QUART (U.S.—LIQUID) (cont'd)

0.0009454	tons (metric) water @ 62° F.
0.00104213	tons (short) water @ 62° F.
0.9454	kilograms water @ 62° F.
2.08425	pounds (Avoir.) water @ 62° F.
2.532943	pounds (Troy) water @ 62° F.
9.455	hektograms water @ 62° F.
94.55	dekagrams water @ 62° F.
30.39531	ounces (Troy) water @ 62° F.
33.348	ounces (Avoir.) water @ 62° F.
243.16248	drams (Troy) water @ 62° F.
533.568	drams (Avoir.) water @ 62° F.
607.9062	pennyweights water @ 62° F.
729.48744	scruples water @ 62° F.
945.5	grams water @ 62° F.
9,455	decigrams water @ 62° F.
14,589.75	grains water @ 62° F.
94,550	centigrams water @ 62° F.
945,500	milligrams water @ 62° F.

RADIAN: =

206,265	seconds or inches
3,437.75	minutes
57.29578	degrees
0.637	quadrants
0.159155	circumference or revolutions
0.5	pi (π)
57° 17′ 44.8″	(In degrees, minutes and seconds)

REVOLUTION: =

1,296,000	seconds or inches
21,600	minutes
360	degrees
6.2832	radians
4	quadrants
2	Pi (π)
1	circumference

SACK CEMENT: =

0.19592	barrels
94	pounds (Avoir.)
8.22857	gallons (U.S.—liquid)
1.1	cubic feet (set)
1,900.8	cubic inches
3.15	specific gravity
0.484	cubic feet (absolute volume)

SEAWATER GRAVITY: =

1.02 to 1.03

SQUARE YARD: =

0.000000322831	square miles or sections
0.000000836131	square kilometers
0.0000206612	square furlongs
0.000206612	acres
0.0000836131	square hektometers or hectares
0.00206612	square chains
0.00836131	square dekameters or acres
0.0330579	square rods
0.836131	square meters or centares
1	square yards
1.166382	square varas (Texas)
9	square feet
20.66112	square links
83.61306	square decimeters
8,361.306	square centimeters
1,296	square inches
836,131	square millimeters
1,296,000,000	square mils
1,650,119,040	circular mils
1.064,565	circular millimeters

TEMPERATURE, ABSOLUTE IN CENTIGRADE OR KELVIN: =

temperature in C° + 273.18°

TEMPERATURE, ABSOLUTE IN FAHRENHEIT OR RANKIN: =

temperature in F° + 459.59°

TEMPERATURE, DEGREES CENTIGRADE: =

5/9 (Temp. F°-32°)
5/4 (Temp. Reaumur)

TEMPERATURE, DEGREES FAHRENHEIT: =

9/5 (Temp. C° + 32°)
9/4 (Temp. Reaumur + 32°)

TEMPERATURE, DEGREES REAUMUR: =

4/9 (Temp. F°-32°)
4/5 (Temp. C°)

Degree Centigrade: =

0.8 or 4/5 degree Reaumur
1.00 degrees absolute, Kelvin
1.8 or 9/5 degrees Fahrenheit

Degree Fahrenheit: =

0.44444 or 4/9 degree Reaumur
0.55556 or 5/9 degree Centigrade

Degree Reaumur: =

1.25 or 5/4 degrees Centigrade
2.25 or 9/4 degrees Fahrenheit

TONS (LONG): =

1	tons (long)
1.0160470	tons (metric)
1.12	tons (net)
1,016.0470	kilograms
2,722.22	pounds (Troy)
2,240	pounds (Avoir.)
10,160.470	hektograms
101,605	dekagrams
32,667	ounces (Troy)
35,840	ounces (Avoir.)
1,016,047	grams
10,160,470	decigrams
101,604,700	centigrams
1,016,047,000	milligrams
15,680,000	grains
261,333	drams (Troy)
573,440	drams (Avoir.)
653,333	pennyweights
784,022	scruples
5,080,430	carats (metric)
6.19755	barrels of water @ 60° F.
7.33627	barrels of oil @ 36° API
28.607	cubic feet
260.02971	gallons (U.S.—liquid)

TONS (METRIC): =

0.984206	tons (long)
1	tons (metric)
1.10231	tons (net)
1,000	kilograms
2,679.23	pounds (Troy)
2,204.622341	pounds (Avoir.)
10,000	hektograms
100,000	dekagrams
32,150.76	ounces (Troy)
35,273.96	ounces (Avoir.)
1,000,000	grams
10,000,000	decigrams
100,000,000	centigrams
1,000,000,000	milligrams
15,432,365	grains
257,206	drams (Troy)
564,384	drams (Avoir.)
643,015	pennyweights

TONS (METRIC): (cont'd)

```
771,618 ...................................... scruples
5,000,086 ................................ carats (metric)
6.297 ........................... barrels of water @ 60° F.
7.454 ............................ barrels of oil @ 36⁰ API
29.0662 ...................................... cubic feet
264.474 ............................. gallons (U.S.—liquid)
```

TONS (NET): =

```
0.892858 .................................... tons (long)
0.907185 .................................... tons (metric)
1 ............................................ tons (net)
907.184872 .................................. kilograms
2,430.56 ................................... pounds (Troy)
2,000 ..................................... pounds (Avoir.)
9,071.84872 ................................. hektograms
90,718.4872 ................................ dekagrams
29,166.66 ................................. ounces (Troy)
32,000 ................................... ounces (Avoir.)
907,185 .......................................... grams
9,701,849 ................................... decigrams
90,718,487 .................................. centigrams
907,184,872 ................................. miligrams
14,000,000 ..................................... grains
233,333 .................................... drams (Troy)
512,000 ................................... drams (Avoir.)
583,333 ................................... pennyweights
700,020 ..................................... scruples
4,536,000 ................................. carats (metric)
5.71255 ......................... barrels of water @ 60° F.
6.76216 ........................... barrels of oil @ 36° API
32.04 ........................................ cubic feet
239.9271 ............................. gallons (U.S.—liquid)
```

YARD: =

```
0.000483387 .............................. miles (nautical)
0.000568182 .............................. miles (statute)
0.000914404 ................................ kilometers
0.00454545 .................................. furlongs
0.00914404 ................................. hektometers
0.0454545 ..................................... chains
0.0914404 .................................. dekameters
0.181818 ....................................... rods
0.914404 ..................................... meters
1 ............................................ yards
1.08 ..................................... varas (Texas)
3 ............................................. feet
4 ............................................. spans
4.54545 ........................................ links
9 ............................................. hands
9.144036 ................................... centimeters
```

YARD: (cont'd)

36 . . . . inches
914.40360 . . . . millimeters
36,000 . . . . mils
914,404 . . . . microns
914,403,600 . . . . millimicrons
914,403,600 . . . . micromillimeters
1,420,212 . . . . wave lengths of red line of cadmium
9,144.036345 . . . . Angstrom Units